The Fish Finder

by

Kevin Callahan

Dedicated to my father, a life giver,
and to the unborn who were never
given the chance to live or give life.

Publishing with J.A.M. makes your words stick...
Callahan Services, LLC

Printed in the United States of America
Published September 2017

ISBN: 0-9990372-4-2
ISBN-13: 978-0-9990372-4-9

Cover Design: Joseph A. Martino
Interior Layout Design: Joseph A. Martino

For more information on this title please visit:
www.PUBLISHwithJAM.com and
www.CallahanServices.us

Acknowledgements

With sincere appreciation I thank Tom Burgoyne, Jakki Clarke, Chas DeFeo, Ed Hastings, Evan Marcus, and A Prominent Philadelphia Attorney who wrote reviews for *The Fish Finder*.

Special thanks to my brother, Rich, for bravely giving the earliest form of *The Fish Finder* its first read over 20 years ago and to my friends and neighbors, Baz, for enduring the read of a later try and Sid, for encouraging me to keep trying.

Thanks to my father for being a life giver and for the support of my brothers, John and Paul, and sister, Liz.

I appreciate the effort and expertise of publisher Joseph Martino. My continued thanks to editor Dennis Mathis, who worked with me on *The Black Rose*. I highly recommend them.

An extra special thanks to my wonderful children, Mary and Jackson, truly Gifts from God, and my brave little wife, Donna.

And with love for my mother, who when I first

started *The Black Rose* trilogy, read the first draft of *The Fish Finder* and wrote a loving one-page note to tell me everything that was right with the story - like only a mother could - before appropriately concluding, “Kevin, this was a very nice try.”

This is my next nicest try...

Book Reviews

With the soundtrack of Rolling Stones tunes playing throughout the book and Cape May, New Jersey shining brightly, Kevin Callahan artfully weaves a story of love, loss and the sanctity of life. And just like a super hero's quest for truth and justice, *The Fish Finder* is on a mission to make the world more compassionate, especially for the ones who can't defend themselves. Simply a beautiful, sometimes trippy, tale.

Tom Burgoyne, The Best Friend of the Phillie Phanatic, Co-Author of Pheel the Love!

The Fish Finder is a slam dunk! Kevin Callahan has made the transition from college athlete to professional sportswriter to now prolific author like few others have. He understands that if you don't know Philly-South Jersey area pickup basketball then you really don't know basketball. Kevin knows how to write and develop characters and paint a scenic picture like few do! For those of us who understand - The Jersey Shore is a slice of paradise! Finally, Kevin is fearless and adept at dribbling through the hot button issues of our day as he did with racism in his first book, *The Black Rose*, and now ball handling abortion in *The Fish Finder*. As a devout and practicing Catholic blogger and author who stands against racism and for protecting life at all stages, I thank you Kevin Callahan for inspiring me! Keep writing, and keep up the magnificent work! God's work! God bless you and everyone who reads *The Fish Finder*!

Mr. Charles DeFeo, O.P., Author of Walk by Faith to Live Joyfully, and Radio Host for oremuscomms.com and prolifeamericaradio.com

You needn't be from the Delaware Valley nor a sports fan to enjoy Kevin Callahan's engrossing story, but those attributes add to make *The Fish Finder* even more delightful.

Jakki Clarke, Author of Flyer Lives: Philadelphia Hockey Greats Share Their Personal Stories, and Death by a Thousand Cuts

Author Kevin Callahan utilizes familiar sights and landscape in Cape May, New Jersey to explore deep topics and questions. Humorous, clever, thought provoking, ripe with basketball analogies and Rolling Stones' lyrics, this second part of a trilogy moves one to appreciate and defend all of creation.

Edward Hastings, PhD, Director of the Graduate Program in Theology and Ministry, Villanova University

Kevin Callahan is a wonderful story teller. *The Fish Finder* draws you into his characters' lives and in so doing, he expertly makes his message come alive!

Evan Marcus, Co-Author of Pheel the Love! and It's Ok to Play, Co-Founder of DillonMarcus

Kevin Callahan captures a grisly business grown commonplace beneath the idyllic tranquility of the Jersey shore. The journey from the "gray area" passive acceptance of a culture of death to an affirmation of life will haunt you. Echoes of Greek philosophers, Nietzsche, Goethe and Einstein underpin these relatable characters' struggle of conscience. You "can't be in the middle" after reading *The Fish Finder*.

A Prominent Philadelphia Attorney

Table of Contents

Prologue

My view has changed from *The Black Rose.* I should have stopped Cali-holi from beating the man in the first story of this trilogy. I should've known he was breaking... that the beating was coming.

The fear came before the guilt. Don't know which destroyed me first. Do know both come from the same damn dark place inside where not even booze or basketball could penetrate, could kill. Guilt is a powerful seducer. Expands silently like the unknown dark energy that pushes the universe.

Rationalization worked for a while. I didn't stop the beating when I should've known it was coming, probably because I knew the cop knew about Andie… he knew about my daughter's plumbing, as she would say to me and mock her sex status to soothe the situation, as if to tell me she was OK with her life.

In my life, basketball, drinking and rationalizing was the mixture, the tonic, I used to live with, well, shielding the guilt of how I should've saved the poor cop from the eventual beating... but he... he just knew about the wrong guy's daughter. I was a fearful façade of a ballsy man who wouldn't do the right thing.

How could I ever wash my hands of not doing

right? How could I ever cleanse that damn spot on my soul?

Now, almost two years later, from this view, I do see life is about choices and not Rochambeau as says my daughter, Andie, and Byrdie, I mean Cresty and Choker, their aliases here in the second story of the trilogy, which plays out during three or four months or so, inside the two years after I was gone in *The Black Rose*.

But, since I'm finally being truthful, I didn't care if I did die diving that day... or any day.

I suppose there is a difference. I do think there is a difference between wanting to die and not caring if you do. But what difference did it really make I thought back then?

I do know much more now how guilt wrecks, ruins and riddles your head worse than any mixture of drinks I ever employed on any night to kill the demon dancing in my thoughts.

What happened, I kept thinking, if God didn't forgive you?

I mean, I believed in forgiveness as a Catholic, but I worried what happened if the sin was just too great to be forgiven? Or what happened, I feared, if God just didn't want to... or just couldn't forgive you? I would never see my mom…

The thought of it all was enough to just kill me.

You see, or at least I did, that you would live the rest your life, every waking minute, every unfulfilled hour, every empty drink, every meaningless jump shot, thinking you were doomed.

You think nothing will ever change your destination.

You are on the Highway to Hell with AC/DC is what I thought when the last song on the jukebox played again, ending another wonderfully torturous weekend day with my sincere wish to only stop thinking.

So, I thought, isn't it easier not to be around? Not to think that's where you're going? Just to go there? Just to go right to hell? Get the trip started, to get the eternal doom on...

And wouldn't life be easier knowing that you were never going to sin again because you weren't around to sin? Wouldn't existence be such a good feeling knowing you would never sin again? And without sinning again, wasn't there just a chance maybe God eventually would forgive you?

I mean, when you're on your deathbed, whether it is for a glorious short hour or for woeful weeks, and you are saying to yourself, "Damn, this is it, I'm going to meet God and he knows I sinned big and I know he knows I know it's a big sin and still did it," well, who wants to be lying and dying thinking this?

The thought of just thinking about this all over again, rehashing the guilt, just makes me glad I did go for the dive two summers ago... even though I do horribly miss Andie and Byrd... Choker and Cresty. I do miss them more than they know.

But going diving was my choice. I had a choice.

You know Byrd, here I go again, I mean Choker was all choked up and ripped apart not knowing to go out fishing or not on a gray day yesterday morning, or was it the day before? Time really does stand still. Anyway, just think how much more torn apart he would be if every minute of every day he worried about not being forgiven by God? Not knowing where you are going makes fear and guilt feel like your childhood drinking buddies. You can't drown fear and guilt with booze when they have learned to tread whiskey.

How could anyone be happy?

From my view now, like a lifeguard looking down, Cape May seems to be a happy town. Yes, a friendly, interesting town with a history worth saving. A vacation town with each new day as inviting as Cape May's past, unlike Camden... which is where Cresty and Choker go one day during the three months, or is it four… again I'm not really into time anymore… of *The Fish Finder*.

And that day in the middle of June is the third part of this trilogy, but a different person tells *The Chess Game*... with a different viewpoint... and a different angle of view.

As the saying goes, however, that's another story for another time. The gestation of this story is now – that's my choice.

I remember, too, when I was younger and couldn't get work one summer, but at least I was given the chance to not find work… and at least I was given the chance to see if God really does forgive the big sins…

Chapter 1

The rich man's boat is docked. Tied-up at the end of a nine-slip pier and under the nauseating cloak of air that smells like a seagull burped out its morning clam.

The bow drifts into the waterway like it owns the canal, floating freely without consequence and blocking the half dozen or so other boats from entering the safety of the harbor. Or leaving if the owner needed. Or if a passenger wanted.

The ring porthole windows are hatched tight, shielding the shifting evening breeze from the comforting innards of the blood red 30-foot yacht that is moored to a bent, flimsy cleat with just one nail banged securely in the wooden pier and latched by only a single nylon line, as if the boat is clinging to life on an umbilical cord from the impending storm.

A modern nautical lantern, encased with fake rusted antique aluminum, hangs from a twisted hook on the second deck of the luxurious BABE ON BOARD, bouncing with the outgoing tide and reflecting on the rippling brackish water like a regretful reveler looking into a broken, foggy bathroom mirror in the morning after St. Patrick's Day.

The oncoming wake increases from an approaching boat in the eastern end of the canal, dividing the water evenly. The ripples roll on, touching both sides equally, like a conflict between right and wrong, as if stirring and soothing one of life's controversies at the same time.

Ahh, it's a raft. An elongated rubber aqua-green and gray inflatable flotation device, like a rescue raft from a cruise ship. Standing and paddling is a pirate, humming and growling. A gray-bearded middle-aged man with a curved knife clenched between his teeth and an unbuttoned ashen vest flapping over a baggy long-sleeve white shirt with a thick collar and a v-neckline untied by a thin hanging cloud-colored string.

"Ahoy, matey," snarls the pirate out of the cocked left side of his mouth and into the seagull-burp bay night air.

A tall, thick man, dressed in all black like Bono at a wake, thumps up on deck of the moored boat while sipping from a red plastic party cup.

"Who goes there?" he says before taking another sip.

"Welcome to Cape May," the pirate slurs, wiping his sabre, called a cutlass I believe, on his floppy gray knickers with black stripes that are tucked into his knee-high black boots, "welcome to the Jersey Riviera."

"You must be *the* old Blackbeard now that your whiskers are pale. I heard your treasure is buried here, down here on the most southern tip of New Jersey."

"Actually, I'm the Welcome Chairman of the Cape May Chamber of Commerce, you can call me The Duke," the pirate says, "Welcome… and say hello to The Dolphin."

Behind the raft, a dolphin flops out of the water and plops next to The Duke. The Dolphin stands up with its blue-gray tail fin drooping between two tan lower legs with shaved, but muscular calves and small feet wearing white converse sneakers.

The Dolphin flips between the rope rails and onto the deck of the drinking man's yacht. Out of the fish's mouth spits and envelope printed on the outside with the words:

WE ENJOY PLAYING & TO DO
BUSINESS WITH YOU
IN CAPE MAY TOO.

Taking another sip, the rich man opens the envelope with his right hand, flashing an oversized gold ring on his middle finger.

"Hey thanks for the lottery tickets," he says without a hint of appreciation. "I can always use more money... I hear the mega-million is Wednesday."

Holding on to his Aviator sunglasses with one hand and his swashbuckling pirate hat that droops over most of his face, The Duke stumbles and then climbs on board. With the raft line looped around his ankle and rum tucked under his arm, he hands the bottle to the man while singing "ho, ho, ho," sounding more like Santa Claus than Blackbeard.

From the mirrored bar top counter, illuminated by the hanging lamp, the man with the gravelly voice that matches his granite jaw and a rock-faced forehead hands The Duke and The Dolphin two red cups.

"I had a good day, drink up, a profitable one," the rich boater says. "I typically drink just marked-down red wine, but I made some big bank today, so I will drink rum… it makes me dumb."

"Dumber," The Duke snarls harmlessly.

The man swigs from the bottle of white rum like a junior high kid stealing his first drink. He offers the bottle to the The Duke and The Dolphin.

"Nah, only drink seagull milk… you drink up… since before we go, you must walk the plank," The

Duke orders like a tyrant. "You're guilty of… of treason."

"Treason?"

"Treason."

"Against who?"

"Mankind."

"OK… I've done worse," the drunken rich man says.

The Dolphin pulls a red bandana from inside the rubber suit and wraps the man's aggressive eyes. The fake fish in sneakers walks the man, now stumbling and giggling, toward the bow.

The Duke hustles below beck. He targets the bathroom. Using the cutlass clenched in his mouth, he flips open the lid of an over-sized red metallic cooler on the toilet seat, nudged securely against the walls by two orange life jackets. With both arms, he pulls hard from the packed ice, then soft and then hard again. With his baggy, long-sleeve white shirt with the thick collar, he covers a small metallic-gray cooler. He uses the untied cloud-colored string to knot around the cooler.

The rich man slowly maneuvers on the bow and tiptoes over to the precipice of the pulpit. He looks up and takes a step into the night air, plunging into the black water of the bay.

With his vest flapping, The Duke lunges into the

raft. Reaching back, he grabs the disguised metal cooler off the boat's stern deck.

"I needed a bath anyway," the rich man yells. He clumsily climbs the rope ladder back on board of his cooler-less blood red yacht.

Paddling with sudden urgency, The Duke huffs a gasp of air, as if the breath is his first, between the enclosed handled knife still clenched between his teeth. The Dolphin flaps its blue-gray tail farewell.

"Ahoy matey," The Duke sings with fake friendliness while paddling away into the water's darkness and the unknown night. The Dolphin curls up, lying on the raft… over the shirt-covered, small-sized red metallic cooler.

From my perch, there is always a dawn somewhere.

Below, in the stormy morning, a TV blinks on a commercial fishing boat - its outriggers tucked straight up while docked by the sloping bend towards the midpoint of the Cape May Canal. First a quick burst of a black screen. Then rapid blinks on the TV.

A frayed cable stretches from the back of the small flat screen mounted on the captain's chair. The wire, with splats of sea gull scat, loops below to the main deck and then across to the boat in the next slip.

The middle section of the cable dips into the dark green bay water.

The TV only can be seen as a reflection looking down through the boat's windshield, like a mirror, off the clear plastic rain cover draped from above and behind the captain's chair.

The TV flashes faster. An episode of Modern Family crackles on the screen like machine gun fire.

A hard cover black book, The Ramayana, cocks half open on the captain's chair seat, resting on top of a frayed paperback, Kurt Vonnegut's Tomorrow and Tomorrow and Tomorrow. Chunks of pages from The Ramayana flap in the circular wind, telegraphing the impending storm like a sloppy basketball player staring at his wingman on a 2-on-1 fast break.

A good number of pages have been torn out, probably to wrap bait. The gaps leave pages space to flap without consequence in the wind, as if not caring which way to blow.

Ominously ashen clouds hover above this bobbing fishing boat. The American Skyper episode continues to blink on the TV. A page of the Hindu Sanskrit book tears away and another piece of The Ramayana floats stiff against the wind before drifting placidly in the canal water.

A news flash interrupts the blinking of Modern

Family… msirorret… gnitoohs... notselrahC… leunammE… nacirfA... tsidohteM… lapocsipE… hcruhC… nalyD… fooR… msirorret… etihw… ycamerpus… msirorret… rolls on the bottom banner.

Huh?

Could the news be real? Could this still be happening in 2015?

Looking at the reflection doesn't make it real, does it? Being dead doesn't mean I still don't feel, does it?

The boat rocks. The wind whips the fishing vessel like a whip. The captain's chair spins opposite of bouncing bow. The TV - with Modern Family on the screen - blinks like Morse code. The storm surge pops the screen around and straight up.

The blinking crawl scroll on the bottom of the screen reads:

> terrorism… shooting… Charleston… Emmanuel… African… Methodist… Episcopal… Church… Dylan… Roof… terrorism… white… supremacy… terrorism…

Further down the canal, at the western end where the tide pulls stronger into the Delaware Bay, the concrete Sunken Ship keeps sinking.

But my mind drifts back up the canal. No. Life

couldn't have changed this much since I've been gone. Could it have? A shooting in church can't be real. The reflection was real, just jumbled letters flashing on a TV with a pirate hookup.

The morning will bring the light and the truth.

But a new day here in Cape May won't bring back the concrete SS Atlantus, which is spelled only a bit differently than Atlantis, the fictional island that pissed off the ancient Greek gods and rests on the bottom of the Atlantic Ocean.

The water surrounding the fishing boat below is unusually dark. And still. The stern, already rigged with fishing rods, is swamped by low, disappointing clouds. The gray damp clouds just sing of rain, taunting you to reach out and squeeze the sorrow out of them like the ones you once loved.

The wind is loud. Whipping. Relentless. Wicked. A fisherman could pick his own word telling him not to go out. Wind like this threatens to rip one's judgment as easily as the screaming seams on the flapping sails make the harbor here ring of harm.

The lanky Byrd - at least the name I called him when he was skinnier - screams louder than the wind - he flaps back and forth, too.

The once fearfully quiet boy, who was afraid to say the wrong word at the courts two summers ago, after he just graduated high school, now screams while whipping rubber straps and thick ropes around the open deck. The cords, only moments before, were neatly tucked in organized rows inside orderly compartments. How everything changes in a moment. Just like the direction of this whirling wind.

Dressed in yellow rain bottoms, his shoulder straps snug his muscular upper torso, pinching his soaking wet Los Angeles Clippers powder blue jersey. The No. 32, of his favorite player, I do remember, Blake Griffin, clings to his chest like the fresh paint in the lane at the Avalon courts last summer. He turns his Yankees baseball hat frontwards with a swift flip, ruffling his regrown dreds.

"Je-ter… Der-ek… Je-ter," he hushes in a whisper voice, jumping up on a side compartment where the straps once were wrapped, taking practice swings as if he is holding a baseball bat.

"We should go to a game this summer," he says, poking his head into the open hatch leading down below. "This summer, we should go to a game. This is the Captain's last season. "

He swings the fake bat.

"We can get to Yankee Stadium in two hours from here, just straight up the Garden State Parkway. We could take the ferry to Staten Island, the one my dad takes to Wall Street. Then just a jump, stop, and hop on the subway to the D-train. A breeze."

Nothing is a breeze, I want to yell down and tell him. But he should know this already. Life is more like the winds are now. Shifting on you in an instant like a friend you made on vacation. Living right is choppy at best.

"Maybe my dear captain will let us take the boat up the East River into the Bronx?" he declares more than asking a question. "Or we can dock at the Intrepid and hop the D-train to Theeee Stadium to see Theeee Yankees win. We gots to go bro."

With his oversized hands, he pulls down on both sides of the soggy hat bill No doubt to try and keep some of the rain out of his intense eyes, which are already squinted mostly shut, but probably more so to make him look a bit like Derek Jeter. They do both have the same skin color. And both are athletes. Both are 6-foot-2 or so. The Yankees shortstop packs a bit more muscle and money. The Yankee Captain went right to the minors, so he isn't a college washout either like my man without a plan down there …

I wish I could help. I wish now I were standing on deck, watching him sway back on top of the compartment with the cords, acting like he is stepping out of the batter's box, pretending he isn't on a boat up the canal a bit from the bay.

He whips off the hat and with the same arm he wipes his eyes, using the wet, long-sleeved t-shirt under the Griffin jersey and draped on his forearms. Yeah, he wipes his eyes the way Jeter does.

He isn't trying to keep dry his matted dreads – or is it dreds? He is officially a wet head like I used to be playing ball at the courts on weekend mornings for all those years. I know him well enough to know he doesn't dig the look.

I don't know if he likes his new life now. But who really does? Well, besides Jeter? Really, who truly loves their life besides the Yankees captain? That's why it is called life.

Well, my man's new life, and Andie, my girl's new story beats on, unfolding here in cozy Cape May on this cruddy boat. They are both 20-year-olds now… or are they 21? I've been gone almost two summers. For a summer, we did everything together.

They changed.

They don't say foo-king, as far as I can tell.

He stands on the top deck of this fishing - more wishing if you ask me - boat docked at this private pier snugged where the canal curves in this southernmost Jersey vacation town. The canal, dug by the Army Corps of Engineers during World War

II for an escape route in case German U-boats invaded the bay, splits Cape May in two, just like the geographically divided state New Jersey.

Cape May is only a half hour drive from the Sea Isle bars and the Avalon Courts, but a lifetime for me away.

The kids even go by new names now. Or nicknames. They must want to go back to Go.

Byrd is now Choker. Andie is now Cresty.

Yeah, starting anew must be their grand plan. Some cross the mighty ocean to start new lives, some stay and just change, while some folks just change friends for a fresh forward in life. Maybe the lads will cross the bay to Delaware someday to start again. Perhaps Byrd, err Choker, and Andie, oops Cresty, will indeed cross the bridge.

I hope, if they learned anything from me, that they have faith in the cross.

We all need plans in life. We all need to follow our own personal legend, like young Santiago did in the Alchemist. I wish I were young like Santiago. But I had my shot to see the pyramids. I had my shot to build my own personal pyramid like Imhotep. And really, a shot is all you can ask from life.

However, like in basketball, the shot doesn't always go in. Sometimes the shot doesn't even hit rim. Sometimes the shot is blocked.

I'm hoping the shot Byrd and Andie now are taking at least draws iron, hits rim.

Until then, I will do my best to call them by their wishes, to refer to them Choker and Cresty as I tell their next chapter in their new story.

While chucking a knotted rope from the deck against the cabin door... Choker... mutters something about something. Sounds like he doesn't know what to do. He continues his reckless slamming of compartment lids and hatches. He opens one and then shuts the top of another without the hatch every opening. Not masking his confusion, he grimaces up to the ghost-gray skies.

The fishing lines stringing up the outrigger poles bang in the wind, snapping like an angry whip. The red flag clanks on the rooftop pole above the white tower building, a shack really, overlooking the boats.

My man should see the flag isn't green, or even yellow. Red is red.

Like the blinking TV, only a staccato of his ranting can be even heard. The wind roars louder when he stops slamming the hatches and lids of the oversized coolers onboard, the giant hopeful ones to hold large fish, as if telling him to stay in the safety of this harbor.

He tries to open one hatch, but the white top is stuck. Or his wet hands are just too wet to hold the handle.

He grunts up at the swirling clouds. The wind kicks up more. A white lid flies open. A clear plastic bag used to pack the fish filets disappears into the angry air. Another bag sails back into Choker's pale face. Well, pale for a black guy, or half black guy.

"You soo-ck," he yells to the clouds. The bag wrapped around his mouth doesn't muffle his anger.

Choker peels off the wet bag, revealing a scowl not seen by me the first time we met around two Memorial Day weekends back. That was a life ago for me.

He gives the double-fisted middle finger to the skies. He stands right there in the middle of chaos pointing both arms up with both fingers extended in the air for a good minute.

The rains fall harder. There is no letting up. Nature knows when to push, when to pull. She is pushing now.

A splat of rain bounces off his cheek. He tucks his chin. He doesn't look up any longer. He reaches down and tosses a black hose over the port side. He throws fishing gear out of one compartment. He throws himself around the boat more.

Byr... Choker finds the manual bilge pump. He sets the rusted hunk of metal up to the hose. I wish I was there to tell him to just pull out the plugs of the scuppers on deck so the trapped rain water would just flow from the holes on the side of the boat into the salt water. I used to tell him everything… until I took the dark dive.

Madly, he starts pumping, using his thin, but much more muscular arms than when he showed up at the courts the first time right out of high school.

The rainwater on the deck deepens even with his mad pumping. His rising madness scares a lone sea gull off a pier post. The disturbed bird flaps into the untamed wind. He knocks his Yankee hat off into a good two inches of water trapped topside. His matted hair drips like a soaked sponge. The drops splash, rather bounce off his tense jaw.

"This blows big foo-kin time," he barks at the flapping bird going nowhere.

The cabin door below deck crashes open. Then slams shut. It opens and shuts again. The wooden door blows open again. A hand pushes up.

With another shove, the door stays opened. A yellow rain slicker sails out. The flying jacket pins up against Choker. He slips around the deck like a cartoon character.

He falls. He laughs. How life can change in a moment.

"Ahhhhh, what a beautiful soo-king, foo-kin day," Byr… Choker yells.

My girl, Andie, ahh Cresty, jumps up from below deck. She is wearing my old No. 24 jersey, cutoff to show her firm, taut side delts and clinging to her lean mid thighs. Her backwards baseball cap hides her lovely red hair like her thoughts these days without me.

"The weather is a bit much, and so were you last night, enjoy this beautiful foo-kin day, hey, hey, hey," he says splashing in the rainwater. "Hey where is the cooler of beer you said you stole?"

"You are just searching or holding on," she spits, "or both bro."

"Bony a bit," Choker says spitting rain water, "but beautiful and at least you don't have scabs all over your ankles from basketball anymore."

Cresty straightens up, tossing the hat below deck while slipping on a surfing wet suit top over the No. 24 jersey. She slides her bare, tanned feet - without scabs from taping her ankles to play basketball - into a surfer's stance, pointed toward Choker on the deck.

Her tangled long hair, naturally red, dangles in the wind, exposing its mid-back length. Her sunburned nose is ready to peel. She is beautiful. She is a beauty in her own way.

She is my beauty.

But I guess all dads say the same about their girls, especially when they are gone. And I'm good and gone. Not across the bay either. Gone like a sunken ship.

Bending low at the knees, she jumps on Choker's back. Her gray knee-length gym shorts jack up to her hair on her back.

"Lay down on deck as if you are a surf board," she says kicking him in the ankle, splashing water in his eyes.

"The sun should've been out for an hour now," he says rubbing his eyes.

"Yeahhhh, what a beautiful surfing day," she sings with a laugh.

Cresty hops from his back to the top of a cooler while staying in the surfer stance. She bounces onto another cooler without breaking the pose. She holds the stance as if she is riding waves. She looks, sounds happy.

Not amused, Choker pushes himself to his knees. He doesn't look up. He grabs the handle of the pump. He churns like a locomotive's wheels with his arms, pumping and pumping and pumping. He pumps possessed.

"Choker, you didn't pump that hard, last night." Cresty says laughing while still posing. "Choker not Poker, I hope you choke out your opponent harder."

"I'm not thinking about judo now," he says between huffs. "I'm thinking, I never know if I should go out on these wet days. I mean I know I got to make some squid if I'm going to go back and pay for college. You know, catch no foo-kin fish means no foo-kin cash to pay tuition. You know my parents are done with me for dropping out."

"At least you still have a dad... and a mom who is around and not an ocean away."

They hug, a long loving one, the one when you really care about someone, not the hug at the end of night drinking at the bar, or after a quick session on the beach with someone.

Choker playfully pushes Cresty with one hand. She hops onto her left leg and resumes her one-legged surfing pose. Choker paces in half circles around the deck. He squints with one at the skies.

"No wonder you can't decide if you should go back to college or not, you can't even decide if you should work or not today," Cresty says, adjusting her shorts. "Just make a choice. It ain't that difficult, Chokey, baby."

Choker squeezes his eyes tighter toward the skies. He doesn't squint, but he squeezes both his eyes. He is an odd sort. I love him like a son.

He kicks the ice chest - the one Cresty mounts like a surfboard. She jumps up on the side rail of the boat. She lands still in her pose. The wind whips up sideways from the bay. The rain whittles to a drizzle.

"God, man, why can't it just rain or just stop," Choker says, looking upwards again. "How am I supposed to know what to do? Big boss man, Mr. Hallward, doesn't tell me, he lets me decide, but I know nothing, like I knew nothing about basketball until… where are you Pete?"

I hear this. I could cry. I could drop more tears now than all of my life, more than this rain drenching…

Andi… Cresty pounds her chest twice and points to the sky.

"He should just tell me about fishing like your dad taught me about basketball," Choker whispers. "But Mr. Hallward just says, 'you make the call.' That's foo-kin it. The skies are gray. It looks like rain. I don't know what to do... I hate not knowing... I hate not being told what to do."

Back on the boat rail, Cresty drops into a deeper tuck pose. She leaps onto the deck. Splash. She is in deep.

There is another splash when the water hits the decking sides. The splash hits one side before the other. With a swift reach, she swoops up his drenched hat floating on the deck, wrings it out, puts it on Choker's head. She spins the hat backwards.

"Hey, surfer girl, can't be no surprises, at least," Choker says. "I love you and all and wish there could be surprises, but you know we are not ready…"

Smiling, Cresty hooks her hands around his shoulders.

"You say, ask s-surprises? Sadly no. You know, just the way it is... looks like it will rain all day..."

"It's a beautiful day yeah, yeah, yeah," she screams like the great Bono himself before adding, "In Cape May, a beautiful day means the best waves where the bay meets the ocean at Devil's Reach."

Choker grabs her wrists, both of them, kisses her forward while swinging her arms over her head.

"I mean any surprises with you... not the weather or the waves… you know, we've never ever, ever never talked about…"

"Oh, you mean about last night? Or was it this morning? Or both?" she says half smiling. "You know my plumbing has too many parts, or not the right bits."

Gently, with ease, Choker pins her arms behind her back. He head-butts her lightly. Lovingly, like.

"Rock on."

"No Rochambeau," Cresty says.

"Ro show what?" he asks. "I know I've heard you, and Pete, say Ro-shoo-boo before, but I forget. I forget so much from, from the summer before last... when we first met. When we connected on those beautiful basketball courts."

Cresty juts out her hand, making a solid fist.

"Rock."

Then, she makes two fingers into a 'V' and closes them like scissors.

"Scissors," she says.

She holds her hand flat out.

"Paper."

She slaps the top of his head, knocking off his droopy hat.

"You know, Rochambeau. Like rock, scissors, paper. You know, Rochambeau - the luck of the draw," she says.

"Ro-shoo-boo, huh?"

Choker snatches up his hat, smacking her lightly over the head. Cresty takes off her wet suit top. Her arms are still strong, her shoulders still square.

I worried she got soft like paper in Rochambeau with her new life. I worried she was no longer a rock like in her old one, her old life.

She changed her name but not her body. Not the body I gave her, just the name. Names don't matter anyway. They come and go like friends, loved ones and bartenders.

"I wish we would be lucky then," he says, turning away.

Cresty lunges at him. Her No. 24 jersey rolls up high towards her ribs. She bites his chin a little bit. She bites lovingly.

"What's that mean, Poker?" she says. She is not smiling anymore.

Choker tightens his grip on her shoulders, moving his hands down to her bare belly, squeezing and smiling somewhat.

"Well, I wish we could get lucky, but not now, you know," he says squeezing her tighter, then letting Cresty go as if he didn't know her.

"We could name the baby Petey, or Petie, works for both a girl and boy."

"But if you did get lucky now, then we'll take care of it, you know?" he says, faking a punch to her belly, then hugging her tight again. "We just aren't ready…"

Cresty knees him in the groin. Just like Andie would've had done. Kneed Choker hard enough for him to let go. She hops back on the ice cooler. She slides a bit on the wet top. She jumps back in her surfing pose.

"First, you can't decide whether to go fishing or not because it looks like rain, but you can make that decision just like that without even... without even foo-king thinking… you didn't even think about it, dopey.

"Second, you know I don't have all the right parts in the right places to bake the bread. So, stop."

He jumps up on the cooler with her, bumping her a bit. Choker makes a mock surfing pose.

"Sorry, I know," he says, "I know I don't have to worry about it, Crest."

"But if I did, there is nothing gray about it. These skies, they are gray. You got to think what to do, if you got to go out and fish. You can get all foo-ked up if you make the wrong call. About that... you know, you don't even have to think about that, not at our age."

"And we aren't really Catholic anymore…"

Choker jumps down, punctuating his declaration like a judge swinging a fateful gavel with his arm smacking the top of the ice cooler. Water sprays in their faces.

"I wish we did have to think about it," she says. "Why can't I be foo-kin normal? Why did God have to foo-k me up?"

He climbs the ladder to the upper deck, brushes the water off the captain's seat with his hat while sitting in the same motion. He turns the key. Nothing. Turns again. A sputter. He turns it again. The engine sputters again.

Cresty looks up to the sky. She looks mad. Actually, she looks pissed. She is mad and pissed for the first time in a while. She doesn't show much of anything either way anymore.

"Maybe, the Big Man doesn't want you to go out," she says. "He might be saving your life. Maybe my dad is looking after you, too…"

"Anyway, it will clear up. I know it. If not, we'll surf."

"I can't swim, not in water anyway," he says lowering his voice. "My *sea*-men can swim but they got nowhere to go, bro."

Choker slumps his head on the steering wheel. He spins the wheel, rocking his head.

"All I know is my boss, he wants me to fish, but he doesn't want me ripping out in a storm," he says loudly while spinning the wheel with his head. "Life is like roulette, I guess. I can't win, I guess. My life soo-cks sea gull shee-et."

"Bay gull, remember?" she says, rising out of her surfer pose on the deck. "No such bird as seagull. We should grub. We should eat bagels at the ferry launch until you hear from the Boss."

Cresty climbs up the ladder as Choker slumps in the captain's chair with the TV still blinking fuzz. She whacks his head again, knocking his hat off onto the steering wheel.

"You soo-ck, you know. I'm not talking about your boss... God, man. Maybe God Himself doesn't want you going out.

"And maybe Pete doesn't either. He is up there losing it, laughing, making the rain mess you up like he used to play with your head at the courts, making you air ball shots without any wind even."

"I miss your dad, you know how much, please don't say his name," he pleads, making me feel damn guilty. "And, you say God? He's been out my whole life lately. Every time I needed God, he is a no show. What is up with His plan?

"Foo-k where was He when your Dad needed him?"

Cresty spins the steering wheel. When the wheel stops she spins it again. The hat falls on her feet.

"And foo-kin please don't be talking that God being good and all the spiritual stuff around me. I ain't your surfing buddies all high, going dipping, coming up from the water like they met the Man Himself, like they know the meaning of everything, like they know all.

"Pete knew it all and he's gone. What does it all matter any foo-kin how? Each day is just a spin of the wheel without anyone steering the ship."

Putting her hands on her lips, covering them like she swallowed the devil, she jumps down to the lower deck. She reaches with both arms like making a quick bounce pass and takes off the engine cover hatch. She pours a squirt of gas from a tank next to the engine into her cupped hand. She splashes the gas into the top of the engine.

"Better not blow this boat up," Choker says.

Cresty bounces up the ladder like hustling back on defense. She reaches around Choker. Moves the throttle stick straight up. Turns the key.

The engine roars.

So, does Cresty. She roars with sudden laugher. Good to see she takes control. Good to see she isn't sinking still.

"A little gas into the carb starts it right up, especially an Evinrude. You can't do that to a Mercury engine, it could start a fire. But, Evinrude engines you can. The E's need less air mixture and so make a lot less fumes. Remember that, judo boy. You might want to know when you start your own fishing business since it isn't looking like you'll get back into college.

"You would be great at feeding fish for a living anyway."

"Foo-k," he stretches out. "I want to find fish, like Pete did with me, like Pete found me."

Chapter 2

The Emerald Canal Marina nudges in the lone bend of the blue-green water on the strait from the ocean to the bay. All 12 slips are filled with rigged up fishing boats. The only life above the greenish water is Choker and Cresty. Not even the sea gulls – well bay gulls here by the bay - are stirring.

For the last 24 minutes or so, Choker has been reading Kurt Vonnegut's Tomorrow and Tomorrow and Tomorrow. He looks at the skies with every page turn.

"You know if no one ever died, there wouldn't be enough fish to feed everyone," he says, looking up to the low clouds… or to me.

The dozen fishing boats here are smaller, not nearly as large as the hundred or so commercial vessels up the canal in the harbor to the east. The big boats are docked at the other port alongside the only causeway into downtown, tied up under the trendy Lobster Shack restaurant sign.

The view down the canal and across the water is always grander than the shore you stand upon. The promising life beyond invites even more if you must look down a long, dark, unknowing canal.

Seeing the water open into the blue-gray bay excites those who feel in need of a new beginning. The opinion of what is best does depend on the view.

There are no laws to say you can't dream of a better life on the other side.

Especially in this early morning haze under soft sprinkling skies. Specifically, when life is indeed gray.

Choker looks like he is going to puke - like he did the first day at the courts.

"Bait or fate?"

"Huh?" Cresty asks.

"I mean some college gots to take me, I'm reading thinking-man books like Pete did before he took the big trip up yonder," he yells with his head down, looking in a compartment. "You are the one who should start the fishing business since you know so much about engines."

"No fookin way, too many haunts down here, this is really the Devil's Reach. I'm out of here, maybe a Florida college where the waters are warm for surfing."

"Maybe, just maybe I will take up free diving."

"Let's just go out... out," he agonizes. "We got the engine started, or you did."

"Right on. Fish on. The clouds will clear up, go away."

The sky smiles on them. The sun sneaks out of a crack in the clouds like a mom peeking in the bedroom door for one last goodnight glimpse of her sleeping infant.

The engine idles. The small marina parking lot above the wooden steps on a hill where the canal angles like a hockey stick at the end of Bayshore Road suddenly fills up with pick-up trucks and jeeps. Fishermen arrive on cue, as if a siren went off in town screaming it is all clear for bathers to go back in the ocean - the shark fin is gone.

Byrd and Andie – Choker and Cresty - are down here at Exit 0 of the Jersey Parkway. There is just one way to ride – up. They can't go south anymore.

This small port, or marina, was named Riverdell back when I was their age and came down here to drink, to see the sunset and think about going into town and meet the artsy mom types. I was feeling artsy one night, painting the marina sign, making the 'r' in Riverdell into a 'n" using a can of white boat paint left on the deck of a small boat named "The Hobbit."

I thought it was funny, you know clever, changing the name. Anyway, all these years later, someone changed the name of the marina entirely. The canal seems wider, too.

The fishermen enjoy a better sightline down the canal now. The end opens into a splendid view of the beautiful bay, perhaps with hopes to match. I hope contentment finds them, just contentment for Choker and Cresty with their new names and lives.

I feel I taught Andie and Byrdie, you know Cresty and Choker now, to "buy the ticket, to take the ride" as the visionary Hunter S. Thompson preached… now I don't think "the ride" is the path.

If you don't know me, well that's OK because I'm gone. I wasn't important enough to know. I was just a guy who played too much basketball for a 50-year-old, drank too much beer for any age and had too many friends, but not enough who I made feel close.

The older I got the wider the gap between close friends became. Like the canal here, I guess.

My prayer, my hope is my daughter and her friend, I guess boyfriend now, don't turn out like me...

First, I'll see if they will take the ride on the boat...

The fishing boat, the one with the butterfly painted on the side instead of a name, shakes in the water with its motor running. Choker and Cresty lounge, idle on deck. The brief showing of the sun vanishes.

A man in his mid-50's - around the same as age as I was before splitting from the race to the tomb - hustles down the steep steps and onto the uneven pier. His tan face says he spends more time than he should outdoors. His mostly salt and some pepper beard and wire rimmed glasses forecast him as smart, or he smartly wants to look that way. He wears a good look that doesn't match his boiling temperament.

"Stop."

The wavy letters A-L-I are inscribed in black ink on his yellow rain hooded jacket. The slicker is unzipped, revealing a wool sweater and a man in a hurry. He sports blue jeans and untied boots.

"What the hell are you doing?" the head-bobbing man, a few yards from the boat, yells at them.

"Gramps," Choker mutters.

Choker must pretend he can't hear the raging, angry man. He grabs the bilge pump and hose. He scurries below deck. Cresty leans over the side of the boat, smiling like this is the first hour of the first day of her new life.

"Choker is below," she says. "He is discussing with himself whether to fly like the butterfly on the side of the boat... your boat I presume, Sir? Or is it Bir? I see the letters ALI on your slicker."

Stitched inside the black and yellow butterfly are the wavy ALI letters, matching the man's jacket.

"Butterflies, the Monarch here in Cape May, don't decide whether to fly," the man says. "Their migration is programmed internally. Like clockwork. The annual late summer into autumn flight to Mexico isn't guesswork for the Monarch Butterfly.

"The Greatest. Muhammad Ali didn't decide to 'float like a butterfly and sting like a bee." Ali just did it. He was born that way."

"Neat, Choker should hear this," Cresty says with an arch in her neck.

She flaps her arms effortlessly. Her hands float out of the No. 24 jersey.

"He shouldn't be going out," the slumping man says while tying his boots. "Who are you? No baby dolls are allowed on the boat. This is a working fishing vessel. Turn off my engine."

Cresty cuts the engine. The tall man stands up straight next to the boat.

"He thinks thinking, like stretching out common sense, in the morning is work," he says.

She hesitates before reaching out her hand. She says, "Hi. I'm just a friend of Choke's."

"I thought he only liked... himself," he says with half a smile. "All he talks about is playing basketball in the good old days."

"We went to school together, we just took a year off from college, maybe more."

"Go back to college and major in pre-law," the man says, stroking the label with ALI inside a butterfly illuminating his rain jacket cracks. "Maybe after a few years you can get your boy here out of jail."

"Call me Cresty," she says shaking his hand.

"Call me Ishmael," he says with another half-smile.

"You are *clever-Ish*," she smiles. "What is the 'Ali' for then?"

"The Greatest."

Choker pops up from below, wearing rubber black boats up to his knees and yellow pants up to his chest showing the top of his Clippers jersey. A black raincoat with a yellow "B' clings over one arm.

"Morning Mr. Hallward."

"Who would wear a Clippers jersey?" Mr. Hallward says. "If I was still in law enforcement, I'd lock you up."

Choker shrugs. He adjusts the jersey under the straps of the pants.

"Didn't you hear what the owner, Donald Sterling just said, well about how he doesn't want his girlfriend to bring black guys to the games?"

Choker double shrugs, clearly showing he doesn't care.

"Who would support him?"

"What happened to the engine?" Choker asks, turning up his palms, walking to the back… the stern of the boat.

He stops when seeing Mr. Hallward staring at him with piercing eyes behind his specs dotted with raindrops.

"My Clippers jersey was cleansed by the sand."

Mr. Hallward looks interested in Choker. No, not interested. Maybe the look is confusion.

"Choke, you know I like you," he says in a sympathetic tone. "I told your mom and dad I'd help you out, you know that, but you're in some deep seas now. The sun is coming out but you can't go out. There are storms circling all around, from Delaware Bay to the Chesapeake Bay. The weather isn't moving off the coast.

"I'd thought it would stop raining, so I'm getting ready to go. Last week, when I didn't go out on a day, even grayer than this, man, you ripped me a new can."

"A different day. This is a different weather pattern. You need to know the difference. Life isn't just about working hard. Living well means living smart."

"Well I just heard you ranting about butterflies. They fly in bad weather south to Mexico, right? Or else they would never get there, right?

"They don't all make it to Central America. In fact, many don't. None of them return until their third or fourth generation anyway. Why are we talking butterflies?

"Are you going through a metamorphosis?"

"I read Kafka's book," Choker said.

"Really, you read Franz Kafka's Metamorphosis? It is considered one of the seminal works of the 20th century, well for fiction."

"I only read half of it, I never finished, it was my second semester," Choker says chuckling while looking down. "Why bring semen into this?"

"Yeah," Cresty says. "My dad loved to talk about Kafka. How he always wanted to visit his grave in Prague when he lived in Turkey. He also said the former Northwestern quarterback was named Kafka and he bet on the Wildcats to cover the spread against Penn State his junior year, but Kafka was knocked out of the game. He said he should've known since Kafka, the writer, never finished his novels."

Mr. Hallward wipes his glasses, spitting on each lens.

"Actually, he burned ninety percent of his writings and yes, he didn't finish the rest," he says. "But he left us with some introspective words, like: 'man cannot live without a permanent trust in something indestructible within himself, though both that indestructible something and his own trust in it may remain permanently concealed by him.'

"But we can't be talking butterflies and Kafka, not now. I can't let you self-destruct."

Plopping on board, Mr. Hallward slips on the wet deck. Choker reaches to help. The well-read man bangs his hip against the side of the boat.

"You know a lot," Choker says.

"I went to Michigan," he says, "back when they ran the football… and won games."

He grabs the black raincoat out of Choker's arm. He nudges over closer toward Choker, almost like he is going to give him a man-hug.

"Where's the yellow top? Forget it... you speared another dolphin, didn't you?"

"What? Who said?"

"Said? The Coast Guard said. My man there, we used to fly planes over this bay here as college kids in the summer to spot dolphins for the tour boats, called me late last night and said another one washed up on shore by the lighthouse. Punctured up good."

"You sure it wasn't a porpoise and it wasn't done on purpose?"

Cresty laughs, drawing a death stare from the man. Seeing her laugh is good, though.

"The only ones who hate the killing more than the environmentalist bird-watchers down here and the nude bathers at Higbees Beach when a dolphin washes up on the beaches is our Coast Guard."

"Don't mess with the law, my young man."

Choker opens his arms as if to say he has nothing to hide.

"All the tourist from Canada, who fill up the boardwalk, and the locals, who are forced to ride their bikes in the morning on the street, don't like taking their little kids to the beach and seeing dead Flippers."

Choker raises his arm above his tilted head and pulls like he is tightening a noose.

"Now it is true, Cape Mayers like the Canadian money, they like them spending their bacon in town with all the fancy French names like Marquis De Lafayette restaurant," Mr. Hallward continues, "but no one likes seeing the sea gulls dining on dead dolphins."

Choker posts this defiant look. He lowers his arm and lifts his chin like he is ready to fight.

"Their foo-kin fault."

"The Canadians?"

"The fish."

"How can you killing dolphins be their fault? And why do you swear and curse so much? Your words define you."

"No, having kids, they shouldn't have kids and they wouldn't be here riding their rental bikes on the boardwalk, getting in the town folk's way. Then they wouldn't see the poor dead dolphins either."

Cresty pounces off the boat. She lands soft without stumbling onto the dock.

"Damn, man… that's deep," she says, turning toward a wooden bench with its back painted in a bright white advertisement – "Dolphin Tour Boats in Cape May," but ingenious graffiti makes it read: "Gratefully Dead Dolphin Tour Boats."

"Kids these days can't even spell," Mr. Hallward says, pointing to the clever sign.

"The tours would be a big hit for all the Kafka quoting, depression delivering of your generation," Choker says.

Seemingly disgusted, Mr. Hallward stares at Choker, who stares back. He wasn't this defiant with me back at the courts.

The silence is good for all of them to heal, to calm down. The wind stops blowing. The still is good.

"Hell, it got caught in one of my nets. What else could I do? I didn't want to cut the net. Why lose a net over an animal?"

"That's bull. How could you harpoon a dolphin? Just because the fish lived free?"

"I'd thought it would scare the fish away. I need to catch fish. The dolphin eats the feeder fish meant to feed the strippers."

"You mean stripers? As in striped bass," Mr. Hallward says.

"Them too."

"Yeah, well, it doesn't matter," Mr. Hallward spits. "This isn't working out. Anyway, you're getting wrongly, misguided ready to take my boat out in a gale storm."

"Gale? *Sheeeeet*, skies are calming down," Choker protests.

"Calm before the storm, but it's more than the storm. The Coast Guard said they wouldn't investigate if I dumped you. My friend said he'd file a report saying a propeller chopped the dolphin... if I'd get rid of you. I have no choice. I'll call and tell your mom and dad something like... like you kept getting seasick."

"Will tell her, too, how at least you stopped cursing, and you don't seem as angry anymore. And to give you some more time to find yourself."

"Angry. I'm mad only at a world that cares more when a fish dies in the ocean than when a man dies in the same ocean."

Cresty's face freezes as rain runs down her cheeks.

Choker turns around slowly, like his dopey spin dribble at the courts, strips off the rain gear with a real methodical madness. He throws the pants overboard first. He does the same heave with the jacket. Then he tosses both boots. One misses the water like his jump shot missed at the courts. The boot crashes down below deck.

He follows the boot. His life is seemingly following the boot now.

Choker bounces back up on deck. He slings a black duffel bag with some Oriental letters written on the side over his shoulder.

"Later gator."

"Listen, you can still sleep on The Butterfly Boat until you find a place to stay," Mr. Hallward says. "But first you damn better get my rain gear out of the water."

"Out of luck, can't swim," Choker says with an annoyed stare. "You damn know black guys can't even do a lap in the baby pool. Not to worry, though, Cresty can dive to the bottom of the bay if needed and find them. You won't even have to pay for oxygen for her."

"Don't worry about the rain gear then. I know your parents, well I don't even know anything about them but their names, however when I met them they said you couldn't really afford to stay at my friend's bed and breakfast on Windsor Avenue anymore. So, sleep here, you can even bring back the old gals you catch at the Rusty Nail. You just can't catch fish on my boat. You can't take it out.

"Please, for your parents' sake, you can't self-destruct even if something inside is telling you to destroy yourself young man."

"The rain gear floats," exalts Choker. "I will get the stuff someday."

"Some days aren't always going to be here just like my boat won't always be here," the man says. "Might just follow the butterfly.

"Why didn't you name the boat, just The Boat?" Cresty asks.

"Or, I, well we, once knew a guy you could name the boat after. All the other boats have names here. Why are you being nice to me anyway? I just threw your gear in the canal."

"Names are forgotten, gear can be replaced," Mr. Hallward says. "Butterflies fly forever in kid's eyes and don't we all want to be kids again?"

"Yeah, I'd kill to be a kid again," snaps Choker. "Well not kill."

Mr. Hallward smiles his goofy half grin.

"You know butterflies sort of kill themselves," Mr. Hallward says.

"What?" Choker barks.

"How?" asks Cresty, stoking her belly in a circle.

"Well the Monarchs down here go through four stages of life to complete their metamorphosis."

"Four?" Choker asks.

"Like the Final Four," Cresty says smiling.

"No really, no basketball jokes," Choker says sternly. "Too sad, reminds me of Pete.

"What are the stages? I might be a butterfly."

"Butterflies go through laying eggs cycles on the milkweed plants down here, then the eggs hatch into the larva stage and into caterpillars," Mr. Hallward explains as Cresty and Choker move closer to him. "The caterpillars then hang upside down during the pupa stage before forming into the adult stage."

"I'm in the pupa stage, I guess," Choker says. "I feel like I'm hanging myself upside down."

Choker chucks the duffel on the dock. He strolls past Mr. Hallward's pointed finger.

"What's those Chinese letters mean on your gear bag? You going to China?"

"It's Japanese," Choker declares. He jumps off the boat.

"Tell me, why do you revere this Pete?" Mr. Hallward whispers loud enough for Cresty to hear. "What stage in life is he?"

Choker spins around, slaps both of his hands around Mr. Hallward's neck. He squeezes. Mr. Hallward can still breathe. Barely.

"Listen man, I could kill you now if I wanted. You be rotting like that dolphin."

Cresty splits in between them. She grabs Choker's arms. She yanks his trembling arms apart.

"No, no, no," she screams. "Let's just go."

She hip checks them both, making more space between the two.

"You're *fooking* angry because he'll never be Pete. You can't score a basket down the courts now even against kids shooting with their moms. You can't even score with a dolphin."

Without making an expression, his face still as stone, Choker drops his hands as fast as he lifted them. He hops to the side of Mr. Hallward. Cresty follows.

"I thought you were a good Catholic," Mr. Hallward screams. "Haven't you heard Jesus talk about the Good Shepherd? The Good Shepherd protects his flock. The Good Shepherd protects the ones who can't protect themselves. The Good Shepherd is the gate to God."

They walk away, stroll down the wooden pier towards the parking lot. Choker slams the chain-linked fence gate at the end of the dock.

"Now I know why they call you Choker," she says, sounding like her old brash self when they first met at the courts in Avalon, back when the courts were still the courts. "I thought the tag was for another reason."

Choker trips on a stray board, catching himself and leaning forward like he still can play ball… before slipping on the wet wood. He twists on his fall. He lands on his back.

As he fell, he tucked in his neck to his chest. He held his duffel bag high. Where did he learn how to fall so well?

"Good thing you know how to fall like a champion," Cresty smiles nice enough to hide her anger.

"Yeah, after 21 years on this foo-kin earth, falling is the only thing I know how to do all right."

Cresty reaches out with one hand to pull Choker up.

"That's because you get a lot of practice with that judo stuff. If you surfed with me, you would never fall. You wouldn't have to practice falling. Just diving off the board before the wave tosses you from heaven to earth."

Choker brushes her hand away, gently though.

"When you fall, just land on your back," he says standing up on his own and throwing his duffel over his shoulders again, "because if you can look up, you can get up."

"Let's get on up then."

"I'm up all right."

"You don't seem to mind that you just lost your job and place to stay? Well, we could still stay there, I guess…"

Cresty brushes the wet sand off his back.

"Did you really kill a dolphin? You didn't always hate animals, I remember in English comp class freshman year at Ursinus, you did your speech on nursing your pet rabbit as a kid. Now you should be called Croker… if you kill animals."

"Fish aren't animals," Choker says staring at her. He brings a strange look in his eyes.

"How did you remember the speech? Anyway, that was before... before Pete went."

Cresty reaches down to the white stones surrounding the wooden walk as if she sees something. She picks up a broken clamshell. She whispers into the shell and then throws the shell in the water below.

"The past is gone, like that shell… like Pete."

Chapter 3

I know.

I do know how looking across the bay here, where the land across the water can't be seen from the stabbing southern tip of New Jersey, how the captivating view pulls one's dreams. Even more on dark days than on the sunny Cape May mornings kissed with butterflies flying, friends caring and souls sleeping.

New Jersey is two words and two worlds. The state can divide the soles of your feet from your soul. The state itself is two states, like people in conflict with themselves.

The view from North Jersey favors New Yorkers while the view from South Jersey favors Philadelphians. That's just the way it is in a state needing two names.

In the middle is the capital, Trenton, a buffer perhaps with a golden state house dome where the view across the Delaware River is Pennsylvania, making the New Jersey state house the only one where another state can be seen.

Back here, the unseen land across the bay doesn't just look better from the South Jersey shore on this weekend before Memorial Day, all land across from any water always looks better.

The unknown view was better for Brendan the Navigator from Ireland's monastic southwest shore to where the land had no religion, to Columbus leaving the old world to find the New World and for Magellan abandoning luxury to globe-trot for trading routes.

Indeed, leaving for the unknown is always better because you can leave the hurt behind. If your ship sinks, so does the pain. But, like people, ships are built to sail.

Cortes burned the boats when the crazed-colonizing Conquistador landed in the New World. The Spaniard wasn't going back across the ocean. Not unlike a baby leaving the water of the womb, a sunken ship being raised or a broken friendship salvaged, there was no going back.

Will Byrd and Andie, I mean, Choker and Cresty, go back?

The skies are brighter, clearer. It's not gray any more. Will they go ahead?

"See I was right, it's not going to rain." she says.

"How did you know? Are you that mystic, the one Pete told the joke about how does a thermos know to keep cold drinks cold and hot drinks hot?"

"Haha, that was good, but no, Rochambeau," she says with a warming, soft smile.

"Really?"

“Yeah, that and from surfing.”

With her red hair flowing on one side and knotted in a ponytail on the left side, Cresty strikes the surfing pose again. Choker tries to make the pose, too, but stumbles like he did the first day on the courts while backpedaling on defense.

“I now know what to look for from that weather and tree guy, dude I told you about. Remember, the guy who has all those gadgets and machines and computers in his truck?”

After another attempt, Choker falls out of his pose.

“He prints out the weather forecast and then faxes it to all the surf and dive shops and food places on the beach and bay. He taught me to read the clouds. That's how come you didn't know it wasn't going to rain. You ain’t me.

“Seriously, bro, why did you agonize so long over the decision? You are washy like the weak undertow in Lewes, Delaware, where the pacifist Mennonites first settled to avoid persecution from the Catholics and Protestants… and to live a simple life without modern means.”

“I love when you sound like Pete, but I hate choices now. I just hate them. Everything should be like judo. No thinking, just reacting. You think, you miss your move or you are splattered on your back.

"And, I mean, what the fook is modern means?"

"Maybe… and what's up with the cussin again… you should train more for life and not judo. It doesn't look like bouncing around in your pajamas will get you back into school. So, so really what good is judo?"

"What good was being a pacifist for the Mennonites when they couldn't defend themselves against the Catholics… when they had no modern means?" questions Choker as he grabs Cresty by her lower arm and upper shoulder. "No means, no beans."

With a snatch, he picks her up. Holds her on his hip.

"See, no thinking, like when Pete was around making all the right choices for us. Just grab and react. Game, set, match over."

"Now what," she injects with disgust, "what are you my boss?"

With a sudden concern look, Choker puts her down gently.

"No, I'm no boss," he says. "Just remember me when I'm gone too."

"Unless I go first."

Tugging on her ponytail, Choker nods like he understands.

"Teach me the hold first," she says, brushing away his hand and unknotting the ponytail.

With a gentle glance of a second-grade teacher at a kid asking for help, Choker grabs her again.

"This is an ogoshi, one little torque and you would be falling like a blacked-out surfer hitting bottom," he says as if he is the judo founder, Kano, himself. "I hit him with a juji-jime, a front choke, anyone can learn."

"There are back chokes too, like the okureri-game, where the person will never see you while you are putting their lights out. You should learn to protect yourself from those leftover hippies at The Devil's Reach who you surf with now."

"Like Pete, I might not always be around."

"Me neither, like I said."

With his left heel, Choker kicks the gray stones in the parking lot. An arm's length apart, they trudge on the slippery slope to Cresty's motorcycle, an old green Triumph with a wobbly headlight. I know she wanted a new yellow Volkswagen bug convertible, but I'm glad she used some of the money I left her on something cool. And practical.

"Well, you better stop choking people and start thinking now. The only place we have to live is on the Butterfly Boat, if we choose. You don't have a job. I'd invite you to live with my mother in Turkey but she has paddled down river in life, too," Cresty says as she adjusts the headlight to point straight ahead.

Choker laughs as he slaps the round glass globe on the steering wheel, saying, "just messing."

"Mess with your FeFe," Cresty says as she kick-starts the motorcycle. Choker slings his bag back over his shoulder and sits behind her, sliding up against her on the wet seat.

"The bike is drier when it doesn't rain," Choker shrugs. "Still have any of Pete's money? You can buy a motorcycle with a canopy."

"Don't know they made bikes with canopies. Where to now?"

"Take me to East Cape May, to our dojo near the Coast Guard base… we can live there forever."

"No such fairyland… the only forever is the word."

"There are other guys who don't work, who sleep there," Choker continues, ignoring her while pressing up tighter against Cresty. "Doesn't matter to Master Uwrenski. A fresh body is always needed for the elite guys he is training. I'll fit right in."

"If you don't like it there why don't you go live at Devil's Reach on the beach with the old hippie surfers and divers."

"You would fit right in there," Cresty smiles. "They haven't bathed since the day you were born."

"Yeah, I would fit right in. They smell better than my judo mates."

"Then, then why don't I take you up to Richard Stockton College, talk to the coach, again," Cresty says. "Maybe, maybe he'll change his mind and give you that scholarship. After all, you beat the state 189-pound high school stud, the three-time state champ in the Open tourney. How, bro, can you not land a scholarship?"

"He won two straight at 189 pounds, and one at 172 as a sophomore. They don't give judo schollies anyway. They don't even give wrestling ones anymore."

"Let's try. Go. Do it bro. Do it for Pete. Show your pissed-off parents you can earn a schollie."

"Yeah, but Uwrenski talks to the Stockton coach all the time. He said I 'don't respect the sport.' To him, *respect* is all that counts, not winning. The coach thinks I just want to choke people out."

"Tell the coach you will change. Tell him you have that respect for the sport now after grinding on a fishing boat. Tell him that you have respect for your opponent. How you would never deliberately hurt anyone again. That happened after Pete…"

Cresty revs up the bike. The headlight shutters before dipping down as she spins out of the lot with the urgency she did sprinting back on defense at the courts. With one arm around her, Choker throws a stone toward the boats. He keeps a shell in the other hand around Cresty's waist.

"Hey, you could've hit someone with that rock," she barks over the rattling headlight against the handlebars. "Listen, you can use Mr. Hallward as a reference. He still likes you."

"Maybe. The dude is interesting like Pete," he says. "Who the foo-k else would quote Kafka?"

"Foo-k, we might need him," she agrees. "Or we will be eating milkweed like the butterflies. If we don't live on the boat, your lame ass will be chewing milkweed in Mirkwood."

"Mirkwood?"

"You know, Middle Earth," Cresty says as she throttles the gas. With her head bobbing, she elbows Choker's ribs. "To Mirkwood…"

Cresty lifts her feet and the thick-treaded tires jump. The Triumph soars past a sign with an arrow pointing east toward downtown Cape May. With her hair flowing, she speeds ahead of a mini-van on Sandman Boulevard, alongside the bottom half of the canal. The blue bay spreads in front of them. Without downshifting, the bike stops after passing the turn off to the left for the parking lot of the Cape May-Lewes ferry. Cars are backed up ready to go to the other side already. The bike stalls. She turns the key to off.

"Maybe, man, maybe we should just go to the other side, start over," she says, turning the key and kick starting the bike. "Maybe Mr. Hallward won't, won't take you back?"

"He knows when to let go, he let me go softly, that's all," Choker yells in her ear. "He is always trying to be nice to my m-m-m… her since my dad… left her. He doesn't even need help, the fishing money. He is cool. He says, 'you got to know when to let go' and that is what he is doing with a bit of a push."

Cresty elbows him. Choker puts the bag between them.

"And even though he is cool, he is going to tell Uwrenski he fired me because I kept killing dolphins for kicks. That would help a real lot for a schollie. I might as well go up to the Stockton coach and kick him in the nuts."

Cresty steers straight toward the dunes. She curls to the right, downshifting, slowing down on Lincoln Avenue when seeing a lady planting flowers in a wooden rowboat filled with dirt, rotting in the side yard. The blue house with pink trim faces, well, on an angle to the bay, as if with its arms open waiting for a lost fisherman, or sailor, or a daughter to come home from playing hoops all day with the boys at Aronimink Swim Club, back in Drexel Hill.

"The sun sets in her face," Cresty yells making the left into David Douglas Memorial Rotary Park. "The house is welcoming, like the face of a father."

The dunes, a bump to the right of us, block the view of the bay. The triple-decked white ferry building with a blue slanting roof rises beyond a spacious parking lot to the left. A smaller parking lot at the end of the park's entrance road opens up to welcome the bay.

Two pavilions with burnt red picnic benches face the end of the canal entrance. An old pavilion, a wooden one on the beach, interests no one. Two jetties with black boulders flank both sides of the canal.

Choker and Cresty wander toward the north jetty holding outstretched hands. Their arms stretch like a clothesline as they look down where one - must have been massive - rock is missing near the front side middle of the jetty. She leaps down into the hole, rather space where the rock is missing, and grabs a handful of sand.

She hops hack on top of the jetty and slides into a surfer's pose. She whirls the sand into the wind coming off the canal. Half of the sand blows back into her face, the other half into the water while Choker leans against a yellow SLOW NO WAKE sign.

Hopping from one rock to the next, they stop at the front end of the jetty where a sign explains how 'Officer Douglas died in the line of duty 1994.' The sign leans toward a decrepit concrete structure with four pillars of rusted steel lodged in the middle and frayed at the ends.

"The poor officer died the year we were born," Cresty hushes.

"Life, that's foo-kin life" Choker says as he straightens the sign pole.

A half of a basketball court away, two teenagers are making out in a car parked on the dirt embankment overlooking the canal.

"Kids," Choker says, letting go of the sign and tugging on Cresty's droopy hair.

With his feet wrapped around Cresty, the motorcycle and the rattling headlamp speed east past a railroad bridge over the canal that is swung open sideways, past Tranquility and Spun Avenues and south around a curve onto the Garden State Parkway, over the causeway bridge and into creeping traffic toward Cape May, where legend boasts Abe Lincoln once stayed. The loose headlight is pressed behind a SUV rack bent by the weight of four bicycles toward the beaches.

Tucked on the eastern-most ocean side of this picturesque vacation town, which ranks right behind San Francisco for the most Victorian style homes, is the United States Coast Guard Center.

Cresty bangs a left toward the nation's only Coast Guard recruit training facility. During prohibition, several cutters were stationed at the base to cut off rumrunners.

She then makes a right down a street with a NO OUTLET sign and swerves to the left of middle on a sandy road rimmed by high dune grass.

With the headlight swaying sideways, Cresty steers the Triumph on the winding path like she has been riding motorcycles all her life, but not even the rough Upper Darby dudes rode cycles where we lived in Drexel Hill, not with four-way stop signs on every corner.

She hooks a quick left onto the grassy field behind the old Coast Guard building with the sign: Uwrenski's Judo Club.

"How did you know about the bat cave entrance?" Choker asks, sliding his right leg over the seat. "Even the judo guys who drive drop me off at the main entrance to the base."

"Rochambeau."

"Sorry I asked," he says shaking her by the shoulders with both hands as she sits and adjusts the headlight, "you shouldn't go in the back. This is where we drink after workouts. No one is supposed to know about this path."

"I know," she says standing on one leg, "I almost ran over a bottle of old Captain Morgan's Rum."

"When?"

"Last week, after I took a job with that weather guy on the beach I told you about."

"Yeah, right that is how you knew it wouldn't rain today. And now you know about the good Captain Morgan's back here. Rum makes me dumb, that's our judo motto."

"Dumber for you."

"Dumbest."

"My friend will smarten you up, like Pete did. He is an arborist. He is looking for more business."

"A-a-a what? He starts foo-kin fires? He isn't going to burn down the damn dojo… I hope… judo is all I have besides you. I'll kill him."

"No, bro, an arborist."

"Oh, he kills babies before they are born. Do we need him? None of us are having babies anyway. Are we?"

Hunched, she peels off the bike. Cresty slams the kickstand to the sandy ground.

"No! An arborist. He takes care of dying trees, not dead babies. Maybe, baby bro, you shouldn't go to college, you don't know any words these days besides ogoshi and Uganda anyway."

"Ogoshi and Ukuri-ere-gami, Get them right. Uganda is a country somewhere in Central America where all those… those short people are coming from the middle of nowhere and taking over the grass cutting business here."

Choker plucks his duffel bag of the bike. He edges up to her with the bag between them and stand in back of the bike. They hug around the duffle.

"What are you doing with this tree terrorist anyway?" Choker blurts.

"I need to work this summer after not doing anything last summer. I can't be surfing all day while waiting to see if my dad's friend can get me in Princeton."

"Pete still lives."

With the bag falling between them, they hug tighter.

"With all those surfing freaks, how did you meet this King Freaky tree dude again?"

"He was standing on the roof of his truck while pruning a tree outside my gyno's office last week. He said he was down, down like good, on my Harvard crew T-shirt. We talked. He was real nice.

Real, real smart, well for a tree doc. He asked me what I was doing in the summer. I told him reading surfing magazines, Vonnegut and medical books to get ready for school. He must have thought I was serious about the medical books, so he said, 'so it goes' and offered me a job."

"He was trying to get into your surf suit, that's all."

"No, he is an old guy. He must be around 50. He does have a dolphin rubber suit and a pirate outfit."

"Creepy."

"Yeah, but he is harmless. Plus, he needs help. He couldn't get this spanking new chain saw started, so I told him to prime the carburetor with some gas. He did and the cranky saw started right up. His surprised face, well he looked like he never cut a tree in his life. His equipment is all shiny new and he has all that weather stuff in the cab of his truck… and he said to me 'we must be careful what we pretend to be."

"He's interesting, in a strange way."

"Like Pete?"

"No one is that madly, crazed fooking interesting… but he did steal a cooler from a boat wearing the pirate outfit and I was the dolphin."

Choker wades his way through the three-foot high bendy grass. He slices toward the back steps with wood grayed from the elements. Cresty rests on the bike – sideways. She balances and crosses her legs in a yoga pose.

"Why did you drive up here last week?" Choker asks while looking back with the seriousness as if he is questioning if all life is purely coincidental.

"We came looking for you. You said your fishing soo-ked. He asked me if I could find him more help. He said he, he was new to the area, but then told me, explained how he really isn't and just doesn't know people, or know people he can trust."

"Anyway, he told me he would come back here tomorrow to pick you up if you want to work with us. I told him you would cut with us if you didn't disappear up your own a-a-a… ego-hole."

"No way, Felipe. I ain't never cut anything but classes," he says shaking his dreds like helicopter blades.

"Not when you get back to school." Cresty says laughing, walking over to a yellow Volkswagen car parked near the ashen steps with the sunroof open.

"You can't be worse, bro, worse than him. You just won't ever know if you should cut any trees… if the skies are too gray… if only you were Derek Jeter."

"Je-ter, De-rek Je-ter," Choker howls while bouncing up the creaking steps.

Cresty spins her right leg over the bike and with the left one kick starts the engine. She revs the throttle. Choker looks back all the way up the steps.

"Don't ever look back," she hollers over the roar of the engine.

"That's what Mr. Hallward says," Choker hollers back at her.

Cresty peels away. At the end of the sandy path, she pauses and looks back. The rain starts.

"Maybe," she yells back at Choker, "my Rochambeau isn't working today."

"Maybe, maybe not until…" he screams back at her, "tomorrow and tomorrow and tomorrow."

Chapter 4

With a hard lean to her left, Cresty spins the revving motorcycle in a half circle. The parking lot stones, mixed with broken seashells and dried by the overnight muggy air, scatter into the bay, disturbing the greenish water.

This arborist man, Marion Francis, and Cresty climb on board a sailboat at the marina under the main bridge arching into town. He unhooks the dinghy on the stern and lowers the engineless boat into the shadow of the mast from the rising sun on the water. Brennan jumps on board, sliding on a tarp. Whimpering, the dog pulls the plastic cover half off. Holding his Aviator sunglasses with both hands, Marion plops on board and spreads the tarp back over the deflated aqua gray rubber raft and the blue gray rubber dolphin.

With his head steady, not allowing his double-bridged wired sunglasses to tilt, he rows across the canal toward the house with the swimming pool in the front yard. He ties the dinghy to the dock. Casually, with both arms, he bear-hugs the tarp wrapped around the raft and dolphin. He carries the goods to the pool house in the side yard and places the rubber toys in the back corner and tucks the tarp over them.

Inside the pool house, he sits and picks at his toenails. He peels the top of each toenail, trimming them with his thumb and forefinger. He cups the clippings in his right hand.

Marion fumbles untying the knot with his one hand balled up before biting a bulging piece of the rope and freeing the dinghy. A thick plank floats in the canal. He drops the toenail clippings into the bay and scoops the wood onboard.

In the parking lot, he helps Cresty wheel the motorcycle up the plank and into the back of his F-150 truck, tilting the steering wheel so the bike fits under the cap and between tools. Cresty slides into the front seat as Marion stares across the canal.

I wonder what he is thinking… why is he here?

Cape May is a peninsula stretching 20 miles out to sea where the Atlantic Ocean meets the Delaware Bay. The Pointe, at the peninsula tip in the south, points straight down, as my life did after not preventing…

What is Marion doing in this slow-poking, snoozing seashore town, which claims to be the nation's oldest seaside resort. Abraham Lincoln, Robert E. Lee and Ulysses Grant all stayed in Cape May, which is designated a National Landmark City, only one of five in the country. Marion Francis isn't Lincoln, Lee or Grant.

But being a National Landmark City means trees. Lots of leaves covering lives.

And lots of trees mean lots of money for an arborist where homeowners want to enjoy the birds, butterflies and beauty. Makes sense. Just like how Byrd and Andie replaced their names and their lives of beer, basketball and my bleakness with birds, butterflies and foo-kin beauty here at the bottom of New Jersey.

But now Cresty is with Marion, not me.

Under Aviator sunglasses, Marion squints as he makes a hard left onto Delaware Avenue, the first street in town closest to the harbor. He meticulously misses each patched pothole, swerving into the other lane at times to avoid a slight bump. He slows to a halt at each stop sign as he drives past blocks of identical drab green, yellow and gray two-story military houses on the Coast Guard Base.

At the access road to the base, where an imposing guardhouse stands in the middle of the entrance, Marion turns the truck around, hitting the curbs twice while backing up and inching forward. He swerves his way back down the block streets with the identical houses toward the ocean, weaving around the patched potholes as if they are land mines and slowing to stops at each intersection.

At the end of Delaware Avenue, he hops a curb making a left onto a street lined with mansions. At the cul-de-sac end is a chain spanning two posts, blocking access to a private street with a half-dozen even larger mansions. Straightening his sunglasses, he drives around the chain on the soft sand to the right. The two of them bounce down the street made of crushed seashells.

"The Grand Canyon has less crevices than this path," he says, pulling tight his brown John Deere baseball cap with a black bill. "Older, too, this road."

His age is hard to tell with his face draped by the hat and the droopy-lensed sunglasses. Marion must be in his late 50's, maybe early, as he shoulders already are hunched. Yeah, maybe he is closer to 50 than 60… like I was. For sure, though, he is closer to the end than the beginning.

The man is rail thin with a thick crop of brown, messy hair under the hat. He wears an immaculate clean white jump suit. The outfit doesn't match the hat or the man.

The pickup truck fails to match the man, too. Another white Ford F150. There are so many white Ford F150 trucks pulling boats and turning houses into duplexes down here, multiplying like seashells. A white cap splattered with sea gull scat covers the

8-foot bed. The truck looks more the part for a tree cutter than he does.

Hope Cresty knows what she is doing. There is no sense of me worrying. Fear, guilt and worrying got me gone.

They bounce in the truck over the shell path as Marion declares again how "the Grand Canyon has less holes." They pull into a back parking-lot. Or what looks like where cars park.

They probably can't even see the one-story building right in front of them since the sun is so bright and reflecting off the metal weather vane at the point of the roof. Although surely used at one time since the weather in Cape May changes from day-to-day like my dreams and dread used to swap places in my head, the rusty pointer doesn't look like it has budged in decades.

The sunlight also reflects off the white judo outfits draped like college banners in Sea Isle and Avalon on both railings of the building. Cresty points to the clothing as Marion spins around. She says, "A judo suit, both the pants and jacket, are called a gi… or at least that is what Choker calls them."

They sit in the truck like we use to do at the courts in Avalon on weekend mornings waiting for the sun to come up. Waiting to play ball. Waiting to be alive.

With an embarrassed look, she says, "Sorry, this place smells even worse than his old fishing boat."

Lifting his sunglasses, Marion, not looking too awake, rubs his eyes. His eyes are sad and still. He rubs real hard. Then soft. Then hard again.

"What do we have here, what is all this?" he asks like a confused college professor who does really know but is faking ignorance to his students. "It looks like a quasar exploded and it smells like a comet hit a port-o-john. These poor cypress trees have to smell the stench from these… what did you call them? Zoot suits? No wonder they are dying."

"They are judo gis," Cresty tells him again, "at least they always wear white, just like you, tree bro."

Marion spits on his hands. He rubs them real hard. Then soft. Then even harder than the first time. The sun sparkles off his shiny watch.

"They must have dirty souls then," he says. "Much like meself."

"Don't we all, bro."

"Their minds must be dirt, too, much like one's self when one doesn't know."

"Now, Doctor Tree, I don't know about that, not about their minds or your mind either, and I don't want to foo-for-nothing know," Cresty says, catching herself, like a mother weary of her kid's bad behavior.

"I do know they don't have clean bodies. The guy's gis hang out back here after workouts. As soon as they wake up, they come out here half buck naked and put them back on for the morning practice.

"I know Choker is here. He said he needed a late-night workout so he slept over. We aren't working here anyway, right? Aren't we here to just pickup Choker?"

Using his left shoulder, Marion shoves open the door of the truck while he holds on his sunglasses with his right hand. He jumps out like a gung-ho paratrooper, but his right foot catches one of the webs of wires from all these instruments on and under and around the dashboard.

The man with the clean outfit falls hard on his left shoulder. The sand must be soft. He rolls like he has fallen many times before. Marion bounces back up like nothing happened, like no one saw his lunacy.

He seems likeable.

"Almost lost my breakfast," he says while holding his hand over his mouth real tight, like he isn't kidding. "Those wires are hard to see in this bright sun."

Cresty reaches over the seat and grabs a really, really small guitar tipped on its side under the dashboard. She grips the neck.

"Are you sure you can see all right?" she asks. "You went through another traffic light already this morning and then you slow down way before the stop signs. Maybe you should drink coffee instead of Coke."

"Pepsi, or maybe it is Coke, and anyway I see better than a fine eagle flying above the conservatory in West Cape May," he says, giving Cresty a crisp geography lesson as well as his b.s. optical report. "It's my foot. I tore my Achilles tendon last summer, falling out of a tree. Don't want to do it again. It's hard to brake, so it is hard to stop."

She strums the tiny guitar.

"Brake, give me a break, there are no brakes in life, just gas, gas, gas," Cresty sort of sings. "You gots to make your own break to quote… me old self."

"Yeah, life is a mask, mask, mask as Jumpin Jack Flash says," Marion sort of sings, replacing the words gas, gas, gas.

Marion's white headband from under the hat and his John Deere cap lay on the sandy ground. His hair is a mess, like mine used to look back in high school. He picks the headband up, pulls up a few strands of grass from the sandy spot where the headband landed, puts both the headband and a strand of grass in each side of his mouth.

"Besides the trees, they need the grass trimmed here too," he mumbles, tugging his hat back over his hair, "but at least they have fine, fine, really fine grass."

From the two-story white barracks next to the judo hut, a voice echoes. A light-skin Oriental man in his early 40's, maybe 50, with black bushy hair and a mustache looking in style from the early 1980's, stands straight as the second-story beans on the balcony.

"Here in New Jersey, we can't smoke it, not even for medical use," he hisses. "You can't even toke if you're dying."

Marion plucks the grass from his mouth and then puts the strand up to his lips, faking taking a puff. He slips on his headband over the hat and then takes it off, biting the headband as he reaches into the truck. He clutches an over-sized plastic soda cup and stirs his drink with a Snickers bar he takes out of his jumpsuit chest pocket. Looking up, he takes the headband and grass out of his mouth and squints behind the sunglasses towards the balcony. He lifts his cup, with the Snickers bar somehow floating upright, in a toast gesture.

"Marion doesn't smoke anything anymore, especially since I wouldn't want to ruin such a fine, fine breakfast with smoke."

"You could use some dope for your eyes, bro." Cresty says. "Medical marijuana is like a miracle drug for dying."

"I know all about mary jane, I was a picker back in Mendocino during the late summers and early autumn… back in high school," he says lifting both arms over his head and making a cutting scissors motion with his index and middle fingers. "There is no miracle. Just like there is no miracle in stem cells or even God's gift of Snickers bars.

"The miracle is in the universe."

The man on the balcony turns around. Going back inside, he passes Choker, who stands in his boxer underwear on the top step.

"Breakfast of champions? Who is this? Don't tell me this is your mad weatherman, wild tree man," Choker yells, sounding as crazed as me back at the courts on a peaceful Sunday morn.

Choker slides down a pole next to the steps. It looks like a firehouse pole. Or maybe it is a stripper's pole. He approaches the truck walking on his toes.

The front of his boxer shorts is wet from the morning dew on the pole.

Marion dips the Snickers bar into the soda and stirs while reaching to shake Choker's hand. Choker nods, gives him a fist pump and walks to the side of the truck where Cresty is halfway out the door.

As he looks in, he leans forward, pinning Cresty inside.

“Where is this weather station?” Choker asks, grabbing the neck of the baby guitar. “Hey, you play the axe now?”

She strums the tiny guitar.

Marion hurries around the truck. He slaps my man on the back.

“No, baby bro, it is a sitar,” he says. “Much smaller than a guitar. It fits in the cab with my other gear. A tighter fit with you two.”

“Grab some clothes. Let’s doctor-up some trees today.”

Marion opens the back door of the truck cap as Choker and Cresty stroll around to him with amused grins. Choker scratches the inside of his wet underwear.

The inside of the back of the truck is insanely clean.

There are two chain saws lined neatly on one side. There are handsaws of various sizes packed on the other side. Hanging from the roof is a long silver pole saw and two bow saws, one blue and one black.

There are three plastic trashcans stacked inside one another. Another long pole with a saw at the end hangs from hooks on the far side of the cap. On the other side of the cap are shelves of neatly stacked books.

The only piece out of place is a couple of plastic pink and blue trash bags hanging randomly from a hook near the open cab door.

"Shee-t, compared to the fishing boat, this looks like the inside of an operating room," Choker says. "Foo-k what are you a tree surgeon for the rich folk?"

Choker pulls his head out of the truck, looking at the ground as if he knows I am around to know he did something wrong. He looks up to see the Asian-looking guy again, standing on the porch of the second floor.

"Sorry for swearing, Master Uwrenski," Choker says as respectfully as he used to talk to me.

Master Uwrenski throws a judo-gi down from the balcony. Choker sprints over to catch both the pants and jacket.

"Hey, Phelge," he says, "Hang up your wet gear on the line like the rest of the guys. Just because you are throwing everyone one and choking them out on the mat, kicking ass now, doesn't mean you can act like one around here."

Marion rushes to Choker. He lifts his sunglasses and squints into his eyes. He wipes the Snickers-Coke combo from around his mouth. He cocks one eye and bites one side of his mouth, looking like someone just elbowed him in the gut going for a rebound while asking him the meaning of life.

"Phelge? Why does he call you Phelge? What does he mean?"

With a huff, Choker turns away. He hangs up both the top and the bottom on the line, evenly distributing the weight of the garments so not to use the clothespins like the other gis.

Cresty grabs Marion's arm, "why do you care what he is called?"

In a swift motion, Choker snatches them both by their necks.

"Master Uwrenski says he knows Choker isn't my real name and says I don't deserve it until I win a tournament, so he made up a name, saying Phelge is what comes up out of my mouth after I am the one choked out."

Marion plops in the sand while holding his sunglasses with both hands. His neatly trimmed fingernails dig into the flaps. He rises to a squat, shaking his head. He picks at the few strands of grass. He rocks his head as if someone just told him the meaning of life. He slouches back in the sand.

Choker leans on the truck casually, as if not any names or anything matters. He picks up the pink and blue plastic bag that must have blown on the ground. He walks over to the truck, putting the bags back on the hook.

"What are the books for?" he asks, scratching his privates again.

"We should be reading more," Cresty says. "Read me something prophetic."

Marion stands up chewing on a long strand of grass. He reaches into the truck, takes out a red, plastic gas can with a yellow nozzle. The nozzle is cut in half and topped with duct tape.

"Be careful with the equipment," Marion says. "And, bend your knees when lowering the gear so you don't get hurt, even though you look pretty strong."

Choker puts back the book he opened on the shelf in the exact spot.

"Don't get hurt? Me? I'm not working with this cartoon. I'm going back inside the dojo to work-out."

Cresty points to the sweaty judo gear hanging on the line, saying, "Your gear is wet, like your drawers, bro. You poking around with yourself in there…"

She pinches her nose again with one hand and points to the judo hut, or dojo, with the free left hand.

"You can't stay in that judo flat forever, and I can't stay there," she says. "I stayed alone on the Butterfly Boat last night. Creepy. Come with us."

"I thought you would sleep on the surfer's beach," Choker says, looking concerned. "Or with him."

"I did... nah, just poking you a bit."

"It worked."

"The only downside to working with us is you will have to wear more clothes. I probably could get you one of those jumpsuits he is wearing. At least it looks a bit like your judo gi."

Choker grabs her hands with both of his.

"I'll go buck naked first."

Marion circles to the side of the truck, extends his hand to Choker, who doesn't reach to shake.

"You can't wear any less than you have now unless you were in your baby suit," Marion says.

"Talking about being nude, dude? Are you a dirty, old surfing groupie?"

"I'm dirty and I'm old. But I run a very clean… clean operation here."

"It doesn't matter if you are. At least you have a great job. Not many 50-year-olds have their own landscaping business in New Jersey. You're doing all right, sir."

"I'm just 51, and, it's not a lawn business. I'm an artist. I practice the art of arboriculture. Saying this is only work is like saying Mick and Keith only enjoy listening to music when they are undoubtedly the world's greatest rock 'n roll writers, singers, players, band. Ever. And, this world has been around a long, long time."

Marion prances toward the front of the truck and strums the baby guitar.

Choker scratches down low.

"Easy on your privates," Cresty says.

"Just 51, huh?" Choker mocks. "How many more days left you got?"

"I'll answer you if you adjust your wears around so the hole in the middle isn't so strategically placed for viewing. We don't need to see your wand."

"I thought you liked the view," Choker says in the sort of ambivalent voice that must tip off Marion he really doesn't mean what he is saying.

"Who are Mick and Keith?" he asks.

Marion rubs his eyes. He looks like he is in the bull's eye of life. Using both hands, he gives Choker an unfolded blue plastic bag with the steady sureness of a surgeon.

"Hold this in front of that hole in your pants."

Marion pulls on white surgical gloves, the kind you see right before a dentist digs in for the kill shot. He opens the gas can with the taped leaky nozzle he had pulled out before ranting about the Stones.

He turns the gas can upside down. Nothing. The can is dry… Empty as a man thinking of taking the dive.

“There is no gas, man,” Choker declares, clapping his hands once and spreading them like a magician trying to make a rabbit appear.

“Arrr,” the forgetful man growls, looking mad at himself and not Choker mocking him.

“Who is freaking Mick and Keith?” Marion growls.

Marion tosses the empty gas can back in the truck. He slams both doors with a thump, thump. He rubs his eyes hard, then soft and then hard again as he suddenly skips happily toward the front of the truck. He slides in and revs the engine.

“Start me up,” he yells, “Come on, come on, both of you. You have a large bit to learn.”

Marion shakes his head. Rubs his eyes real hard. Then soft. Then hard again, saying, “who is Mick and Keith?

“Incredulous,” he adds.

“Easy Mr. Myopee,” Choker rips. “I’m not driving with a nut who can’t see.”

Cresty turns to Choker, grabs his arm, and pulls him to the truck.

"We are going with Marion to get more than gas."

She yanks him with the command of telling Choker they are going to follow the myopic Marion where ever he goes, as if he is now pointing the way for their wandering inners.

"You know who they are, remember my dad telling the cop, John Rage, about Keith's spiritual soothing 'you were there and now you're here' story?"

"Of course, it was another Pete Parable that I used to live by, just accepting people as they come in and out of your life, not asking where they have been, not caring why they have not been.

"Yeah I remember. I remember like the first day at the courts when he told me how to shoot the ball into the wind."

"Why then act like you don't know? Why not just let Marion know you know? Why not let him know you are as smart as he pretends to be?"

"I don't want him to know what I know."

"Why?"

"The guy is whacked," Choker says. "How can you forget to bring gas to a job? And why is he here when no one here will pay him to cut these trees? We rent from the Coast Guard base."

Choker hugs the rusting flagpole, which rises higher than the two-story building, but doesn't have a rope. The clothesline that is used to hang the judo gis had to be the pole's rope since there are rusted pulley marks on both sides of the line sagging under the weight of the gis.

"And I don't want to get close to anyone again," Choker spits. "Life changes too quick, pulling at you from both sides, wearing you down… down to where you're about to break yourself."

Cresty gives him a playful two-handed shove. She pushes him between his shoulders, now a good two fingers wider than two summers ago when the bay breeze blew him around the courts.

"He is a good whacked. Just hop in the truck, he'll take you. And, anytime he asks you a question or you don't know what the foo-kin, foo-kly foo-k he is talking about, just answer the Rolling Stones. I learned to say the Rolling Stones to everything at the beach. Just roll with him, bro."

"I guess, I should put on some clothes, I got to see this guy in action. Plus, maybe I'll get some more from you in the back of the truck… it is cleaner than the boat."

Choker returns wearing his Clippers jersey and baggy bright yellow shorts with black spider web stripes. Cresty pulls him in the front of the truck as she slides in the middle, just like how we used to drive from the Avalon courts back to Sea Isle in my truck. Marion reaches across her to shake his hand.

"All you need to know is Mick and Keith are Jagger and Richards. The Glimmer Twins, sparkling and shiny like your shorts. Hang with me, you'll learn."

"I'm not learning nothing, I don't need to know. I'm going to sleep… anyway… I'm a black dude, how would I know about the Stones?

"I'm not learning nothing."

"Anything, not nothing," he bristles. "And the Stones have a black bass player… Darryl Jones replaced Billy Wyman…"

"C'mon Choker, you need to learn a lot, like the old days," Cresty said. "Like with Pete. Like to learn again."

"I want to sleep more than learn. Sleeping doesn't shove you into the middle of making more mistakes."

Choker bolts out of the truck like he suddenly needs to finish taking a dump. He slams the door, rattling the wires under the dash. He walks away, circles and then goes back to the dojo. He bounces up the stairs. He softly shuts the door.

"He is not going to sleep. He can sleep when he is expired, not before," Marion says. "We are meant to be together."

"You mean, Rochambeau," Cresty nods.

Marion spins his wristwatch real hard around his wrist, then soft and then hard. He spins the shiny watch like he rubs his eyes.

"No, this isn't by chance. Not a bit."

Marion hops out of the truck as if gas suddenly appeared in the can with the taped-up nozzle.

"All can and will be fixed," he says. "We'll wake his sleepy soul up."

Crazy man hustles around the back of the truck and opens the cap door with a hard tug. He pulls out a chain saw. He fills it up by dumping the gas from another chain saw into it. He uses a funnel. The funnel also has gray duct tape around the pointed end. Not one drop spills on the new HomeLite. He yanks the starter rope with a hard tug. Then a soft one. And then a hard long one.

The machine revs up on the third pull as if on cue. Smiling, he starts cutting branches from a low-lying tree. The first branch, which is touching the flagpole, drops. He starts cutting the next branch before the first branch hits the sand.

As if the roaring engine isn't enough to keep Choker from sleeping, Marion sings, "I once worked in a cross-wire hospital and I howled at the ma in the skulling pain, but it's ain't right now, in fact it is a mask. But it's ain't right, I'm Finder Jack Fish."

Marion prances around the tree with the chain saw ripping like he is Jagger himself at Madison Square Garden.

Choker leans over the side of the upper porch. The railing doesn't seem like it can hold his weight He cups his ears.

Marion keeps cutting. He whacks away at all overhanging branches in the far back of this yard. Choker watches every swipe of the saw from the porch. Cresty sits inside the truck. She looks tired. They both look tired.

She used to bounce up in the morning before the sun, ready to play ball with her old man at the courts every weekend over every summer up in Avalon… and that was after drinking at nights in old Sea Isle.

Marion carefully turns off his saw, studying the switch as if to make sure it is truly off. He sings again, woofing up to Choker, "Finder Jack Fish, it's a mask, mask, mask."

Marion dodges over to the front of the truck in his Jagger prance. He picks a Snickers bar off the top of the dashboard. He chomps a bite. He picks up his

Wawa soda, a small cup without a lid, and he sways to the back of the truck.

"My haunting flavor cherry red," he sings, poking his arm in rhythm out the window.

Choker bounces down the steps and over to Marion, who rips a fart.

"It's a gas, gas… mask," he sings, laughing silly.

Cresty howls with a throaty, "haa, haa haa." I haven't heard… or seen her laugh so hard since was kid at St. Bernadette's School back on The Hill, before she knew about her plumbing… before being cursed by loving to play pickup basketball with her old dad and his friends. She stumbles out of the truck and melts onto the ground. Choker stands above her, like Ali over Liston, not offering to help her up.

"It's not that foo-kin funny. And you never fall, I thought."

"Just hungry," she mumbles, "I guess."

Marion snatches a smaller saw from the truck. He shows Cresty, who is still on the ground, and the defiant Choker how to start it with one hard pull, a soft one and then another hard one.

The saw sparks to life. With the same suddenness, he shuts the purring engine down.

"Why do you pull hard, soft and then hard?" Choker yells over the fading buzz of the saw.

"You will learn," Marion says, ripping a long fart out his squeezed butt again.

"Some more gas, gas, gas?" she asks.

"Just having fun."

"Why not have fun with us Choke?" Cresty says, popping up and pushing him between the shoulders again.

"Indeed, you got to manufacture fun, just last week one of my friends got drunk and fell down his basement steps, broke his rigid neck, and another friend checked his bendy butt into the hospital for the DTs," Marion says.

"You got friends here?" Choker pokes.

"Well back in California, where me and the Beach Boys rose and where the Stones played at Altamont."

Choker seems like his old sympathetic self from back in our Sea Isle days when he shakes his head looking at Cresty, who slumps again to the sandy ground.

"We absorbed our share of left hooks and right crosses, too, from life," Choker says. "Just because we are younger doesn't mean we don't bleed."

"Let it bleed, the Stones say," Marion smiles. "Just let it bleed. Indeed."

"Or just bleed out," Choker barks, sounding like he wants an answer to life's unfairness.

"Got to stay on the edge, live life on the ledge," Marion says, lifting the sunglasses and staring both of the lads down. "You got this chance to live large… many never get the shot."

The tree man makes a goofy basketball pose like he is going to shoot. His shot would be swatted at the Avalon courts, back across the Townsends Inlet Bridge into Sea Isle, if this *is* the way he really shoots.

"I know Cresty played basketball, and you too, even though you look like you still play, so it's like you have this shot, you might be covered, but either you are going to take the shot or you are not."

"Right," Choker says. "And either you are going to make the shot or not."

Marion reaches in the back of the F150, picking out a roll of toilet paper. He shoots the toilet paper like a basketball. He hits the flagpole with the roll.

Scooping up the toilet paper, he shuffles toward the trees that circle the property on three sides. His legs squeeze together. He climbs a tree - the one with the most branches that he just pruned - with his legs still squeezed.

The canopy of the tree shakes. There is a laugh. He stays up there a few minutes before he strolls back to the truck. Legs loose.

He places the used toilet roll on the shelf with the plastic bags. The white-ish brown paper in one hand is tossed it into the high weeds.

"Now, that felt great. Anything that comes out of the human body is great. But, that my friends was special. Yahoo the day is on."

"Why don't you use one of those pink or blue trash bags?" Cresty asks in anger. "Why litter? You just trashed the earth, nature man."

"Yeah, you are supposed to be Mr. Clean with your perfect jumpsuit outfit," Choker piles on. "You know what Pete would call you. He would call you Captain Crazy, Colonel Cockeye, Commander Coo-Coo."

"Crazy people…" he says. "I like the names. I'd use them all if I didn't already have my new name… my alias, like you guys."

"Why don't you use the can, a toilet?" Cresty asks.

"Fertilizer my friends," Marion offers, "plus it's nature."

Marion struts to the front of the truck with the satisfaction of a man who knows he is empty. He jumps in the driver's seat. He sings again, "I'm all right, all right now. I'm all right" in his Jagger voice.

Cresty plops in the middle of the bench seat. Her foot snags on a wire. Kicking the wires with his left foot to free Cresty, Choker slides in next to her.

"Be careful, you know this is my office," Marion says.

"You looked like you were going to explode," Choker mocks with a degree of delight. "You were squeezing so tight. Do you need underwear? I have sweaty ones from my workout last night that must smell better than what you are bagging."

Marion sings out: "I'm all right now, I just had the big bang."

"Is that what you call it?" Cresty says amused. "You sure talk a lot about crap."

"Scatological," he declares with the determination to make his scat not smell. "I graduated from Scatological University at Berkeley."

"Figures, the science of sheee-t," she screeches.

"You like my squeeze move, huh?" Marion says in a surprisingly declarative voice. He is not waiting for a response. "Learned that in college. That is the big crush. The big bang always comes after the big crush."

Choker shakes his head; his budding dread locks are matted, but not wet like yesterday on the boat. He laughs, putting his arm around Cresty. So good to see them laugh again, even if the laughs are just in bits.

"You went to college, there is hope for me then," Choker does say with more sincerity than bite. "But, I'm not sure if I want to go now if all you learn is to call a dump the big crush before the big bang.

"Foo-k I learned that after eating Wawa hotdogs in Rumson when on preschool trips to Ellis Island."

"You didn't learn how the universe started in kindergarten, did you?" Marion says, continuing without waiting for an answer, "do you know about the Big Bang and then the Big Crush, or the Big Crush and then the Big Bang?

"Really, how the foo-k, as you say, do you look at creation, or Intelligent Design, as the Pennsylvania public schools now call creationism?"

Choker grabs his groin, giving him the defiant pose of an angry NBA player who just got posterized.

"Had a big bang the other night," he says.

Cresty elbows him in the side. "Me too," she says playfully.

"Who cares how the universe started?" Choker says without hesitation and conviction. "The world ended for us two summers ago. That's why we just hack around now. I don't even care if the universe is still around when I'm done hacking.

"After Pete, nothing matters much."

Marion squeezes his face as if he has to go again.

"I had heard about Pete, sorry, but still you should, everyone should care," Marion preaches. "Cause if you know how the universe started, you will know how the world ceases. There is an end game to the pain. Cool, huh?

"Anyway, you'll learn someday soon. Just like you'll learn about Mick and Keith now. I know that now."

"If you know all this, then why technology? What are all these machines for under the dash?" Choker asks. "Are you trying to find aliens? We can go to the Cape May airport and go search for ET."

"Just fishes, only trying to find fishes," Marion says.

"I tried catching them, too," Choker adds with an embarrassed grin. "Not easy like the Alaskan Bush people make it look on the Discovery Channel."

"Nope. Not at all, but found my first one the other night," Marion says, starting up the truck as he finishes pontificating.

He speeds away, swerving around the chain at the end of the sand alley as he sings to himself, "The Fish Finder, that's who I am." He makes a left on Pennsylvania Avenue, which is one of the larger roadways in the cape. He makes a right before slowing down at one of the seven red lights in town.

We – yeah we, I feel I'm with them again – drive east on Pittsburgh Avenue, another busy street for sleepy Cape May. The wide street runs straight up to the ocean.

Two kids run across the street with surfboards, but Marion doesn't stop or even slow down as two cars skid. The drivers both beep in disbelief more than anger that Marion blew a stop sign.

Marion waves and smiles away as the horns blare.

He makes a right on Missouri Avenue before slowing down even though no cars or kids are in sight. He comes to a stop in the middle of the road.

"That machine is to turn on my weather satellite in orbit, it's my eye in the sky," Marion says real serious as he points under the dash.

"Marion, you better tell him the truth, he doesn't understand humor anymore," Cresty pleas. "No more foo-kin fooling."

"All right then, it's not a satellite, it's just a Doppler radar," Marion says sneezing. "It's nothing more than a basic weather radar."

"That's how he knows where the big waves are going to be," Cresty says. "That's how he knows what beaches are cranking out tubes. He knows if

Devils Reach is calm for fishing or roaring for surfing. He tells us all, where it is flat and where the big ones are."

"The big waves, or the big dump?" Choker jokes. "Maybe it is how he tells another one of his dumps are coming?"

"The machines really work," Cresty huffs while planting a solid elbow in Choker's ribs. "You should see how he does it. All last winter, when leftover El Nino swells were rolling up thirteen footers, he used the Doppler to mark his maritime charts. He strung an antenna over a tree at the beach and he sent out faxes to all the surf and shops and eat joints along South Jersey, from Cape May to Barnegat Bay."

Cresty shakes Choker, who is faking being a sleep, with both hands around his head. Choker rips a long fake snore.

"El Nino?" Choker asks with another snort. "Even I know that system is on the West Coast."

"See you are smart," Cresty says with a sudden perk in her voice. "He did this out West first. He's a legend. He sent a fax to Mark Foo in Hawaii back in '94 and he was up there the next day and caught the wave of the century in Half Moon Bay at Pillar Point."

Marion squirms. His foot slides off the brake. Poking his foot for the gas pedal, he starts driving again.

"After Foo's body was found washed up on shore two days later, he only would let locals know about where the mountain waves were," Cresty continues, obviously impressed with the story she is telling. "That's why he really doesn't do the surf stuff anymore. He looks for calm seas for fisherman and for free divers. But he tells me where the waves are…"

"He just started with the tree stuff."

Holding his sunglasses tight with his left hand instead of using both hands to turn swiftly, Marion bounces over the curb on a bend in the road. Bang. Everyone bounces, banging heads on the roof of the cab. Marion's soda splashes and spills a bit on his under-dash equipment.

With both feet planted on the brakes, he finally stops the truck right before hitting a statue of a mom with two young boys looking out into the foggy Cape May Harbor. He pulls himself up straight as if to see the odd bronze figures better.

"I didn't mean to kill him," Marion says. "I never meant to kill anything.

"Not Foo…"

I think Marion knows how I feel. Exactly.

Lunging with his right hand, Choker reaches around Cresty and squeezes Marion's throat.

"I'll kill you if you don't stop at the next light, the next stop sign, the next time kids are crossing the road," Choker screams. "I'll kill you if you jump another foo-kin curb."

Gasping, Marion turns the truck off. Reluctantly, Choker eases his grip. He lets go.

"I guess that is why they call you Choker," Marion coughs. "Is that the real reason Master Uwrenski calls you Phelge? You choke your opponents so tight, they spit up Phelge?"

Cresty pushes the two apart.

"Why are we here at the Fisherman's Memorial?" she asks after catching her breath.

Marion rubs his neck with one hand real hard. Then soft. And hard again. With his sunglasses drooped on his nose from Choker's big squeeze, Marion squints real hard. He doesn't look across the harbor where the fishing fleets are docked, the slacker boats not out pulling in fish to feed the Cape May masses. He isn't drawn to the old schooner with Christmas lights illuminating a looping line from the bow to the mast and then the stern. He stares up the harbor.

"If only the past could come back," he laments.

He points to the gadget next to the Doppler with his right hand.

"That's my cesium atomic clock," he boasts as if he invented the machine. "It uses atoms to clock time. Simple. The element of cesium stimulates one another to make a continuous wave of precise frequency. And, this frequency is used to measure time on earth and in space."

"I call it my rock clock."

"Yeah, right," Choker says grabbing his groin with both hands, "Rock this whacko."

"I don't joke about time," Marion protests. "No not time. Time is not on my side like the Stones."

Choker takes one hand off his privates and points to the oldest looking piece of equipment in the cab. It is a dusty brown box with a slot in the middle.

"That's my Fish Finder," Marion says in a proud manner. "You were a fisherman, right? You should know what they are for."

"I know what a fish finder looks like, and this ain't one," Choker barks.

"Isn't, come on Choke, don't start talking dumb now," Cresty injects with a tone that sides with Marion. "And you know. Pete used to have a portable 8-track player at the courts. Remember the Who and Who Are You?"

Choker looks away and rubs his eyes with both hands as if he is wiping away the memory. Memories are maddening, he is learning.

"He just calls it a Fish Finder for some silly reason," she continues.

Marion reaches down and pushes a button on the old box. The cab fills up with music. Marion turns it up. He starts up the truck.

"Yeah some might call this an 8-track player, but to me it is a Fish Finder," Marion says. "When I play music, good things happen ..."

"Rochambeau," Cresty agrees.

Backing off the grass, bouncing over the curb, he almost sideswipes a shiny SUV. The elderly lady driver swears while yelling thanks to God for keeping her safe. I don't know if God can hear her. The music pounding out of the truck blares the Stones' Jumpin Jack Flash.

Marion sings again: "I was raised by a speechless, bearded gag, I was schooled with a law right now to attack. But it ain't right now, in fact it is a mask. But it's ain't right, I'm Finder Jack Fish."

Choker reaches to turn the music down. With his right arm flashing like a hockey goalie, Marion blocks him. The truck swerves off the road at the curve near the row of gray condos that all look the same on Texas Avenue. Humming Jack Flash, he skids on a sandy patch of a driveway.

"You might be a Findin' Jack flasher, all right, dude man," Choker unleashes, "but, you can't drive. And that is no Fish Finder. You are no Fish Finder."

The truck's wheels spin like Choker's confused, angry mind.

The wheels keep spinning. Looking like he doesn't know anything else to do, Marion keeps hitting the gas. The wheels spin with more anger. Not able to hit the gas more, Marion reaches toward the music box. He turns the music up louder. It is the Rolling Stones' "Can't You Hear Me Knocking" with Bobby Keys wailing on the sax as Choker and Cresty begin to push, trying to help the spinning wheels.

"Weatherman, hey old, deaf man, you got to rock the truck and that music won't do it," Choker says rather calmly.

"What? Wait, can you, until this one song is over?" Marion questions, but without listening.

Choker grabs Cresty by the arm. He adds a twist and a pull. Then, he stares. He never looked at her with so much intensity two summers ago.

"What's up with him and that music?" he asks. "What is that music box called, I mean why does he have one?"

Cresty hits downward, pounding on his arm. Choker holds his grip. He is getting stronger.

"You know, really you know as much as you know… you are acting foo-ked up, but you have nothing to worry about the other night," she says. "Pete had one, like I said, it is an 8-track player."

"Never knew your inner parts could work," Choker snarls. "But nothing is clear anymore."

"I know you are trying to move past Pete, me too, bro."

"I can't. This guy reminds me in a weird way of him. Even the old school music."

"I know, I'm trying too, like I said," she says sadly, making me sadder. "There are just too many reminders of him, which is why we came here to Cape May, made up new names, starting new lives.

"And with Marion."

"Does he listen to The Who, too?"

"I told you, everything is the Rolling Stones with him, unlike Pete," Cresty says. "Every foo-kin thing."

"It is only rock n roll," Marion screams out the window. "But I like it, like it, yes I do . . ."

"We'd better roll this truck out of here or I won't be rolling anyone in judo tonight," Choker says.

"This is bad, Rochambeau," Cresty nods.

With a grin and then a grimace, Choker and Cresty squat lower and push harder from the back. The truck jumps a bit forward, but rolls back in the rut. The music still roars. Choker makes a hand signal to try again. They both push. The truck jumps forward again. The truck pops out.

Cresty falls.

"You've been falling all day, sister," Choker says. "You better stay off the waves for a while or you'll end up like that Foo guy."

"At least I will be with Pete."

"Take me."

"I'm just a little sick, like in my stomach. Let's go. I need something to eat."

They both hop back in the truck, playfully pushing at each other like kids. Choker squishes Cresty in the middle. He flicks the air freshener dangling in front of them from the rearview mirror of the truck. It is a tongue sticking out of a mouth. The red tongue is old and dusty. The man must never clean the air freshener like he cleans the back of the truck.

Choker continues flicking the tongue for some reason.

"Be careful, I have to get another summer out of my air freshener and we got a few months to go,"

Marion says. “I know you know what the air freshener is, Choker. You do, don't you?”

Choker shakes his head in mock stupidity. He lurches toward Marion with his hands out to choke him. He kicks the Fish Finder. The music stops. So, does the truck.

“Aw, man, you booted a wire loose,” Marion says, but not mad a little bit, as if it happens all the time. “Kick it again.”

Choker gives the box a solid kick. The music starts. Marion drives again.

“Don't tell me the foo-kin Fish Finder is hooked up to the motor?” Choker asks.

“It is connected to everything, the universe all the way wired to my soul,” Marion says.

Marion pumps the brakes on a hard curve at the end of Texas Avenue and onto Lafayette Street, on the way into down town Cape May. He manages to stay on the road with the help of Cresty holding the wheel.

He drives slowly pass the one story, white brick school on the right. He stares out over the baseball fields where a dad is throwing pitches to a young boy and yells, “swing batter, batter.”

“Swing like Je-ter… De-rek Je-ter,” Choker yells out the other window.

"Swing like Je-ter... De-rek Je-ter hitting to right field boy," Cresty yells from the middle seat. "Right out of Yankee Stadium..."

"Back in my day, the man for the Yankees was Bobby Murcer," Marion says. "I had a poster of him on my wall with his quote, 'You decide you will wait for your pitch. Then as the ball starts toward the plate, you think about your stance. And then you think about your swing. And then you realize the ball that went past you for a strike was your pitch.

"We can't swing and miss when our pitch is here this summer."

Choker twirls his index finger around his ear, rolling his eyes. He keeps twirling like a crazy man as Marion runs a stop sign.

Marion never looks over as he sings "Hey, hey, hey Vance, it's a gas, gas, gas," driving past Vance's Bar, an old run-down brick place, jutting out oddly in tidy Cape May with all the pink and yellow Victorian Homes.

But the rest of this stretch of street doesn't really fit in either - like Marion – in tidy Cape May.

Across from Vance's beat down bar, where I would've fit in nicely back in my day, are rows of brick two story homes, which were erected by the Cape May Housing Authority. This is the low-income part of town. On the right side rise more

1950-ish houses on Lafayette Court. The run-down homes stand out as much as the obtuse statue of the woman with the kids at Fisherman's Wharf.

Suddenly, swerving to miss freshly paved potholes again, Marion drives on, crossing over the railroad tracks into down town.

The tracks were used to haul the rich vacationers to Cape May from Philadelphia, before the Atlantic City Expressway and Garden State Parkway. I know my grandfather worked on the luggage car for 48 years. He would never let me play near trains, always telling me about the kids he saw hopping to first base on one leg while playing stick ball.

"If only you could get on a train and go back," Marion says rubbing his eyes. "Go back in time and do a do-over…

Marion stops and backs over the train tracks, stopping in the middle as he says, "I was at the main lodge in the Grand Canyon and there was a fire place built with flat stones from the same strata of the Grand Canyon… you couldn't go back in time but you could see time…"

What good is seeing time gone, or time going bye? What is gone is gone. Hopefully, Cresty and Choker know this now and will just roll forward.

"You can, you can go back, like the Prodigal Son did," Cresty says, rubbing the top of Marion's head.

"The Prodigal Son," Marion interrupts. "The Rolling Stones played it with Brian Jones! It was written by Blues guitarist Robert Wilkins and the Stones covered it on Beggars Banquet, the only cover on the classic album."

"Huh? The Prodigal Son, you can always go back to the Father," Cresty stops him. "I prayed to Him, or Her, that you would ride into our lives."

"And, you did," Choker huffs, "like all Four Horsemen of the foo-kin apocalypse in one saddle."

"Well, the Lord works in mysterious ways," Marion says.

"Indeed, Psalm 23," adds Choker, tugging on Cresty's long red ponytail.

Chapter 5

Marion weaves around the patched potholes in front of the decrepit train station that has been converted into the Cape May Chamber of Commerce while humming The Prodigal Son.

He slows down in the no parking lane of the bus station to Atlantic City, which backs up against the tracks there, as if he is looking for someone.

Shouting, “I was lost and is found,” Marion makes a right turn on Elmyra Street, going wide and scraping the historically converted building. He makes another quick right, pulls into a driveway, but is wide again, scraping the mailbox in front of a house with a wrap-around porch that backs up to a branch of the bay running under the railroad tracks. The house’s blinking light out front flashes: “Palm Reading.”

He doesn’t shut off the truck as he hops out with a purpose, like he won a free palm reading, and disappears into the backyard of the shuttered house while whistling sideways out of his mouth.

“Great, foo-k, we’re visiting Madame Palm, she'll tell us we're foo-kin nuts for working with this foo-kin, flaming crazed hole of a man,” Choker barks.

Marion returns some trash in his hands. His serious face is alarming.

"All right, my dear Lady Jane," Marion sort of sings.

"Why are you calling her Jane and dear?" Choker barks with a swat at the hanging tongue. "Why the foo-k are we here?"

"Just another great Stones song," Marion says, shutting off the truck. "Now, listen up, my first rule on any job is to pick up any paper so it doesn't get caught in the shredder. Cups from the outdoor Bella Vida Cafe over on Broadway blow over here when the wind comes from the west. The cups, man, they get shredded up and make a mess.

"A real mess. I hate that. It never should happen, so don't let it. Nothing goes through the shedder, but small tree limbs. The big stuff I cut up later."

Marion springs to the back of the truck and pulls out a portable shredder. He shows Choker how to operate the choke. He starts the engine with one hard pull, a short one and then another hard one.

"Don't let any of your clothes get caught on the branches, you could get your hand pulled into the teeth of this and you… then you wouldn't be able to choke me anymore," the man says grinning like he is about to eat a fatted calf.

Cresty splits around to the side of the house. She picks up a cardboard box lying under a tree. She dumps trash from the box into a can near the back steps below an old sign without some letters reading 'alm ading.' Holding the box, she cleans up discarded paper cups mixed in the twisted uncut grass near the railroad tracks.

Marion shows Choker how to place the shredder so the wood chips will land in a green plastic trash can. Marion places a brown tarp over the chute. He tells him "this way no chips can fly anywhere but in the can, man." Choker is looking at Cresty as he says, "Huh?"

"It's like taking a dump, you want it in the can," Marion says patting his own butt. "Unless, of course, you are up, discreetly up in a tree.

"I'm going to trim some branches here for Madame Palm."

"No way, bro. Is that really her name?" Choker asks, "I was joking when I said it."

Marion turns at him quickly, spinning wildly off-balance, "is Phelge really your nickname now?"

Tapping his own neck, Choker fake coughs as if he is spitting up.

"You do know the word is phlegm, the thick yellow stuff that comes out of your throat, don't you?" Marion adds. "Doesn't Uwrenski know?"

"What does anyone know?" Choker retorts and then adds, "Pete said he once played basketball in Istanbul with a psychic who was hit by a bus that he said he never saw coming."

Shaking his head, Marion strides over to an overgrown tree. He digs his hand into the sandy soil and pulls up a root. From the root, he plucks off a smaller stem. He tucks the big root back into the ground.

"Perfect. This is phellem, a secondary meristem coming from the periderm, or main root," he says holding up the hairy little root. "Are you sure Uwrenski doesn't mean to call you phellem? You seem to me to be like a secondary stem living off the memory of this man Pete."

"Whatever, man, I know you are trying to show us how smart you are with the Latin and the botany, but we already learned from the best, Pete," Choker says while tapping his heart. "And just don't use Uwrenski's nickname… and don't use that English Lady Jane crap and call me Sir Choker. Why you call my Cresty, Lady Jane? She is my lady, bro."

"Lady Jane is one of the Stones great early tunes. Brian Jones is splendid on the dulcimer, which is like the sitar. That is why I play it. Why do they really call you Choker? That can't be your real name either."

Choker leaps forward, spins toward Marion, and jams him in a chokehold.

"This is why they call me choker. I'll choke your fuzzy brains out."

"I'm back, no slaughtering each other while I'm here," orders Cresty as she edges in between them, dropping the box. She pulls on them with equal disdain – knowing they are both wrong in this fight. Choker lets go. Marion drops to the ground coughing.

"With a regal grip like that, I should call you Sir Choker, indeed. You'll do just fine plucking tree limbs to be shredded into mulch."

Cresty kicks the box, sending cups sailing.

"Maybe Madame Palm can tell me my future," Cresty says smacking Choker's clenched hands. "Or us, our future. We don't want her to know our past, though."

Picking up the cups, Cresty playfully kicks Choker behind his knees. He nods and with his outstretched right hand helps Marion stand.

"That is why we have these nicknames," Choker nods again looking up at the high sun reflecting off the rusting railroad tracks. "The past is too painful. The past makes me wish I wasn't even born."

Marion yanks out a chain saw from the truck. He grabs protective clear plastic glasses from a hook on the door.

"You should wear those glasses all the time instead of your dark sun specs," Choker says. "You are going to kill us driving."

"I'll never kill anybody, ever… ever again," Marion says while sliding on the clear glasses. "Don't mess up, brother, don't destroy my shredder, if you do, you surely better vanish to the nearest black hole to escape me."

"Ever again? Oh yeah, you killed Foo," Choker digs. "And what's a foo-kin black hole?"

"Mark wasn't the last I killed," Marion says, shoving the smaller root he had dug up back into the ground. "If only people could grow back, or comeback from Middle Earth, comeback more loved, like a hobbit."

Choker and Cresty look at each other with the shock as if they both saw me again. He shakes his head, alternating rocks between sideways and up and down. Cresty shrugs her sun-tanned shoulders and says, "If only, fashure… if only."

With his arms extended, Marion adjusts the choke on the chain saw. He squeezes the trigger, giving it gas.

"A black hole isn't mysterious, although we don't know much more about the holes in space as the ones in Middle Earth," he says in a professorial tone. "We do know that there are giant black holes in our universe and on their extreme edges, there time actually stands still."

Cresty makes a surfing pose and says, "It is a mystery what was in the cooler, too, but no one is asking." She holds the stance.

"You should go there, you're getting old, man, and that music you blast is ancient," Choker says without sounding mean. "And, so is that music box.

"Yeah… what the fook is in the cooler, or was…?"

"Your ignorance is not your fault. You can't learn about the universe and how time stands still unless you understand whom are the people who make time stand still. You can think about it as you run the shredder. Think music, like in the world's greatest rock n roll band.

"Time is on their side, too."

Choker twirls over to the shredder, like he is dancing and fakes putting his hands in the teeth. The opening looks like a shark's mouth.

"Hey, I want you to pick up only the *dead* limbs," Marion says, well orders. "Any live trees will be green leaves in the shredder pile so I'll know.

"Fingers come out red."

"Aren't you here to cut down trees?' Choker asks. "Aren't trees alive, Doctor dude?"

"I only trim the dead branches off live trees so they can survive. I would never cut down a living tree. I do move trees, and that's where you can help, with your strong grip. It's heavy lifting to transplant a live tree. But today, I will only trim and keep the living trees living.

"Oh yeah, I do plant tree saplings, too… I will need your help with the little trees, too."

With his arms still out, Marion gives the chain saw a hard pull, then a short pull and then a long one. It starts up on cue. He has the touch. Three pulls.

"Like delivering a baby," Marion seems to say under the rising roar of the chain saw.

Choker hits the green button on the shredder, start the machine right up. No magic touch needed. He grabs a limb Marion had just cut. He stuffs the branch through the shredder. The lifeless limb turns into small dead chips.

He does this only a few times before a white rabbit with big ears appears. The bunny bounces out of a hole, like it tunneled from Middle Earth. The rabbit inches up to him like Choker feeds him every day.

"Get the foo-k out of here silly rabbit."

The rabbit is too young to know.

"Peter… Peter foo-kin rabbit. I'll call you Pete. Are you Pete? Is that you Pete?"

The rabbit stares curiously.

"Shoo, Pete, you are spooking me."

The rabbit inches closer to Choker, who fakes an aggressive charge at the bunny.

The rabbit flashes its stubby teeth and hops sideways, away from Choker.

Choker charges the bunny. The rabbit lunges between his legs. He kicks the bunny in the head, pins it against the shredder with his foot.

The rabbit drops still.

"Foo-kin, fook rabbit."

Choker picks the dead rabbit up with two sticks. He throws the lifeless bunny into the shredder.

Crunch.

The pile of chips is covered with blood.

Choker feeds the chipper more dead branches before casually walking back to the truck.

Marion turns off his saw and walks back to Choker. Looking at the saw, he says, "I need to sharpen the teeth on this chain," and quickly adds, "where you going?"

"The teeth on your shredder are just fine, maybe too sharp," Choker says. "I need to get a beer out of your cooler in the back of your truck. You must make a ton of money to pack a metallic cooler like that. You could've picked a better color, pops. Blood red? And what's up with the key lock on top?"

"Don't touch the cooler, ever," Marion snaps.

Then, shuddering looking at the pile, he drops the saw. He lunges to turn off the shredder.

"You all right, man, did you cut yourself?" he screeches.

Cresty, who is resting in the truck, actually sleeping, hustles over. She screams.

"Oh no, your hand, your judo…"

"A rabbit attacked me so I threw it through the shredder. That is all. No one is hurt."

Cresty clutches her stomach. She turns toward a bayberry bush and throws up, pukes, like I used to do after a basic hard night drinking.

"How could you?" Marion asks softly, as if he isn't mad, but shaking all over.

"What, you wanted to eat it for dinner?" Choker asks.

Marion kicks the shredder. There is spit coming out of his mouth. He calmly walks to the truck rubbing his eyes and comes back with a shovel, wearing surgical gloves.

Kneeling, he digs a hole next to the blood-splattered woodpile. He shovels the bloody red chips into the hole. He sprints to the back of the truck, pulls out a little tree sapling.

"This cornus florida rubra will grow well here. This partial shade and moist acidic soil will be perfect. The tree will flourish and give comfort."

"The foo-kin flora what?" Choker asks, grabbing the shovel and stabbing it at Marion like a pitchfork.

"The cornus florida rubra is a Red Dogwood. This lovely tree will flower red in the spring and reddish purple in the fall. One of my favorites, yes corny flory ruby will do well in this Northeast Atlantic climate. Our Madame Palm will like the splendid colors and shade, too. No charge either for making life out of death."

Standing, Marion backfills the rest of the hole with some peat moss from a bag in the truck. He kneels down next to the hole, blesses himself.

"Indeed, a holy hole," he whispers.

"C'mon, it's only a fookin rabbit," Choker snarls like I would at him when he didn't box out.

"A rabbit is life and life is sacred."

"OK then, let's drink a beer from your locked cooler to celebrate bunny's life," Choker mocks.

Cupping his ears, Marion looks down toward the tires of the chipper… he reaches into a little hole in the ground. He pulls out two baby rabbits.

"They must be only a few hours old," Cresty whispers.

"Attacked you?" Marion says in a low but stern breath. "The mother was only trying to protect her babies."

"What mother wouldn't protect her baby... born... or unborn?"

Unzipping his top, Marion rips off his t-shirt from under his jumpsuit. He makes a basket with the shirt in his hand. Cresty puts grass in the shirt and then puts the two baby rabbits on top of the grass. Marion cradles the bundle close to his body.

"They should stay warm," he says as if trying to convince himself. "They need to stay warm. They need the warmth of love."

Choker taps Marion's flabby under belly, now hanging over his lowered jumpsuit.

"Yo bro," Choker taunts, "you preggers?"

Marion's face is frozen as he stares at the cooler in the back of the truck.

"And if the rabbits get hungry they can eat the rolls you have on your stomach,' Choker continues poking. "You need to do judo, lose some weight... you baby fat freak."

"We must keep the beautiful bunnies warm, love them," Marion starts rattling. "They lost their mother. We must get them food. We need to buy them toys. We need to get them clothes.

"Off to the pet store, Paw Prints on the Washington Commons Mall, and provide for the beautiful bunnies."

Cresty lifts the cardboard box at her feet. She wipes the inside with the bottom of her shirt, stretching and pulling so hard you can see her… top.

Choker peeks and pokes her playfully in the ribs.

"We can put them in here," she says grabbing Marion's arm. "I feel terrible. This box was on the grass over the hole. I picked it up and you put the chipper there. Their mother ran away. It's my fault."

"It's all our fault, the universe's problem," Marion says. "No… yes, it's all our *fecking* fault."

Marion places the baby rabbits, wrapped by his shirt, in the box. He slings his free arm around Cresty. With heads down, they walk to the truck.

Choker follows, but yards behind them.

"You didn't know. Look, there are a few holes in a row and they are all out of the way." Marion says to her. "How were you supposed to know… how were you supposed to know Row and Way here were under the box?"

"But," she begins to protest, "still… it's always your fault when someone dies and you could've helped.

"The bunny mommy didn't deserve this."

"This has nothing to do with deserves, as the great Clint Eastwood said in "Unforgiven,'" Marion rationalizes for Cresty, cupping his hand over her mouth.

A butterfly circles them. Flapping peacefully. The orange butterfly has thick, black strips like veins in both wings. The butterfly lands on the box.

"This is a female monarch, named after the King of England, the monarch Edward the IV… I believe," an upbeat Marion says while securing the butterfly between his thumb and index finger. "The king liked the butterfly and he was the boss man, the monarch, so the butterfly was named after him.

"In nature's wisdom, the male monarch has much thinner black stripes and doesn't look as manly as the female."

He examines the butterfly up close with Cresty. He lets go. The butterfly circles them once real fast, then slow and then fast again before flying away.

"Let go, just let go," Marion says. "Stop, the guilt will kill you. He is the one that needs to feel some guilt. He's probably never felt the pain before. He probably never has lost anyone close to him."

"You shouldn't judge."

"You are right."

"You don't know."

"What don't I know?"

"My dad, Pete... di... passed a couple of years ago, I think that's why he is the way he is. No, I know..."

"I know, but no excuses," Marion says. "There's no reason to kill. None, baby."

"As Pete would say, 'tell it to Muhammad,'" Cresty retorts with obvious cynicism.

"Muhammed? Sure, the founder of Islam would agree," Marion says, "so would Moses and Judaism, Lao-Tzu and Taoism, Confucius and Confucianism, Krishna and Hinduism, Buddha and Buddhism, Mahavira and Jainism... and your Jesus of Catholicism.

"Of all Christianity," Cresty says.

"Yeah, man," grunts Choker, "not just Catholics."

"Well," Marion continues, "the founders, leaders, or whatever you want to call them of the world's eight great religions would all agree."

"So, would Pete," Cresty says solemnly, "the leader of *Irishism*."

Annoyed, Choker hauls the bloody shredder over to the truck, lifting the machine onto the back tailgate and then banging metal-on-metal like a car crash into the cooler.

"Easy!" screams Marion.

"Hey, I killed a rabbit. So, what? People kill people every other day. I know."

With one hand, Marion gently puts the cooler between the wheels of the shredder and pats the top of the silver-gray key locker. With the other hand, he hands Choker the box with the rabbits, now bouncing around inside.

"Carry this, their lives will help to heal you."

"Heal this," Choker says, grabbing his crotch. "Let me ask you a question Pete would ask." Edging his body between Marion's low-top sneakers, Choker continues, "Tell me, if you raised your kid in one of your so-called Eight Great Religions, and it was the wrong one and your kid went to hell because you raised him in the wrong religion… well, Pete would want to know if you would feel guilty about it?

"I would add, since you only had a 12.5 percent chance of picking the right religion, why should you feel guilty if you raised your kid in the wrong religion?

"I'm hungry, can we eat more than spiritualism for lunch? Are the bunnies grub?" Choker suggests as he backs away from Marion.

"Let's get some food, first for Row and Way," Marion says looking down at his sneakers.

"Row and Way who?" Choker asks, "are they Rolling Stones, bro, too?"

Cresty elbows him in the gut. She suddenly clutches her stomach.

"I like the names," she says. "Which one is Row, which one is Way?"

She pulls one rabbit out of the box. The rabbit is white with a black stripe between its eyes.

"This is Row, see the black stripe?" she says showing a disinterested Choker.

The other rabbit is just white. Absolute white. No marks. No spots.

"This little bunny looks like it knows its Way," she says putting the rabbit in the box and leaning the opening toward Choker to look.

Instead, Choker stuffs the box under the hanging tongue... making sure first that the spot is secure. Marion smiles for the first time since they found the rabbits.

"Hey, they will be all right there. Actually, it's perfect. Andy Warhol drew up this tongue and lips and he liked animals, so they are right under his blessing," Marion says.

"Who the hell is Andy a-hole?" Choker asks. "Does he live in a black hole, or just have one?"

"That's a good, good question, boy. Maybe, just maybe he does live in a black hole since Andy is gone from us."

Up ahead, the traffic light on the corner of Lafayette and Ocean streets is as red as the cooler in the back, but Marion doesn't slow down. He zooms right through the intersection and into the parking lot of Paw Prints, whizzing past a thick-legged mother pushing a baby stroller.

"You can't be in this much of a hurry to get food, toys and clothes for these rabbits… you are bar-bent, to steal a Pete word, you will kill someone," Choker says. "Or, are you just trying to kill us?"

Marion's face is as stoic as the power-squatting mother still standing in the middle of the intersection, who appears uncomplaining and accepting that there are nuts in this world who blow traffic lights in a shore town.

"I will never kill," he says while lifting his sunglasses and with a strange bounce of optimism. "Never… again."

"Again? You keep saying again," Choker says, "who have you foo-kin killed besides Foo?"

"And that was 20-some years ago now. Right?" Cresty says. "And it was a weather, or wave, report. Pull yourself together."

"Time here on earth doesn't heal fast enough," Marion says, "not even a continent away."

Marion turns up the music as he pulls into an open parking spot, over-lapping the right-side tires on the white line. The Stones boom loud from the Fish Finder. He sings: "I saw the green lore and I want it sainted back, no colors anymore I want them to turn black."

Revved up as if by the music, Marion points to a closer parking spot with an apple red jeep pulling out. He swerves the truck at the last moment to avoid hitting a parked car in front of him and pounds the gas. The truck hops a parking cement curb. Cresty screams while clutching the box of rabbits.

With the lady pushing the stroller still frozen, the truck rumbles onto the front lawn of this house-looking store and to a stop near the door of Paw Prints.

"Dude, you just missed whacking a lady and now a car," Choker says. "You might have even hit that car, but you were going so foo-kin fast we couldn't tell for sure."

"You just missed parking in the store, fashure," Cresty says.

Marion waves, like nothing happened, at two tattooed-up young girls, who stop to look at his madness. The one with a black skull and red roses on her left arm points back with her middle finger.

"Who would do that to their bodies?" Marion says more than asks. "I couldn't love… as much… if I had a kid with a tattoo."

Smacking Marion on his forehead, saying, "You need some ink right here, you madman. like Manson," Cresty checks the rabbits cuddled in the box. She strokes the black stripe on Row.

"Are you, all right?" she asks, "You never saw the mom or the parked car ahead of you, did you? I can't take all these bumps; my stomach is queasy or something."

Marion reaches under his seat, pulls out a pair of wraparound sunglasses that old people with cataracts wear … he puts them over his Aviator sunglasses, quipping, "The sun is too spectacular."

"They are meant go over real eyeglasses," Cresty says with her first hint of impatience toward Marion. "You, really, you should get the real ones first. You bought the wrap sunglasses without buying prescription lenses to help you see."

"Just the sun shining off the windshield this time of day," he says. "My vision is quite perfect."

"Vision? You can't see," Cresty asks. "I thought you said it was your Achilles why you couldn't break?"

Real unassuming, polite like customers to each other at Starbucks, Marion backs the truck up off the grass and down the curb.

"You sure scorched the earth here," Choker says. "Good technique, no trees will grow here. You might as well have thrown napalm.

"Did you learn the scorched earth technique in Vietnam?"

"How could I have been in Vietnam, I was born at Altamont," Marion says.

Marion smiles as if he likes his Altamont answer. He straightens the rearview mirror. He adjusts the tongue, which had flipped over the mirror.

"What's Altamont?" Cresty asks, "is it a movie theater or something?"

"No, although Paramount, which is a movie company, made a historic movie about the events of that day there," Marion says. "Altamont is a motor speedway east of Oakland where the Rolling Stones staged their famous free concert in 1969. The Stones hired the Hells' Angels to be their body guards, paid them only all the beer they could drink."

"Pete and the Lids, his boys to you Marion, would've signed up for that job," Cresty says.

"I wish your pay was all the rum I could drink," Choker says. "Rum makes me dumb and I need to be dumb right about now."

"Rum makes you dumber," Cresty pokes him.

Shaking his head in disapproval at the two tattoo girls while tripping into the parking curb, Marion adjusts his wraparound sunglasses while walking to the pet store.

Shortly, he stumbles down the store's two steps with a bag and tosses the goods into the cab and on Choker's lap. Cresty opens the bag and puts some seeds into the Bunny Box. Marion squirts Choker with a small water bottle he pulled from the bag.

"You don't get paid today unless you can tell me what that tongue is… so what is it?" Marion asks. "I already gave you a hint. Think young ones."

Choker wipes the splattered water from his cheek, reaches and touches the tongue, as if wetting parched lips.

"It's the mouth that ate the black hole…" Choker cracks, laughing.

Really, damn good to see him laugh.

"I like how you remember what I tell you about the black hole, but, no. Feed them, Row and Way now."

Cresty is already doing the feeding as Marion starts the truck. He scans the parking lot. Weaving around some potholes, he even stops at the traffic light with a red signal, making a right on Lafayette

Street. Cresty pets Row and Way as the 25-mile per hour speed limit is obeyed.

He slows down below the limit passing the field where the dad, holding his Starbucks coffee cup inside the baseball glove, is still pitching to his son.

"Ball four!" Marion yells out the window, "take yer base! Son"

Cresty cracks, "The kid drew a walk like the great De-rek Je-ter."

Choker relaxes as well, saying "Je-ter… De-rek… Je-ter."

Marion drives toward the South Jersey Marina where the famous Lobster House rises above the fishing boats like a prison tower.

"The dead fish look over their killers," Marion says, taking both hands off the wheel and pointing at the Lobster House on Fisherman's Wharf. "The dead shall indeed one day judge their killers."

Cresty grabs his hands and puts them on the wheel.

"Maybe you can get a job there fishing Choker. You think maybe?" Marion says.

Choker sticks his right middle finger out the window and the left toward Marion.

"Testing the wind?" Marion asks. "Just dial up the Fish Finder for the weather, my friend."

Ahead, the Cape May Bridge stretches out of town to the mainland and onto Route 9. Marion makes a hard left turn at the foot of the concrete structure, which rises high enough to allow even the fishing ships with the tall masts to go under. The box of rabbits, slide hard on the sharp turn, but Cresty keeps them from falling.

On the downslope on the street, without slowing down, he turns right on a stony road. He stops in front of a row of boats with tall mainsail masts. The sign UTSCH'S MARINA also serves as a perch for two adult seagulls and three little ones.

The air is clogged with the smell of fresh meat as someone is grilling burgers on their boat's stove.

"Are we trimming sails today or trees?" Choker asks.

Marion clutches the box with the rabbits. He points to Choker, motioning to carry the bag of food. Cresty follows holding her stomach and looking at the pudgy sailor flipping two burgers.

They walk down the broken seashell driveway and onto the pier. Marion leads the way past perhaps a half-dozen boats.

After locking the back of the pickup, and going back to double check he locked the cap, he jumps onto a disheveled sailboat with a main mast and two smaller ones. The boat must be 40 feet in length.

With some work, the boat could be ocean worthy. But not now. No way. Not with a tree rising from the bow.

Sniffing the meaty air, Cresty slides on the deck rails over to a two-foot or so Colorado Blue Spruce sapling, which stands upright in a tin pan tied on both sides by the lifeline on the rail of the forward pulpit. A pink and light blue ribbon tied to a branch of the sapling is half tangled with the support cord. The other half blows lightly in the bay breeze.

A few feet or so from the baby blue spruce, Marion stares over the bow and across the canal. He rubs his eyes, hard, then slow, then hard again.

He opens a hatch and slides the box down. He pulls out antique binoculars and goes back to the bow. He squints through the glasses before taking off the caps.

Choker leaps, but before both feet are on board, Marion swipes the bag from him.

Choker snatches the binoculars. He aims across the bay from the bow. He can see a middle-aged woman with weathered skin and graying blonde hair getting out of a pool in the front yard of the house facing the canal.

"You dog," Choker says, flipping the glasses to Cresty, who drops them.

Marion places the rabbit feed down the hatch. On the other side of the boat, a window hatch opens. A stream of yellow water squirts through. Piss.

"Don't worry, that's just Brennan," Marion says, "You can also call him C.J. He never goes until I come back."

"C.J., that's the blessed-breast chick from Bay Watch, we watch all the reruns at the dojo," Choker says. "If that mutt pisses on me, I'll throw poochy in the shredder, too."

Cresty whispers to Marion, "we lost our dog, too, Scoob, so he doesn't like any other dogs either."

Marion spits overboard as he sits down on the boat side rail with both legs up. Brennan rushes to his side and hops between his Buddha crossed legs. Picking up the binoculars, Cresty sits next to them. She pets the dog. Choker walks around the boat muttering and doing judo foot sweeps.

"C'mon we need to go cut some trees, I need the money," Choker pleads. "We need to get cutting."

"We don't cut trees. We doctor them. Never threaten Brennan, either. He is all the family I have."

"You got us," Cresty says laughing. "We are like a normal dysfunctional family, like that TV show Modern Family… along with Baywatch, Choker watches reruns."

"She's blessed double, too," Choker says, "that Gloria is glorious."

"G-L-O-R-I-A," Marion sings and nods.

Brennan squeezes his hind legs while hobbling past Choker. He hops off the deck of the boat, barely making the distance - maybe two feet in the air - to the dock. The shaggy brown dog trots down the pier and up the driveway before squatting under a large tree with one extended branch over the parking lot casting a shadow all the way to the boat cooking burgers.

He poops and then lets out an agreeable bark.

"He dumps just like you do, except he doesn't climb the tree," Choker says.

"Yeah, I taught him about the Big Squeeze before the Big Bang, but he doesn't have to climb a tree, no one cares if he goes there. It's his spot. The Utsch's do care if I go there, but not him. He goes there all the time. It's fertilizer heaven there. Look how big that dogwood canopy, well one limb, spreads."

Marion dips below deck, which leaves Cresty and Choker flashing each other looks like "what the foo-k are we doing here?"

The half-blind crazy man below yells, "It's hot as Hades down here," while making a myriad of crashing noises moving things underneath. He returns on deck and scurries to the back of the boat. He shuffles some more gear around. He throws a pair of surgical gloves on top of a hardback textbook about butterflies on the captain's perch.

Choker teases, rather taunts, Brennan with his hand, making circular motions like he did in the truck mocking Marion, but this time around the dog's head. With a throat slash, Cresty motions for him to stop. Choker grabs the box of rabbit food. He pretends he is going to feed Brennan and the two baby rabbits.

"What are you looking for?" Choker asks.

"I need something to put water in," Marion says, "for Row and Way, our new friends."

Marion throws gear around on board now, knocking over the butterfly book.

He rushes to put the book on top of the hatch below. He stuffs the surgical gloves in his back pocket.

"Who-a-here's boat?" Choker asks without sounding like he cares, "I see there's that, that old tongue on the side. Is this Andy War Hole's old ship?'

"This is home, where we live," Marion says. "You can stay when you know the mystery to the red tongue and black hole."

"I won't be coming around here no mo'… the dojo doesn't even smell this bad… and I just want to know what's in the cooler?"

Marion dashes over to him and puts his finger over Choker's lips as if to hush him.

"Hey, Boss Man, if we aren't going to work, I'm going to do some surfing or start up my long awaited free diving career," Cresty says. "I want to be more than a surfer chick. I gots to work on my breathing."

I like it when she says gots like the old days.

"Why do you read a book on butterflies?" Choker asks while flapping the books front and back covers like wings.

"Simple, butterflies change," Marion says. "You, we, all of us can learn from butterflies. And they migrate too like birds. People need to learn to migrate, boy, too. At a certain point in your life you need to leave before your friends leave you… or as Keith says, 'you better walk before they make you run.'"

Marion jumps off the boat, saying "Ahh, the wisdom of Keith Richards." Quickly, Choker follows him onto the dock. He fakes pushing Marion into the swampy-green like bay water.

"The boat is kind of cute, much better than the wreck you were working on," Cresty says to Choker, grabbing him by his budding stubs of hair. "And be nice, he told me we could stay on the boat until we got settled a bit more."

"What did you name it?" Choker turns to Marion. "You name everything else and the only thing I see is the tongue. You name rabbits, but you don't name a boat and everyone names their boat."

"Even my old boss, who liked butterflies, too, even had 'The Boat' as the name for his boat?"

Choker looks around on the port side of the boat. He stops as if he is shot with a stun gun. He yells the name: "Thomas Byrd."

"More Rochambeau… Byrdie," Cresty says laughing.

"Maybe not," Marion says.

Brennan sniffs around a small pile of dead saplings in the corner of the parking lot. As Marion picks up the old pooch, Cresty tells Choker how a couple of weeks ago he left the other boat owners here each a Colorado Blue Spruce sapling with the pink and blue ribbon. But she said the trees just sat on the dock before the marina owner piled them near the blue recycling containers. She said the ribbons had already blown into the harbor.

Nodding over to the burger cooker, Marion carries Brennan back on board.

"He doesn't jump on the boat as well as he jumps off for some reason. I don't think he can get the spring he needs anymore. He is 12-years-old now."

"We know all about old dogs, like I said," Cresty says.

From a hose on board, Marion pours Brennan some water in a dented metal bowl. He places the silver bowl carefully by the main hatch. He pulls the box with Row and Way out of the hatch and carries the box, gently, with him.

"Maybe Brennan might eat Row and Way," Marion says. "He doesn't know. Sometimes you just don't know. I can't take a chance. They'll ride with us for now."

"Really, how did you get those names?" Choker asked. "Way and Row, don't tell me they were born at Altamont with you? Or is it sailing terms, like wade in the water and row your boat gently down the stream?

"Or did King Edward the Monarch name his butterflies Row and Way?"

"Man, no wonder you can't get in college. Row v. Way is the famous court case when they let black kids into public schools down south," Cresty says… embarrassing me for not teaching her about… "And, how do you know baby lullabies, row, row your boat, you hate kids more than seals… and rabbits."

"No, man that is Brown v. Board of Education," Choker says. "I'm black, I know that case."

"Indeed, you are."

"I want to know, genius girl, what's in the red cooler?"

Marion looks over to see if the guy cooking burgers is listening. Walking over toward him, Marion says something, but the guy can't hear him. Looking relieved, Marion motions with his hand to his mouth.

The guy gives a burger to Marion, who hands the overcooked grub to Cresty. She swallows the burnt burger in two bites as they all flop into the truck. Marion pulls out a box of 8-track tapes from under the seat. The musty black box with a flap holds the tapes in neat rows. He reaches to put one in the Fish Finder.

"Plenty of fish out there today," he says.

Choker yanks the 8-track tape out of Marion's hands. He stares at the picture on the front of five heads - all turned sideways with the words "Rolling Stones - Hot Rocks" and the tongue.

"Got it, the tongue is some sort of symbol for the Rolling Stones."

"Right, Andy Warhol drew the tongue. It is the Stones everlasting symbol. Each and every soul needs an everlasting symbol… cause we will all be good and gone someday."

"We know all about loving goners." Cresty says.

Waving to the burger guy, Marion pats Choker on the back as he turns the truck out of the marina. Choker fakes like he is going to choke him. He reaches to put his arm around both Cresty and Choker.

"Don't touch me man."

Cresty glares at Choker and then looks over to Marion saying, "he's not homophobic, he is actually open to people's sexuality, but we both think you should keep both hands on the wheel."

Cresty and Choker both brace themselves against the dashboard with one arm. Cresty clutches the rabbits with her free arm. Choker wraps his left arm around her.

Marion just misses hitting the marina sign, scattering the family of seagulls. Looking straight ahead, he puts on those large sunglasses from the dashboard over his Aviator sunglasses.

"Let's climb the mountain," Marion yells louder with each syllable." To the mountain top and beyond."

"Been there," Cresty says with emphasis.

"Done that," declares Choker. "The crash is just harder than from a mole hill, or a rabbit hill for us."

Marion cranks a hard left going toward the Cape May Bridge. He passes the shiny new boats of the Cape May Whale Watcher and the Spirit of Cape May Dinner Cruise fleets. He waves at a handful of skyward looking kids outside the Cape May Beach and Kite Shop.

Before the bridge, he stops the truck in the middle of the road and gazes up at a kite, dipping and darting over the canal, attached on a string held by three boys along the walkway at the highest point of the bridge. He crosses over the bridge real slow, saying, "A kite is safe on a store shelf, but that is not why kites have wings."

On the other side of the bridge, going north toward Sea Isle, the concrete road turns into the asphalt paved Garden State Parkway. There is a grass median strip separating the traffic where he makes an immediate U-turn. Marion's stare fixates over toward Cape Liquors, an older wooden-sided building next to a new vinyl-sided structure with an italic red-lettered sign: *MEDICAL CLINIC OF CAPE MAY.*

With the suddenness and subtlety of a mad man, Marion cuts over the grass median strip. They all bounce inside the cab until he pounds the brake in the Cape Liquor driveway, next door to the clinic.

The lot is crowded with SUVs packed with kids. He finds a parking spot in the rear of the store near tall weeds. He turns off the truck and swiftly grabs the old music tape out of Choker's hand, pushing the tape into the 8-track player.

He sings: "I look inside myself and see my soul is black, I see my red door and I must have it turned back, maybe then guilt will fade away and not have to face the faces. It's not easy facing up when your sold soul is black."

Choker nudges Cresty to get out of the truck with him. Marion keeps singing while getting out real slow.

"Your world is green too," Cresty says to him after the first verse, "let's cut some trees here and make money or go eat."

Choker slouches toward the back of the truck. With his shoulders hunched, he unloads the shredder. He tries to wipe the dried blood from his hand with a pink plastic bag. He can't. The blood is caked dry.

He tries to open the cooler, even though it is key-locked. He shakes the cooler.

"No beer bottles in here," Choker announces.

Marion stops singing. He is completely still. He stares over at the shiny medical clinic, and then stumbles toward Choker.

"Whoa," Marion cautions, putting a tarp over the cooler. "Easy now, Nellie."

Choker shields his body between the clinic and the cooler.

"Got gas for the saws? Or did you forget? Leave them in the black hole?" Choker asks in mocking rapid succession. And then he whispers, "Is there a bomb in the cooler?"

"I told you that the black hole is part of the galaxy where Einstein theorized time stands still. The black hole is not in Cape May."

Cresty is picking up bits of trash around the liquor store. She stops, though, when she hears Marion's suddenly raised voice.

"Einstein theorized gravity affects time," Marion barks. "He said the gravitational pull at the edge of a black hole is so strong that time stands still there."

"So, how does that tug on us?" Choker asks, motioning with both hands for Marion to lower his voice. "I don't feel a pull."

He lifts his hands toward Marion's neck and says, "My life sucks but I'm not blowing up a clinic… I know what type clinic it is."

Cresty drops the trash from her hands and darts toward them.

"Do you think… guess… hope that is where our souls go?" Cresty asks.

"Gravity is everything," Marion says, softly lowering his voice as Choker drops his hands. "Gravity is God."

Choker sits down in a lotus position right next to the trash that Cresty dropped. He turns his hands upright and lifts them up above his shoulders.

"I got to hear this one, man," Choker says.

Marion plops next to him and Cresty kneels on the other side.

The trash scatters in the wind coming from behind them in the west, over the bay.

"Should I get Row and Way out of the truck to hear this one?" she asks.

"Gravity is what causes the Big Bang and the Big Crush… or the Big Squeeze and I'm not talking about my dumps, but the start of the universe," Marion begins to preach. "Gravity rules the whole universe. Like I said, the G-word is God."

"He might be right, I know gravity affects the moon and the moon affects the tides and when we can surf on moving mountains," Cresty says.

"Remember how Pete never understood where the water went when it was low tide?" Choker laughs with sudden amusement. "Now he knows… since he is with God."

"Just think for a moment, the earth and moon orbit around the sun, the sun travels 175 miles a second around the center of the Milky Way galaxy, and our galaxy is circling under the influence of other galaxies in the universe as it expands.

"That's a lot of movement. And, unlike man, which forces laws on people, laws that kill other people, gravity rules not by force, but by inducement, or persuasion.

"Man doesn't rule by anything but force," he continues, kicking both feet in the air.

"Gravity lays convenient paths for planets and galaxies to travel through time. We are traveling through time, just like the planets. It's just that we flow in God's time.

"Pete taught us a Greek word for God's time," Choker says, "Kairos."

Marion stretches his feet out on the ground as he taps his wristwatch.

"A black hole is how God is showing us the power of gravity. God shows us there isn't time at the edge of a black hole. This is His way, I think, to show us there isn't time in heaven either. So, to understand heaven, or to think what it is like, you must understand the black holes in our universe. Then you will know."

Choker pops up. He stands on one foot. He makes the yoga prayer pose.

"Just like a thermos knows to keep food cold when it is hot and hot when it is cold."

"Or is it the other way around?" Cresty asks.

Man, it is good to hear them fooling again.

"After lunch we can talk, we really need, got to get this done here," Choker says. "But I think clearer on at least a half-full stomach. Let's go to Tony's Pizza across from the marina."

"I thought you were losing weight for your July 4th judo tournament… it's just next month," Cresty says. "There should be no lunch for you, I'll eat your share, my stomach is rumbling."

Marion stands up like a creaky board, mostly straight and walks with tempo to the sidewalk. He stops and says hello to a young girl wearing dark sunglasses with her haired tied up under a black skull hat. Her baggy clothes flap as she stumbles toward the clinic.

"Hi, there, Missy Miss."

She walks faster, not even acknowledging Marion.

Marion keeps pace with her long strides. He keeps talking before opening the center door of the building. He gently pats her back.

She doesn't turn around. She doesn't say anything.

A mean-looking lady with sun wrinkled skin under her neck and onto her chest comes out of the door. Maybe she is nice, but she looks mad, making her look mighty mean.

"Hi, there," she says looking hard into Marion's wild eyes. "Can I help you?"

She is in her mid-50s. Maybe 60. Dirty-blond hair wrapped up. She is athletic looking, even in the oversized hospital gear.

"No thanks missy madam, I do not need any help today. I will be on my way, but it was sure splendid to… meet you… "He sings, "Hope you guess my name."

Marion fast-walks back toward the truck. The lady follows him.

"What is your name? What are you doing here?" she asks.

"Yeah, he is too old to be hitting on girls your age," Choker says to her. "I think he digs the girl who went into the clinic."

"Arrest him," Cresty laughs.

"I'm sure he wasn't hitting on her, not in her condition, but he sure looked like he wanted to talk with her," the lady, rubbing her pressed white outfit, says disapprovingly.

Marion nods stupidly.

Cresty sits down back in the truck. She pets the rabbits. The lady peeks inside.

"I love rabbits, can I hold them?" she asks.

"Sure, this is Way and this is Row," Cresty says.

"Oh, oh, what interesting names," the lady says. "Not like row, row, row your boat this way down the…"

She turns and walks away backwards while waving fake politely. Marion follows her.

She stops, whispers something to Marion with her hands over her mouth.

Then she barks, "You know you shouldn't talk to the girls. We have professionals inside to comfort them."

She jogs backwards to the building as Marion joins Cresty and Choker in the truck.

"We aren't eating lunch, yet, not now," Marion says. "I'll pay you for your time. We wait here."

"Good… I need to drop weight anyway," Choker says.

Cresty drifts asleep. Not much later, so does Choker, resting his head on her shoulder.

They wake as the girl in the black skullcap is leaving the clinic. The mean-looking lady in white has her arm around her. She wipes a tissue under the girl's dark sunglasses.

Marion is sitting on top of the truck. He smiles at them as they walk past the truck. The lady grabs her hand. The girl stops. The lady puts her arm back around the girl. They turn toward the clinic's front door. Both are slouched over.

The girl turns back toward the truck. She looks as if she wants to say something to Marion. She turns back before going back into the clinic.

"Lost one," Marion says real soft. "That's one fish that got caught in the net, got out, got caught in the confusion."

Marion slumps down, sliding off the roof. He holds his head with his hands when landing.

"What's that all about, the fish?" Choker asks. "How did the lady know what the names of our rabbits were, or meant. What the hell is going on?"

"Does she know what's in the cooler? I think I hear it ticking."

Marion stares at the Fish Finder.

"It's not easy to explain," he says. "Infanticide."

Marion jumps back on the truck and climbs on the roof. He jumps off the roof.

"I want to be like the butterfly. I want to change. I want to migrate."

Marion starts up the truck, grinding the key past the ignition spot.

After blowing through the red light where Routes 9 and 109 meet, Marion drives as calm as the eye of a storm. He stops at the traffic light at Route 626 as if he is taking a driving test in high school. He makes a textbook left and crosses the canal. He seems to see the stop sign from below the bridge.

After a few seconds of driving along the railroad tracks, he makes a sharp right at the stop sign on New England Road.

Marion pauses to look at an old rusted tow truck. The red and black wrecker on their right hasn't moved for years and will never move again. On the left is Francis Delmar Barns by the Sea with a house like a Mexican villa. There is a house with a wooden sleigh sharing a dirt road with the Bay Springs Alpaca Farm.

The brown alpaca behind a wobbly fence stares back at Marion.

He turns up a gravel road. The road seems to go, well not anywhere. There are plenty of potholes.

Marion somehow misses the potholes. The truck does scrape every tree limb. The road is narrow and the trees are overgrown. The truck spurts to a stop at a dirt parking lot. There is a narrow road to the right, almost looks like a nature trail with white birch trees in heavy growth.

At the end of the road to the right is a parking lot facing the ferry. The hill is high over the canal, allowing them to see over top of the ferries and beyond to North Cape May where houses line the bay.

Across the canal, the blue house with pink trim faces them as if with arms open waiting for a lost fisherman, or sailor, or son to come home.

The two pavilions at the canal entrance are filled with joyful people. It looks like a family is having a reunion. A kid digs with his hands inside the jetty where the huge rock is missing.

Marion sprints to the back of the truck and carries out the cooler. Does he care if the rich man knows the cooler was swiped from his yacht last night? He wraps the cooler with both arms.

"Like turning a key, life changes, life ends," he says while glazing his hand over the key lock and onto the left side of the silver-gray box. "The butterfly changes three times before being an adult."

Lifting both pairs of sunglasses, he squints at small numbers on the side. He rolls the three numerical wheels and opens the cooler, using the combination 6-6-6.

"How the foo-k did you know the combo?" Cresty asks. "Who locks up their beers?"

"I didn't, it was never locked," Marion says. "I reset the combo… and no beers in here."

"You can't detonate a bomb up here," Choker protests as he points to the picnic people.

Under blue ice packs is a plastic bag.

Marion closes the lid and carries the cooler, turning toward where there is a higher dune to the back of them. The dune isn't a dune, though, it is an old landfill covered with Whipporwills, or at least that is what we called the stalks with fuzzy ends.

Marion wanders to the front of the landfill. There is a footpath to the top. They climb the muddy makeshift trail to the top. In the middle of the wavy low grass and surrounded by the Whipporwills, or whatever they are called, is oddly a lone tree sapling tied to a support stake.

The sapling is identical to the one Marion planted at Madame Palms for the mother rabbit.

He treads with his head down. Mixed in the high grass around the Whipporwills and around the sapling are scores of yellow dandelions.

A sudden cold breeze off the bay tilts the Whipporwills toward Marion. The dandelions seem to dance in the wind as, with his trembling hands, Marion digs a hole next to the sapling.

He opens the cooler and takes out the blue bag. Inside the bag, floating in yellowish fluid is an arm, two arms… two legs curled up… a shrunken head with closed eyes…

On the sandy dune overlooking the bay, Marion buries the fetus… the unborn baby.

"What…" Cresty tries to ask. "What was under the other tree sapling?"

Marion falls to his knees and shakes as the ferry's whistle wails like a sad bagpiper in the distance. On his knees, he drives a stake next to the other sapling, the new one, and ties a support cord. The wails get shorter before Marion speaks.

"Gott würfelt nicht."

Back in the truck, the Fish Finder blares and Marion sings: "I see a red floor and I want it painted black, no colors anymore I want time to turn back, I see the girls walk by dressed in their surgery clothes, I have to save the dead until the darkness goes."

Chapter 6

Another month goes by without meaning, like they do. Choker and Cresty constantly grill Marion about the fetus. How he knew where the boat was that night? Why the rich guy never reported it? Who was the rich guy?

Marion just says he will tell them in time… in God's time. "Kairos," he reminds them. "Maybe in a few days for the Summer Solstice."

The only marker in this unretractable racing of time is Marion's untrimmed beard. His crew marks the days by counting the girls who keep going into the clinic with bigger bellies. Each morning, Marion would cut across the grass median strip into the little Cape Liquor store parking lot with Cresty and Choker.

Every day.

But one.

On that day, in the morning, he parked on the median strip and told them he couldn't tell them where the unborn baby in the metal cooler came from, the one he snatched from the red boat as The Duke with the Dolphin.

Early the next morning after the thievery, Cresty had her annual "pre-summer solstice girl doc appointment." Well, that's how I remembered to schedule them, before bathing suit season. Cresty and Choker drove to Camden. I'm not into time now, but I do remember that day because it was different. The day was June 16. Choker kept saying on the ride to Camden how it was cool to take a road trip on Bloom's Day. He was an English major at Ursinus before he and Andie, Cresty, dropped out… after I went for my dive. He was reading Ulysses second semester of this freshman year, his last semester, when he changed paths.

I remember how he said it was so cool to celebrate the 110th anniversary of Bloom's Day with a road trip because he lived in Suite 110 – The Flat – at Ursinus.

Anyway, Cresty had to see a special girl doctor, Dr. Burk, a former baseball player at La Salle, I remember, a catcher. We used to talk a lot about sports when she was little, younger. He would come out into the waiting room to talk the betting line on the college hoops games. He never bet, though. The doc said he didn't believe in taking chances, or leaving fate in someone's hands. Still, he wanted to talk the lines.

It was good she went because Cresty woke up having stomach pains. But she checked out OK, I guess. Choker didn't mind the journey a bit. He walked around Camden like he was Leopold Bloom himself in Dublin. He stopped and watched two older, city-type guys play a game of chess on this run-down row home porch just one and a half blocks down from shiny, sprawling Cooper Hospital.

Cresty did ask Dr. Burk how someone would acquire an unborn fetus. He said it was illegal.

On that morning, Cooper Hospital buzzed with ambulances like the Cape May Clinic lately, but with new SUVs.

Girls, really ladies, visit the Cape May Care clinic as if the facility was an emergency room at a Camden hospital.

The July 4th holiday weekend is coming up and traffic to the shore is heavier on the Parkway. Two girls pull into the clinic lot as if they are stopping to get out of traffic for a few hours. They small talk like at a day spa one afternoon.

Marion muses in the truck for a bit before walking toward the building. He wears a white doctor smock over his white jumpsuit.

"This is weird," Choker says. "Every other day we trim and plant trees in the morning and wait next to the clinic here in the afternoon. Each day whacko talks to a confused chick going inside and then the angry lady.

"They, those two, talk so much they are actually becoming very friendly."

"Yeah, Marion seems to like to talk with the lady, but he never comes back to the truck very jolly," Cresty says. "He isn't getting any nobber, fashure."

"At least it gives us time to rest," Choker says. "You get tired quickly and I'm beat training hard for the Independence Day judo tournament."

"You are in much better spirits when you train hard," Cresty says. "Pete would be proud. I'm proud."

"I'm just fighting back against the world."

Marion returns to the truck with a smock in hand. He plops on the front seat. He twirls the face of his wristwatch backwards. First hard, then soft and hard again. He stares at the watch face as he reaches under the seat, pulling out a drawing book like the pad an artist would use.

He sketches an outline at first of a building. The drawing becomes a picture of the clinic. He stuffs the drawing book under the notebook he now keeps on the dashboard.

"That book is getting thick, like the dust in the front cab of the truck," Choker says faking a sneeze. "Why do you keep the back clean and the front a mess? Makes no sense."

"So… cool… there is methane in the dust," Marion says with a blank face behind the oversized sunglasses.

"Cool? What the foo-k you talking about?" Choker questions.

"There is methane in the dust, so that proves there was life on Mars," Marion says. "NASA has found, or their Curiosity Rover has found, traces of methane gas on the red planet. The report won't be out until the fall, but I have friends at MIT who analyze the data from the Curiosity Rover. We talk."

"I'm talking about the dust on your dashboard," Choker says.

"Oh, never mind, like the Red River flows without minding."

Choker swipes at the dust and sprays Marion. A month ago, the cab of the truck was operating room clean.

"What are all those pictures, or sketches, for anyway?"

"I draw because Charlie Watts sketches his hotel room before every concert," Marion says, twirling his charcoal pencil like a drumstick between his fingers.

"Who is Charlie Watts?" Choker asks, "is he your eye doctor?"

Marion removes the big sunglasses with his free hand, still twirling the drawing pencil with the other.

"Charlie, is the Rolling Stones' drummer," he says looking through the smaller sunglasses right into the back of Choker's ambivalent eyes. "He keeps the band on course with his beat, just like gravity holds the universe and us on our paths. Charlie draws sketches of every hotel room on the afternoon of the show. He says it helps him relax. It works. He never misses a beat, so the drawings work."

"Why don't you draw, sketch the other places we go besides the clinic?" Choker asks reaching for the pencil.

"Let me draw something for you like a slice of pizza," Cresty adds. "I'm starving mister mystery man."

With a quick swipe, Cresty sprays Marion and Choker with dust from the dashboard.

"Do you dig that lady clinic chick?" she asks playfully. "She is nice looking, not perfect, and not nice at all. Or is it all these plump girls that come here each day that you are after?"

Marion smiles and sings: "Don't play with me because you are dusting with fire."

"It's time for me to go play with some wild water," Cresty says. "I don't know what it is, but I've been feeling better in the afternoons of late. I want to go surfing. First we should eat."

"You're hungry, already again," Choker states as if he wants the time of day on record. "You're going to be eating so much you'll look like these chomping down big girls who go for their checkups here."

Marion motions to the rabbits, using the pencil like a pointer. The rabbits both are bigger, so they are now in a cage. The cab is packed with barely enough space for the dust.

A few days ago, Marion removed his little sitar. He put the baby guitar on his boat. The Thomas Byrd now has live music at night.

"First we have to take care of Row and Way. Choker has to clean the cage."

Choker grabs surgical gloves from Marion's top pocket, reaches in the door of the cage with urgent disdain. He has done this before. He scoops up the poop like making an uncontested layup. He throws some of the little pellets at Marion, spreading when hitting his white smock.

"Man, I have a hard-enough time seeing without getting hit by poop missiles."

Not even looking at the damage, Marion takes Row and Way out of the truck and holds each of them in one arm.

He busts over to the liquor store tree. He wraps Row and Way in his doctor smock. Marion climbs the tree as clinic lady, with her full face and pink cheeks so puffy she could store nuts in the winter, darts out of the clinic toward the truck. She must not have seen the nut above her as she turned up her flat nose and then walks right past the trunk of the healthy tree.

"Shit," she yells in a screechy voice when she steps in the shade of the tree.

She reaches her hand on top of her head. The face she makes can't be made unless one is truly disgusted. She throws a piece of poop back up at the tree.

"Shit, shit, shit," she continues, wiping her decorated left hand in the grass. "Bird shit. I hate you bird."

"What do you mean?" Choker protest, "what did I do."

"No birds, not you boy," she says.

Another bomb from above splats her squarely on the head as if GPS is guiding the droppings.

This is all Choker needs to see. He falls out of the truck laughing. Cresty walks over quickly to him, but he motions for her to go over to help the lady.

"Sorry, bird, I love you, I really do," the lady says, "but not this much. This is war. I want him to cut down this tree. Get rid of the problem."

Choker tiptoes behind the lady and Cresty. He winks up toward the tree. Choker looks as happy as when he made his first shot at the courts after a few pickup games in Avalon against us old guys two summers ago. Yeah, he looks even happier than when he saw Taylor Swift on the beach in Stone Harbor that summer.

"I used to like birds, especially the Atlantic Puffin, but then I started to hate all animals, but suddenly I kind of think they are all right," Choker says. "Sometimes they can even do funny… shit."

Cresty hustles back to the truck. She is there for a heartbeat and comes back with some of the diaper wipes Marion hangs on the back rack. He uses them to clean his hands after a messy tree job. He doesn't like pulp on his steering wheel or on his big sunglasses, or little ones.

"Here, we have plenty of these," Cresty says handing the wipe to the lady. "I don't know why, but we have tons. We have so many I clean my surfboards with them after the gulls drop their clams. They break them open on my long board."

"I wondered why his hands are always clean for an arborist," the lady asks while wiping and poking at her head.

She wipes herself all over her body. She cleans top to toe even though she was bombed on just the head and a bit on the shoulder. Still, she looks a mess.

"Where is my bud anyway?" she asks while still wiping places on her not even hit.

"Why? You like him?" Choker asks. "We're hoping someone does. He is a bit lonely and makes animal sounds in his sleep during afternoon nap time."

"He is interesting, I guess. I mean who would name their rabbits Way and Row? It is so obvious. He's weird, but, at least he doesn't trouble any one here. Not like the others."

"What's your name?" Cresty asks, "we want the right spelling on the wedding invitations?"

"I'm Dr. S. Hyde. Not like Dr. Jekyll either. No jokes. I never change. I'm the same person all day. Well unless birds squat on me. I just have one of those names. A name not bad enough or needy enough to make me want to marry."

"So, marry my man Marion," Cresty snaps with a slight smile and a poke of her hand to the doctor's arm.

"Never. Not again. No, it wouldn't be right. Not for my late husband."

"Oh, so sorry," Cresty blushes.

"Hey, who are you guys? What are your names? I see you around but I don't know your names. You don't have a weird name like Marion, do you?"

"We'll tell you... if you tell us what the S. in your name is short for. Well?" Cresty says.

"*Maaarioon*. Did you ever hear of a name so strange? Sounds like the honk some old guy makes when he blows his nose in church before you have to shake hands for the Kiss of Peace. You just want to smack the guy. That is who Marion sounds like."

"I'm Cresty and he's Choker. Just average names at best."

"Don't bite us," Choker adds. "Life is smacking us around enough."

"You say average? Nothing is average about any of you guys. You all are as interesting as your names. Or you seem so. Tell me what Cresty and Choker means. They have to be nicknames too. Or alias.

"Are you kids on the lam?"

"Just from life," Cresty says.

"She is Cresty because when she first started surfing two summers ago, right away she would only ride the crest of the wave and then duck out," Choker says, grabbing the back of his hamstring as if he has a Charley horse. "All the guy surfers started calling her Cresty because she was always on top of the wave, always on the tipping point. She doesn't surf much anymore, though she should. I wish she would."

Cresty shakes her head as if to say don't go there again.

"She is getting into diving without air now, free diving, but the name stuck. It still works because she is on the edge, or the crest, taking those long free dives without any air. I don't get it, really."

"The other surfers said she had a death wish riding on the crest so long, now I really think she does. Runs in the family, I guess."

"At least I like my new name,'' Cresty says poking out her chin, nudging him in the chest. "And no one says, 'hey you're Pete's foo-kin daughter' anymore. But I miss that though more than a bit."

Clenching his fists and teeth, Choker bites his bottom lip. He rubs the back of his hamstring and hops away as Cresty begins talking.

"He is now Choker because in judo he always chokes his opponent out instead of pinning them or arm-barring them. No one likes him in judo because of his choice of *how* to win. He could take the less painful win to beat the opponent, but he wants to make it hurt like he hurts.

“He can't swim either. He’d choked after going under a wave in one foot of water. He would choke to death in the surf while standing in water up to his bony knees.’’

“Hey, I get wet more than most guys like me… who can’t swim, I mean.” he says. now rubbing his gangly hands over his forearms while walking in a circle. “What, now say, what is the S. stand for?”

“Yeah, fess up,” Cresty demands.

“Just Sibyl.”

Choker shrugs his shoulders as the lady doctor leaves wiping her hair. He says, “I can see why she wants to hide her name.”

After the Sibyl lady is back in the building for a few minutes, the thick rich man from the boat pokes his head out the door. The short, but squatty-strong man extends his neck like a turtle looking toward the truck. Seconds later, Marion drops out of the tree. He hits the ground and rolls like a drunken paratrooper. Throughout the fall he holds the two bunnies in his right arm, making fatherly sure neither touches the ground. Marion is choking over his hearty laugh.

“Hey, I heard your expungement, now I know what your names mean, but I had Choker figured out anyway," Marion says rubbing his neck real hard, then soft and then hard again. "And Cresty a little bit.

"Why, anyway, you trying to marry me, The Expunger, off? I've already had my past expunged, my crimes against humanity."

"Who are you? The Fish Finder or The Expunger? You can't be both," Cresty says.

Marion says, "but I am."

"Well, then, she would be a good catch for your Expungeness," Cresty snips.

"Like the catch of the day on my old fishing boat," Choker says. "The best fish of the day, no matter how small, how puny, how smelly, would still be the best catch of the day. The best catch of the day is all you have to take home, or eat for yourself. You can't do any better than the best catch of the day."

"No, you can't," Cresty says. "The best you can catch is all you can go home with ever. No sense thinking or dreaming of any better catch."

"Hyde, a real interesting name," Marion says. "Hyde with a 'y' I guess. I'm sure with a 'y' – why else?"

"Maybe it is with an 'I', she might want to *hide* from you," Choker says grinning.

"Or she might have something to *hide*," Cresty says.

"We all have something to hide," Marion says. "Some hide hurts better. Some hide lies. Some hide the truth. Some make the truth hide.

"Some move on. Some stay still. Some end it all. But we all have something we want to hide. Some want to hide their real names. Expunge the name, like a good dump.

"We all have something inside we want to end."

"Indeed… or somethings," Cresty says, playfully kneeing Choker in the hamstring he was just rubbing.

"You hide to take the big bang in the tree," Choker says. "What else you hiding?

"Man, tell us… whose fookin cooler?"

The squatty rich man from the boat peeks out the door again. He takes a full step outside, as if he is surveying the parking lot filled with SUVs, mostly black or white, except one red Cadillac, when he sees Marion. He stands and stares at the three arborists.

Standing straight, Marion stares back.

The silence is the type of quiet you think you hear someone's soul speak. Choker must hear Marion's soul confession since he starts talking fast, the type of speed talking one does when they don't want to hear an answer they know.

"I'm sure she has a big tree at home that you could doctor everyday just to get in the door with her, so you can stop stalking her at work," Choker spits out. "Her chest is big enough."

"Yeah, we should call her Chesty," laughs Cresty.

"That's why we're here. Right?" Choker asks before adding, "She is a catch for you, a real solid double off the wall in the ninth inning. She is second and short yardage at midfield for you. She is a backdoor layup against a flat-footed zone..."

"You don't get many shots in sports or in life," Cresty injects, "so you need to make the play."

Marion tugs on the back of the pant section of his outfit. He pulls hard as if to keep his lower body from splitting away at his belt.

The rich man long-strides over to them. He points his left hand at Marion. His large gold ring flashes a beam of light from the sun on Marion's chest.

He circles Marion twice before stopping in front of him.

"I didn't mean to bomb her, but Row or Way, probably Row, had to go, you know," Marion says with an apologetic quiver of the right side and holding on both sunglasses with his left hand as he extends the right one. “It’s great that they went, I'm just sorry the deposit was on her head, even if her head is confused.”

The rich man doesn’t shake hands.

Marion puts the two rabbits back in their cage as a siren sounds in the distance. The rich man long-strides back to the building and enters the side door, taking one more look back at Marion.

“Maybe Dr. Hyde is having a heart attack because of you,” Choker says to Marion, who is slumped on the back bumper. “That dude is going to kill you.”

Cresty puts her hands over the rabbit’s ears, but Choker grabs her arms and pulls them away. He taps her on top of the head with both hands. A gentle head butt follows.

“Let… them hear… hear… the real world,” Choker says chopping his words. “The siren is stopping, or going away anyway, probably as soon as the cops get to the projects, I bet.

“Or maybe they are looking for me, the dolphin killer.”

“The marine police drive, or ride or whatever you do, in boats,” Cresty says. “You are safe from the law… not the rich guy, though.”

Sitting up, Marion curls his head close to the intermittent wailing of the sirens.

"No, it is certainly not stopping," Marion says with the complete certainty of predicting the sun will come up tomorrow. "You hear the siren is making a different sound… the change in pitch means the siren is moving farther away… they aren't coming closer… the cops aren't coming for you… or me…

"And the rich man can't hurt us… I just don't want him to stop us."

"Maybe, old man, you hear the siren going away because your ears are getting as bad as your eyes," Choker says walking over toward him and adding, "Rich man… he's not going away."

"No," Marion says, "it happens to everyone, young and old, it's the Doppler effect. I used the same principles in my weather radar."

Cresty and Choker both sit down like a school kid does when the nun eyeballs them for a lecture, or back in my day, for a scolding.

"Here we go again," Choker says not looking disappointed at Cresty. "I wish I could tell him I learned all this is middle school, but I went to Catholic school where science took a back seat to religion class.

"All that religion really helps me now, huh?"

"Religion is science and science is religion," Marion says. He circles in front of them purposefully, as if he has something to say that matters to him.

"You see, sound travels in waves to your ear at a steady speed. When the sound gets closer, it's because the waves get shorter and the pitch rises. When the sound is farther, that is because the waves are wider and the pitch is lower."

With a smooth hand motion like following the sands on a dune, he moves his outstretched arm from one side to the other going up and down. He looks like a surfer, except for the white outfit.

"That is why there is a different sound when the siren comes and when it goes on an ambulance… or a cop car sounds in your case Choker.

"Fashure," Choker emphasizes with a fist pump, "and for what?"

"You should know now, know when the next time you have a bash at your dojo, you can tell if the cops are coming or if they are going to bust the surfers and divers partying at the beach, by the pitch of the siren."

Marion reaches toward Choker's head and peels his ears back.

"Listen. Plus, if you knew how to use a Doppler radar, which works on the same principle, measuring the distance of clouds by bouncing sound waves off of them and checking the pitch, you would still be catching fish and not working for me… the *fooked-up* Fish Finder… you'd be making more catches of the day."

"Who needs fish when you have friends like we do?" Choker asks with a sarcastic high pitch.

"You're right," Marion agrees. "And the rich man likes us, too."

"Sheeeeet," Choker screeches.

"We gots real friends," Cresty declares with a head butt on Choker. "We're going with our boys from college to see the Yankees play this summer and the great De-rek Je-ter. Maybe we could take your boat up the Hudson River?"

"Ahh, on our way to New York we shall stop in Basking Ridge, at the church to see the country's oldest oak tree before it dies and, oh yeah, be careful of friends," Marion says. "Friends at your age travel to you in waves at a steady speed. When they get closer, it is because the waves separating you are shorter and the intensity rises. When they are gone, the waves spread out and you can't ever get the pitch back again.

"Don't get close to anyone… only like people at a distance like you do De-rek Je-ter."

Choker bounces to his feet like a grenade exploded next to him when he sees the rich man stick his head out the door again.

"Come on," Choker says with a discreet nod toward the rich man, "how do you know all this stuff, you're just a tree man? You aren't Pete."

Marion spreads his arms. He pretends to hug a tree. He puts both arms on Choker's shoulders. He gently head butts him.

"I heard about Pete. I look forward to meeting him… I do… I suspect soon."

"At the black hole?" Cresty asks. "Or is it *in* the black hole?"

Marion nods and says "In." His nod is definitive. Like he really knows and then he says, "Both."

"Bring me," Cresty pleas like a two-year-old asking her mom to go food shopping. "Bring me to this beautiful black hole."

He nods again. The nod is slower and longer in its arc this time.

"As I've told you, it is important to know how the universe works," Marion says. "The universe supports by serving goodness and protecting the weak just as the foothills are the foundation of the mountain, the fortress around the peak.

"You can't serve two masters… not both judo master and *the* master."

Choker reaches to grab him, but stops. His arms stay extended.

"OK. I get it, but stop being Pete," Choker says. "And… and… Just don't be telling me about the *droppler* effect when I'm trying to learn about black holes right now. I can't learn everything. This is not college. I'm a dropout, remember?"

"It's Doppler, not droppler," Cresty corrects him in a teasing tone. "And you're not a drop out, you're a *dop* out… you, we, were influenced."

Choker raises his arms slowly overhead and then dropping them swiftly, says, "Oh, I thought the droppler effect was what your boy just did in the tree."

Marion spreads his arms to the sky, making a cross with his body. He joins his hands. He clasps his fingers.

"We're all tied together by one big umbilical cord," he says pulling on his fingers but not releasing. "The universe is tied together, too. Once it stretches too far, it will bounce back.

"And, I think it's about time for a bounce back. Again. I think that's what happened to life on mars. The Big Crush crunched the red planet.

"If only relationships here on earth could bounce back," he adds, looking toward Cresty.

"Then, will the universe then bring Pete back, then?" my girl asks, kneeling.

Marion's stone-faced stare turns soothing as he waves to the rich man.

"You forgot to tell me where the Stones fit into all of this," Choker says. "They do fit in, right?"

Marion whips completely around. He rolls his arms like making a travelling call in basketball.

"You're learning quickly. Like Mick on the guitar," Marion smiles. "The Stones are the umbilical cord who pull people of different generations together. They make the big bang with their music and they pull them together for the big crush at their concerts still."

Choker reaches down to help Cresty up on her feet. She doesn't move as she did on the basketball court. She seems slow and lethargic and not the bouncy basketball girl who I raised.

"Stick with me. You will never need *no* college again," Marion says as he starts up the engine. "I will *learn* you, life and living"

"Huh?" Choker hesitantly asks. "How am I going to make any mullah? I need coin. We don't do much work."

"You can't serve both The Master and mammon," Marion says, adjusting both sunglasses and squinting behind the steering wheel.

"Right, you can't serve God and mannan as you call man, right?" Choker asks.

"Not mannan, that is polysaccharides in plant cell walls," Marion says. "It's mammon.... Wealth... material goods ... money."

"Right, then I'm doing good since I have no mullah," Choker laughs.

Marion makes a sharp right out of the lot and towards the Cape May Bridge into town. At the cross over, however, he circles back. The traffic is lighter. Going easy on the pedal, he makes a sudden left at the dirt crossover used by cops and then turns a hard-left back onto the Parkway toward the somber ocean side town.

Suddenly, at the cross over, he circles back and heads north on the Parkway again.

He drives past the Cape May Clinic without looking and makes a quick left onto Route 109, going toward the Cape May-Lewes, Delaware Ferry. He flies right through the red light.

Choker reaches across Cresty and pushes the mad driver.

"What the foo-k?"

Marion stops. The truck idles in the middle of the road as he says "Cresty wants to take off early, too, from work today. I know she didn't feel well this morning again, but since she has been surfing and diving less after work, she wants to dive today. The ocean is calm, too, I hear."

"I just ask one favor," Marion adds driving again. "I'm too old to dive or surf, but I would like to learn some judo. I never played any sports as a kid. I just studied. I want to try it."

"You aren't mean enough," Choker says. "You can't hurt anything."

"He's crazy enough," Cresty grins.

"Judo is not just a sport, it is a way of life I hear," Marion says. "I did practice some Weng Chun in college and later when I lived in Santa Cruz in my twenties, in between seven days of work building up my practice."

Choker looks startled. He extends his reach and clutches Marion's shoulder.

"How do you know about judo?"

"Judo means the gentle way in Japanese," Marion says. "I like how judo traces its roots definitively to Kato, or is it Kano? Anyway, Wend Chun is too nebulous, going back to a young girl who learned to fight to beat her master in China. I like the tangible. I like to learn and move forward. Life is too painful to go backward, waiting for the past to return."

Marion makes weird touching motions with his fingers, like a mad scientist, in the air.

"I like how both martial arts preach to be flexible," he adds. "You need to be gentle in your everyday life before you can be a judo champion on the mat. Right? Gentle is the way, then it's easy to respect your opponent, to respect life."

He rubs his eyes hard, then soft and then hard again.

"I'm gentle, I haven't eaten Row and Way yet, and I'm starving everyday trying to cut weight for the tournament… but I want to know, really, why do you want to learn judo?

"You want to protect yourself from the rich man, right?"

"There are probably eight great martial arts to choose from, right?" responds Marion with a bemused look. "I choose judo…

"I need to keep up with you. You'll get that scholarship to Stockton State. It's the top-rated judo college on the east coast and you are the best around in your weight and age, I hear. And, Stockton's coach will see your attitude is changing, too, this weekend. I'm going to Pomona, well maybe, to see for myself how you fight and how you've changed."

Choker flashes a pleased smile and says, "You're scared of the rich man."

"Before you go, I also want to learn one or two of those choke holds, especially the one from behind you do," Marion says. "I can't be teaching you with no *reciprocal-action.*

"Reciprocate me, like the universe expands and then comes back."

"I can teach you, I know it all in judo, mastering it in less than two years. Just like you know all that black hole and Rolling Stones stuff.

"But, you have to tell us whose cooler? It's the rich man's cooler, right matey?"

"You never can learn it all in anything," Cresty injects.

"The more you know in anything the more there is to learn," Marion agrees as he turns on the Fish Finder.

"You'll learn more too. I think you'll even love animals someday."

"I used to love Scoob, Pete's dog, but he left too," Choker says. "I'm not St. Francis, dude. You'll never make a saint of me."

"The Fish Finder is already working," Marion yells. "You'll Never Make a Saint of Me is a song off the Stones' Bridges to Babylon, their 8-track in 1997, before A Bigger Bang in 2005."

"Really, A Bigger Bang?" Cresty elbows Marion.

"How big can a bang be.... and don't you mean CD? That was in the nineties." Choker says.

"Somewhere I'm going to find it on 8-track," Marion says. "I will find one at one of these millions of antique stores down here in Cape May. That's one of the reasons why I am here.

"I dig antique stores, how the shops tease you to bring back the past to make the present meaningful," Marion says.

As he slows down on sleepy Route 109, which branches off to Route 9 on the right, less than a half-mile from the Garden State Parkway.

The GSP and Rt. 9 stretch parallel along the South Jersey coast, dividing Atlantic City on the East and Pomona, where Richard Stockton College is, on the west side of the two roads and continues all the way to New York state.

Route 9 intersects Route 109 and crosses Seashore Road, which runs north towards Rio Grande and south into Cape May, ending at the Promenade, where a pavilion faces the bay. The jetty there is where the beach curves toward the opening of the Delaware River Bay and is called Devil's Reach… pulling my Andie, now Cresty, to surf, to dive.

Looking in the rearview mirror, Marion drives west on Route 9 toward the ferry, which brings hope by leaving the past for the other side. He slows down to 15 miles per hour as a red Cadillac SUV creeps closer behind him.

"I thought we are going to eat," Choker says.

"We are," Marion says. "The Peking Palace is up here on the right. And, if that is crowded we can eat at Uncle Bill's Pancake House on Bayshore Road."

But with the red Cadillac SUV slowing to a crawl behind, Marion continues driving to the end of Route 9. He goes through a red light as the road turns into Sandman Boulevard. He speeds across Tranquility and Shun Avenues. Past the sideways railroad bridge on the canal, he blows another red light as Sandman turns into Ferry Road.

The red Cadillac SUV is 12-feet behind the truck when Marion says, "The Cape May-Lewes Delaware Ferry, or CMLD, is celebrating its 50th year."

Marion coasts into the car line for the ferry that launches on the Cape May Canal entrance to the bay. The red Cadillac SUV stops behind them in line.

"The canal runs under the main bridge into town and then into the east harbor," Marion explains nervously as he looks in the rearview mirror. "On the south side of the canal is New England Road, which runs past the Cold Spring Campgrounds and to the bay beach.

"Cape May is spread out. I know the layout since my boys and I used to underage drink 35 years ago, in the summer before medical school, down here on the dunes and look for leftover hippie babes sunbathing nude at Higbees Beach below the ferry."

"What's up, doc?" Choker asks after looking out the side view mirror and seeing the red Cadillac SUV.

"The dunes are high there," Marion says, pointing across from the ferry, "but they don't look like sand dunes anymore."

"We know," Cresty says, "we've been there… and Pete, my dad, took me there as a kid, I think, but there were no trees and bushes."

When I used to take Andie, well Cresty, there the dunes were all sand. They must have been cleared cut. She would roll in the sand and jump off the dunes as a young kid. She was fearless like a boy. Now the second growth covers the tops of the dunes.

Cresty often said it was her favorite place on earth. She would go with friends who I would drive. I didn't even know their names. She would fly into the air like a dude. All the other girls just slid down the dunes. She would land in the soft sand maybe 10 feet below.

Other parent types sat on the dunes without kids and watched the sunset. They sipped wine they bought on the way from Turdo Vineyards, where the ferry's whistle can be heard.

When the sun went down and my six-pack was empty, I would tell her tales of Blackbeard the Pirate and how he buried his bounty near the ferry, above North Cape May in The Villas. I told her friends, too, how some even believed he went all the way up to Burlington, which is north of Philadelphia on the Delaware River and south of Trenton. This hit closer to home for them.

There, I told them, in the river town of Burlington, Blackbeard was said to have buried his treasure. A huge dig there in 1926 revealed no gold, though. But I never told them that spoiler… just like Marion doesn't tell them whose cooler was the fetus in…

"Thankfully, trees and brush now line the dunes," Marion continues. "The dunes are natural again. The landfill even boasts high grass… and you can see the two tree saplings lined up on the hill. Both support lines are tight.

"We need to add a third one, make the mound look like Golgotha," he says with sudden determination.

"You never told us…" Cresty says, "What… who was under the other tree sapling?"

He turns off the truck, which is about 12-deep in line, and starts walking to the jetty. Choker and Cresty follow him. They sit with their legs dangling in the hole left by the missing rock in the jetty. Behind the two sunglasses, Marion keeps his eye on the red SUV.

"My dad used to tell me and my friends about Blackbeard the Pirate and how he buried his bounty near the ferry here, that's how I remember those dunes," Cresty says excitedly. "None was found, though…"

"But Cape May does have diamonds, even if there is no pirate gold, or pirate gold that has been found," Marion says.

"The 'Cape May Diamonds' can be found at Sunset Beach, a couple of miles south of the ferry on the bayside and near the Sunken Ship.

"Diamonds on the beach, you're dreaming Doc,' Choker says with one eye on the red SUV.

"The diamonds are clear quartz pebbles that wash down the Delaware River," Marion explains. "People come from all over the world to collect the diamonds."

Marion slides into the hole and motions for Choker and Cresty to slide down also. They do. Marion takes a peek above the jetty.

"People are coming from all over the world now to Cape May, to collect…" Marion whispers. "Planned Parenthood, the clinic here in Cape May, sold the fetus we buried, I buried… to the rich man.

"The rich man, and Planned Parenthood couldn't call the cops and say someone stole the late termer because it is illegal for abortion clinics to sell unborn babies for parts, for science.

"The rich guy on the boat is an intermediary for the research company. He is used to dealing with 'prolife fanatics' but The Duke and The Dolphin outwitted him.

"No matter, he will just buy another fetus... and another."

Back on top of the jetty, they see the red SUV is gone. They stroll to the truck as Marion tells them, "Cape May is also tops in the northeast United States for bird watching, with over 400 species recorded over the years. The world-famous Cape May Observatory is located in Cape May Point."

Chapter 7

With the ferry debarking behind them, Marion makes a lazy loop at the end of the road, driving past the wide ferry entrance. He loops beyond Uncle Bills and hooks a sharp left into Peking Palace.

With the front bumper, he knocks over a green picnic bench outside. Some Cape May Diamonds, probably left by a collector or a kid, fall to the sand back to where they came.

"Sweet driving," Choker says.

"This is the only Chinese place east and west of Hong Kong that serves Mexican food," Marion boasts.

Cresty orders three bean and cheese burritos as she is being asked what she wants to eat by the elderly lady wearing a black Che Guevara t-shirt behind the counter. Marion orders a chilidog. Choker points to chicken taco on the smeared menu taped to the counter.

From the condiment counter, where a massive green head fly buzzes, Marion loads on extra cheese. He spills half on his hands.

"How can you, Mr. Animal lover of all people, eat meat?" Choker asks. "Can I use your computer in the truck to schedule an angioplasty for you tomorrow?"

Cresty chews with thoughtful bites. Her eating is fierce, like me woofing down a late-night cheese steak at Tony Luke's in Philadelphia when drunk after leaving a Flyers game back in the Stanley Cup days.... forty years ago.

They eat while going back to the truck to eat. Cresty asks if she can finish Marion's grub. He reads a section of the newspaper he took off the picnic table, the one he crushed.

Cresty takes two bites from Marion's chilidog. She drops a Cape May Diamond out of her hand into the rabbit cage.

Marion jumps out of the door singing, "I'm just waiting on a friend."

Cresty and Choker wince to his cracking voice singing, "I'm not waiting on a lady, I'm just waiting on a fiend."

He hums. From the humming, he flows into a lesson.

"I thought we would talk more about our Milky Way galaxy, or Snicker's bar galaxy as I like to call our backyard," Marion says pointing toward the puffy white clouds. "Get it? Milky Way is a candy bar and so is Snickers, the world's most perfect food."

"Huh?" Choker huffs and then closes his eyes. "Let's talk about who was in the red SUV following us."

"There are millions of galaxies," Marion says, sitting back in the truck. "On Saturday, after the judo competition, I'll take you down to Sunset Beach and we can observe M87 galaxy."

"Say what? You're fooked," Choker says. "I'm thinking the rich man from the clinic was in the red SUV. Right?"

"The M87 galaxy was discovered in 1978," he continues when Cresty says, "No. stop with the galaxy… I mean, you said Saturday, after the tournament, are you going to Choker's competition for real?"

"Well, I guess the secret is out. I already said so."

"The only secret I want out," Choker demands, "is the driver of the red SU…" Marion reaches across the seat, rubs him on the head real hard, then soft, then hard again.

"And then we'll check out old M87. A must-see," Marion resumes seamlessly. "M87 is part of the Ungo, or maybe it's the Virgo, Cluster and it is 50 million light years away. Its black hole is massive. A billion times bigger than the sun."

"Our sun?" Choker asks before grumbling, "I don't want you guys coming to the tournament. Not in a light year. If you go, I'm out."

Marion pops out of the cab again and hovers around the driver's side of the truck before sliding in and starting the truck up. He pulls out and scrapes the bench again before both back wheels drop down the curb and onto the street.

"We're going and you better go, you need to win this, to get that scholarship and show that Stockton coach that you've changed and you just aren't out for yourself anymore," Cresty pleads. "I want to be there."

"We want to be there," Marion says, putting on and then taking off his big sunglasses.

"No real need. Nope. I'll win and I haven't changed that much. And why are you so concerned about me and my future the last few weeks?"

Marion doesn't give her time to answer as he taps him with his sunglasses. Cresty snatches the sunglasses and puts them back over the other sunglasses on Marion, who speeds up and blasts through a red light at Seashore Road. He continues speeding toward the Parkway.

"Light travels at 186,000 miles a second," Marion says.

"So, do you," Choker says.

Marion makes a windmill guitar motion while letting go of the wheel.

"A light year means, the simplest way for me to explain is I mean, if a light leaves a star and it takes 66 million years for me and you to see it on earth, it's 66 million light years away. That's why I have to act now. I am losing time. Light years are flying by."

Marion sails up Route 9 toward the intersection where the road splits to the north and before turning back into Route 109. Just before the Parkway, he makes a hard right into the parking lot of the Cape May Clinic. The two-story white building with a red roof stands out next to the dull gray Cape Liquor Store. There is a yellow house with a new clothesline stretched in the backyard between the basketball court and a swing set on the other side of Cape Liquors, which is protected in the back with barbwire.

Out of nowhere, a crowd multiplies in front of the clinic. Two men sit on each of the red benches. The four of them chomp on the bottom of the cones from Villa Bean Creamery down the street. Some ladies with ice cream still smeared on their hands hold signs and chant "It's not freedom of choice when babies have no choice."

"Yeah, baby, this is for girls who want to drop pounds," Choker smirks.

"Yeeee-sssss, Jesus, yeeee-ssssss," Marion says slowly, "this is where they give out haircuts."

"Haircuts?"

"How would you know about haircuts," Choker adds. "Your hair is wild, so is your beard, just like you're driving."

"Errrr," Marion says making a silly pirate sound. "I cut my hair using Keith Richards' `hey, that piece got to go' method. It works for him *a wright.*"

"Hair my ass," Cresty scorns, "rather head cuts for kids."

"So, what's the problem, it's legal, isn't it?" Choker says. "Cresty, and how do you know about that stuff anyway? You are Catholic, too."

"We don't go to mass anymore."

"Pete isn't here to take us, that's why," Choker says.

Marion pulls up in the Cape Liquor lot next to the clinic, near enough to hear the sign people chanting.

"Sympathy for the Devil" clicks on the Fish Finder.

The law is here. The police hang by the side of the crowd. Marion turns up the Fish Finder. The sign people look over.

"Good, they can hear the music" Marion says. "They need to hear the gospel of Mick and the Stones."

"So, can the police," Cresty says. "They can hear the Stones too."

"What goes on inside the building is Stone Age stuff," Marion huffs, shaking his head, putting his arm around Cresty.

Marion makes balled-up fists with his hands. He puts up his dukes like a boxer.

"As the Stones say, it's time to do fish finding in the streets, boy," Marion angrily sings.

Marion grabs Row and Way out of their cage. He hugs them.

"If Row and Way's mommy had an abortion, there would be no Row and Way, and, we would've lost out not knowing them. Never being able to take care of them. Our loss as much as theirs."

"Rabbits can't have abortions, you silly rabbit," Choker says. "Bad argument, allegory, metaphor or whatever the foo-kin-phor…"

The two cops walk across the street toward the truck. One is whistling Stairway to Heaven.

"You better get lost," said the cop with the thick old-school mustache and without humming the Zeppelin song.

"We're here to doctor some trees next to that place, but the driveway is blocked," Marion says. "We not here to bug, as Bono would say, anyone."

The whistling cop smiles and says, "We'll clear an opening if you promise no trouble, not even a fake baby cry."

"Really, we don't want any trouble," the other cop says. "We want to get done our shift and drink at the Ugly Mug… our mug is hooked in the rafter and awaits us… after our shift."

After a quick talk with a lady leader, who could pass for Dr. Hyde's twin sister, in the crowd, the cops clear the driveway just as "Sympathy" ends.

Marion pulls into his usual spot behind the liquor store's side storage shed with the Bud Light summertime Jersey Shore sign showing a bunch of good-looking guys and hot girls drinking with the words 'Here we go' and 'We ID.'

He walks past a white trash bin with long black handle locks. He picks up trash under the picnic table before following a young girl walking to the side door entrance of the clinic.

The crowd in the front can't see her. The door is blocked by a large metal container, which is marked HAZARDOUS WASTE.

"Please, let's talk," Marion begs while stretching his steps.

The girl picks up her pace.

"That's a nice black dress. I'll buy you a matching white one if we can talk a little," Marion says.

"Screw you."

Marion turns, and slumps back to the truck.

He looks like he did when the rabbit's blood was all over the wood chip pile while slumping in the sweaty seat.

A few minutes later, the girl with the black dress walks out of the side door of the building. Dr. Hyde helps her back inside.

The girl leaves again. Holding the door, the girl doctor waves to us in the truck and waits for her to return. Hyde does not walk after the girl.

The girl turns around, and is paralyzed looking at the door. From her hand, she ties a pink sash around her head, making a bow, and goes back in the side door.

"I don't have all day today to sit around," Choker barks.

"Right let's work," Marion says, popping his head up. "You guys wait here. If the cops come over, tell them I'm up high checking out some of those Colorado Blue Spruce trees in the back."

Marion walks to the side door of the clinic. He tries to open the side door, but it doesn't budge. Choker whistles and points to the front door.

Marion nods. He goes over to the blue spruces bordering the back of the clinic like sentry guards. The mustache cop stops at the side door, peeks inside and then watches Marion inspect the blue spruce branches.

"Lovely," Marion says peeling apart a pine needle.

The other cop with drinking on his mind walks with a purpose to the front of the building where the crowd thins.

Marion returns to the truck, sighs and pets Row and Way. Taking off his big sunglasses, he pulls his John Deere hat over his eyes and slumps in the seat.

A few hours later, the girl in the black dress, but without the pink sash bow, slides out the side door. Alone.

She cuts across the liquor store lawn. Stops. Looks where to go. The crowd and signs are gone. She wanders toward the truck. Marion pokes his head out of the window, knocking his hat off and putting both sunglasses on. An earflap breaks off the larger glasses and drops on the stone parking lot.

"Are you all right, OK?" Marion asks softly, reaching with one hand as if to hug her.

"All right? OK?" she says looking upward toward the sky. "I had no choice."

"Do you need a ride? Would you like to talk? How about sit under the big blue spruce with the fine needles."

Trying to run at first, she slowly walks, or more like waddles, away.

Marion slumps in the cab. He rubs his eyes under the sunglasses.

"Are you crying too? You are, aren't you?" Choker asks, "What the foo-kin hell are you crying about? Balls, this is nuts."

"I'm not crying, I don't cry anymore, my eyes are just bothering me," Marion says holding his broken over-sized sunglasses. "Can you see who is walking out the back door of the clinic? Someone is."

"It looks like a doctor or somebody, carrying a bag," Choker says.

The rich man from the boat, the guy who was hoodwinked by The Duke and The Dolphin, is dressed in medical clothes. He stares straight ahead at the medical waste bin. He drops the bag in the dumpster. Marion sits straight up.

"Tell me when the accomplice is inside," Marion says putting on the sunglasses without the broken wing.

The echo from the top of the dumpster slamming rings like a siren. The echo is haunting. The banging sound rolls like the Doppler effect until the rich man enters the building, and without looking behind him, slams shut the glass door.

Marion pops out of the truck. He zips straight toward the dumpster. Looking around quickly to the front, he lifts the lid. He pulls out the green plastic trash bag. He gently lowers the lid. There is no sound when he lets go. There is no echo as he walks quickly to the truck. He runs holding the bag in one hand and steadying the broken sunglasses on his face with the other.

"Hey, you didn't forget the trash bags today?" Choker says with a nervous mock. "We have plenty of the blue and pink ones in the back."

Marion sits in the truck. He opens the bag. Another blood red metallic cooler.

He makes a U-turn on the Parkway crossover before entering Cape May and sits at the traffic light as families pour into the historic village from South Jersey, Philadelphia and beyond.

As the light turns green, the rich man leaves the building and gets into his red Cadillac SUV that is parked in front where the protesters chanted in a handicap space. He pulls around the building.

Marion makes a left through the red light and sees the rich man's SUV stops in front of the dumpster. Marion watches the rich man in the rearview window.

Chapter 8

Pulling off to the side of the road in front of Uncle Bill's, Marion opens the cooler. He lifts the two plastic ice bags. Underneath, in a clear bag with yellow fluid, are two opened eyes.

Marion flips over the bag.

"A lovely girl."

Cresty throws up.

Choker holds his hands over his mouth before falling out the door in front of the lady in the Che t-shirt from the Peking Palace, who is smoking a cigarette in Uncle Bill's parking lot.

"Get me a pink bag from the back," Marion says as detached as ordering his lunch a few hours earlier. "Pink, please.

"Come on, hurry," Marion adds with urgency as he waits for a break in traffic to pull out.

Marion revs the engine and pulls away as Choker leaps in the moving cab.

He politely waves to the families driving west toward the declining sun over the Parkway and into Cape May.

Choker climbs through the back window of the truck as Marion starts driving faster. He hands Marion a pink bag though the window.

Marion holds the pink bag in the hand he is driving with and then with the free hand he puts the ice-wrapped fetus bag into the pink bag while swerving through a red light. His broken sunglasses fall off his face into the bag.

Cresty wipes the puke off Row and Way, who are snuggled on her lap, as Choker climbs back up front. Marion turns on the Fish Finder. Street Fighting Man blares.

He turns the music up louder: “Everywhere I fear the sound of stabbing, changing feat boy, because summer is here and the time is right for fish finding in the street boy, hey, think the time is right for a social revolution, but where I live the law game plays compromise solution, hey said my name is called Deliverance, I'll shout and scream, I'll kill this ring, I'll set bail for all Hell’s servants."

He blows through the red light where Route 9 and 109 meet. Marion stops at the traffic light at Route 626. He makes a left and crosses the canal. After a few seconds driving along the railroad tracks, he makes a right at New England Road and drives past the old rusted tow truck, past the house like a Mexican villa and the one with a wooden sleigh, past the Alpaca Farm.

He turns up the gravel road and stops in the dirt parking lot.

Marion jumps out as the truck stops while holding the pink bag like a sleeping baby in his right arm. He eats a Snickers bar with the free hand. He shoves the Snickers into his mouth.

Marion hurries to the front of the landfill and zags up the footpath to the top. He treads with his head down, making sure to step around the two saplings and patches of yellow dandelions. He digs a hole in the middle of the two saplings, pulling the sand with both hands like a dog digging for a bone.

Marion lays the pink bag in the hole gently. He pushes the sand back into the hole… the grave.

The ferry's whistle wails like a sad bagpiper in the distance. As Marion kneels, the wails are shorter.

"Gott würfelt nicht."

"What…" Cresty ties to ask.

"What?" C'mon tell us what that means?" Choker asks. "What the fook?"

"No," Cresty interrupts. "What… who is under the other tree sapling."

"It's German, it means God does not play dice…" Marion says quickly, "You know who Einstein is?"

Choker flashes him the "You're crazy look." Cresty looks stone-face numb.

"I know you've seen pictures of him, he said that about the universe. How it works. How we work. But he later recanted that theory of saying it was the biggest mistake of his life and that the universe works the way God made it and nothing happens by chance."

Cresty's face brightens up, well her cheeks at least moved.

"You mean it's not like Rochambeau?" She asks. "Not just a roll of the dice?"

Marion rocks his hands like he is rolling dice as Choker turns to him, saying, "It was dumb luck that we met. Wasn't it?"

"I don't think so, Phelge."

Choker edges into Marion's tense face.

"Easy, only Uwrenski can call me by my judo name. Understand. When you get your fifth-degree black belt you can call me anything you want."

"Chill, Phelge is my email... Phelge@gmail.net," he says. "Now that's Rochambeau... huh?"

Marion rambles: "And, I quote, '`There was a time when lifestyle, if you will, were as important as the show itself. A time when it all seemed to be one blur. But eventually it is the music that wins and everything else becomes just a means to the end.' End of quote."

"Einstein said that too?" Choker asks.

"No, another genius, Keith Richards."

Marion scurries down the trail, zips to the back of the truck and grabs a sapling. He unwraps the baby tree from a plastic tube. He stumbles up the hill. He claws with his right hand a narrow groove and plants the tree sapling in the hole above the pink bag. Kneeling on both knees again, Marion gazes beyond the ferry.

"I guess it's fine to quote Einstein and Keith in the same breath. They do have the same chopped-up hair styles," Cresty says. "And Marion's head game is beginning to look like both of them."

"Do you know what he just did?" Choker snaps. "He is foo-kin crazy. We could go to the clink."

"For what? Trash picking?" Cresty asks as she ties a support line to the sapling and Choker wraps the cord twice around a stake.

Marion kneels on one knee next to the hole, now. Choker and Cresty take a knee next to him. Cresty bangs in another stake and Choker ties a second cord around their sapling.

"For the ones, we can't save." Marion prays.

"Is that another red dogwood?" Cresty asks while stroking the sapling.

"No, this is a pink dogwood. It has low branching limbs. It will live a long time up here, all of them will.

"And some day, when you are on the other side of the bay, you will be able to see the trees," Marion says. "And hopefully you will ask yourself, am I doing, right?"

"Are you?" Choker asks.

Marion stands up, pushing off with his hand on the shoulder of Choker and says, "When we go to the Judo match Saturday, I want you to show me that choke hold."

Arm-in-arm, the three descend the hill and walk without words to the truck. Marion turns on the Fish Finder and clicks to another Stones' song, Dandelion:

"Little girls and boys can't come to play, bring their dandy lying to blow away. Dandy lying don't tell but lies, dandy lying will make you die, tell me if she shrieks or cries, blow away dandy lying, blow away dandy lying."

With a resolute head bob, Marion turns down the same path back to the parking lot. The cab is quiet. The only sounds are the slashes of branches against the truck's sides on the way down the hill. He hits every pothole.

Everything inside the cab is bouncing. The truck roof hits a solid tree limb. At the bottom of the shoddy road, the Fish Finder pops out from underneath the dashboard. The wires of the Fish

Finder are exposed. So is the inside of the box. It is cracked. Marion pumps the brakes. He picks up the broken machine and holds his eyes again.

“I got this in high school. I'd listen to it so loud on the way to school I couldn't hear the nuns for the first two periods, class periods.”

As he chooses his words, Marion carefully places the broken pieces on his lap. Silence.

“Are Row and Way all right?”

Cresty nods while petting them as Marion wipes his eyes. He drives past the Alpaca farm, singing, “I don’t want to be your beast of burden,” and past the old rusted tow truck that will never move again. He makes a right at the railroad tracks and drives into West Cape May.

Marion pulls the truck off to the side of the tracks. From under his seat, he hands Choker a piece of paper on cardboard. Cresty turns the paper cardboard around. She looks on the back and then the front again. She flips back to the back where there is a sequence of numbers.

“I want to know what it means that… that God doesn't play dice, or no Rochambeau?” she asks.

“That is Einstein's answer to quantum physics,” Marion says. “Einstein reasoned everything happens for a reason in the universe and he used math to prove it, $E=MC^2$ or energy equals mass times the speed of light twice.

"Quantum physics teaches things just don't happen by chance. I believe Einstein. We. You. Me and you didn't meet by chance."

"We met because of Cresty," Choker says.

Marion taps the side of the broken Fish Finder.

"There is another reason we met, you'll see, just like there is a reason my Fish Finder busted, too. We just need to discover the reason, like Einstein needed to know if resting mass had energy.

"So… now I need to know the reason why Fish Finder broke. I know if I find the answer, I will find other answers. I need to go discover the *why*s. You do, too. Let's go on the road to learn…. and to find a new Fish Finder."

"We'll have to, it's not like we can buy one," Cresty says recognizing they need to get out of Cape May, to lay low after what they just did at the clinic.

Marion drives like a tourist, putt-putting slowly through Cape May before turning around at a circle on Columbia Avenue and Gurney. There is a tall concrete statue in the middle of the plaza. Marion says, "The pointed concrete monument is a memorial to the soldiers and sailors who gave their lives in the Civil War, so we could be free… free to make choices." Across from the statue are kids playing whiffle ball on the green lawn of The Abbey, a Spanish-looking Baptist Church in the middle of all the Victorian Homes in the square. A kid, the pitcher, yells "foul ball" on a hit off the statue.

Pulling his hat down closer to his sunglasses, Marion traces his route back to the bridge by the railroad tracks, which cross the canal. He passes the library across from Hawthorn Cottage with old people playing checkers on the porch without any kids or pets bothering them. He passes the white horse drawn carriage waiting for riders at the mall flagpole in front of the Washington Commons shopping mall and the crowded ACME parking lot. He drives down Lafayette Street and passes in back of the rectory with the statue of Jesus, his arms spread, welcoming vacationers into town.

Marion drives to the fishing boat where Choker worked for Mr. Hallward.

"This is your final, your last chance to go back," Marion states.

Cresty and Choker poke around on board while Marion throws stones into the bay. They grab some clothes and stuff Choker had left just in case "surviving in the judo hut didn't last." They chuck Choker's gear into the truck.

"Let's go to my place," Marion says as gleefully as a fan at a baseball game catching a foul ball. "But first…"

They drive in silence. Fish Finder is quiet.

They drive up the Garden State Parkway toward Sea Isle, past a lake in the middle of the north and south bound lanes near the Rio Grande exit, where Marion suggests, "Blackbeard could bury even more treasure." At the exit before Avalon, which is south of Sea Isle, Marion turns right toward the ocean at Exit 10 - Stone Harbor.

He glides to a stop in front of Our Lady of Lost Angels Roman Catholic Church on 99th Street.

The sign says the church is part of St. Paul's Parish.

"Perhaps this is *our* road to Damascus," Cresty says.

"We should walk then like Paul," Choker says. "Maybe we will be saved, too."

They walk back toward the bay on 99th. They cross Corinthians Drive. "Really, Corinthians Drive, Paul wrote to the Corinthians," Cresty says. "I remember the nuns telling me his words were spoken in plain language with simple metaphors, but he was powerfully pervasive."

"Subtle but strong," Marion says, "like gravity."

They drift with a wide left turn together on Sunset Avenue. The bay, smelling like a pile of sweaty basketball socks, stinks and sinks to the right.

At the dead end of Sunset, they hook a right on Berkley.

"An omen, I went to college at Cal-Berkley," Marion professes. "I was a pre-med major, but freshman year I had to take an English literature class. The only piece, or poem, I remember was by the Welshman Dylan Thomas, I remember because back then we were protesting still to Bob Dylan songs.

"Anyway, Dylan Thomas wrote a poem, Do Not Go Gentle into the Night."

Marion rubs his hands real hard, then soft and then real hard again. He reaches for his broken large sunglasses on top of his John Deere hat since they are not over his eyes with the smaller glasses.

Stopped in the gutter of Berkley, he realizes the glasses dropped into the plastic bag he had buried. Unfazed, he says, "In later college years, when trying to flesh out Creationism and Evolution and delving deep into the Scopes Monkey Trial, I read a quote by H.L. Mencken, who said 'Every normal man must be tempted at times, to spit on his hands, hoist the black flag, and begin slitting throats.'"

Stepping on the curb, Marion spits in his hands, rubs them together real hard, then soft and then real hard again.

"I prefer to call it simply 'delivering the goodness.'"

Chapter 9

They don't hideout for long. The next morning, with the sun already bringing its business, Marion drives through Cape May proper, which is just the downtown. Still, the proper people must call it such.

The cab is quiet like the sleepy streets it covers. He wears a new pair of big sunglasses he bought last night in Stone Harbor after stopping at Fred's Liquors to ask when the Stones' cover band plays. He wears the oversized specs over the Aviator glasses, the same type that old folks wrap over their prescription glasses. He has a backup pair resting on the bill of his JD cap.

A lone newspaper truck, still with its lights on, passes their peaceful truck. Marion checks to make sure his lights are off. The low, early morning haze rising off the bay reflects the headlights like a grainy mirror.

Going away from the beach, Jackson Avenue dips into West Perry Street, where the All Irish Import store and Swains Hardware dip at a low point. Marion slows down at both stores as if he wants to stop, but neither is open.

He turns at Colliers Liquor Store, going west and heading to the old lighthouse. He drives past a 7-11 with fresh newspapers stacked outside still.

Perry's Video Store, Good Mothers Restaurant and a modern CVS Pharmacy stand on the corner of Broadway and Sunset Boulevard. The stores all have outside porch lights on still from last night.

"The locals call this section the *sold-out strip* of their quaint Cape May," Marion says to the sleeping Cresty and Choker. "The proper people don't drive this way to the lighthouse. They make the loop out of town and back over the canal near the railroad tracks, stopping on their way at Turdo Vineyards.

"For the vacationing families, the prices are cheaper here on this commercial strip corner than on the Promenade and the Downtown Mall. So, the stores thrive, even more than up the road on Sunset where a series of antique stores are in the business of just getting older."

A mile or so on Sunset, heading toward the bay, past the Black Duck Restaurant and the West Cape Motel, Marion pumps his breaks at Lighthouse Row, which is a string of identical modern-looking, three-story Victorian homes that he says, "Stand together like a big Irish family with all the kids a year apart and looking the same."

The homes are double homes, split right down the middle. The one side mimics the other half right down to the mailbox.

He waltzes through the red light, continuing down the lonely road past West Cape May to The Pointe.

Ahead, off in the western distance, the ferry's whistle crossing the bay is as loud as the intermittent snores from Choker and Cresty. Row and Way huddle under the dash where the Fish Finder used to hang.

The early morning fog thickens as Marion pulls closer to the bay. Missing is the usual line of trucks with fishing poles poking out of their front grill heading toward the Sunken Ship.

"I thought the roads would be crowded," Choker says, stirring and rubbing his drowsy eyes. "You always hear the same apocalyptic travel warnings on the radio the day before a holiday weekend."

"That is why I don't have a radio," Marion says. "You can't believe what you hear on the radio, not like Einstein and the Stones."

"Yeah," Cresty mumbles with her eyes still shut. Her feet are up on the cage. "Maybe all the drivers are on horses. Maybe they are horsemen," she adds, trying to stretch out even more.

Marion grips the steering wheel, bulging the veins in his strong hands. He drives steady at 35 miles per hour even though the ground fog warns he should cut his speed in half. He flips up his large sunglasses only, though, on top of his hat.

Sunset Boulevard stretches past the Cape May Nature Conservatory on the left. On the right is an asphalt road covered with sand leading to Higbees Beach, which is a Wildlife Management Area stretching off the bay with miles of undeveloped shoreline and as Marion tells the lads next to him, "Higbees was a nudist's beach."

"The half mile or so stretch of sand wasn't officially, or lawfully declared a nude beach," he adds. "Years ago, before syringes and rubbers splashed in the waterline, nudists packed the unmarked wildlife boundary…. and into the complaints around the tea table of the old-time locals."

"How do you know?" Cresty quips.

"I'm told, a narrow stream runs through Higbees and into the bay," Marion chuckles, "dividing even the nudes back in the day into the ones who were really nudists and the ones who were just reading the menu."

Almost missing the entrance of the turnoff to Cape May Pointe, the truck scrapes the painted white concrete fence with black gates. He pumps the brakes at the circle, past houses hidden by trees, where St. Agnes Roman Catholic Church, painted gray with green trim, juts out with its shiny gold cross stabbing skyward on the roof. Across from the church and much less conspicuous is the barn-red Cape May General Store.

"Last January, I had won tickets from American Express to the Super Bowl back in San Francisco, but it was the same weekend as my wedding," Marion says.

"Huh?" Cresty huffs.

"What? Who would marry you?" Choker adds with the disbelief of seeing the fetus in the red cooler.

"I sent an email to my male friends asking if they were interested…." Marion continues. "I wrote whoever was interested would *love* the quaintness of this clapboard church…. and to just ask for the lady wearing the white dress."

Across from the church, dogs do their business in the middle of the open park inside the circle. On a spoke of a road down Pearl Street rises the landmark - St. Mary's by the Sea.

Marion blesses himself going by the old age home for Catholic nuns resting in the shadow of the towering lighthouse, only a block away at the point of the beach. This fortress of a three-story white structure with a red roof boasts a welcoming wrap-around porch lined with empty rocking chairs.

Adjacent from the retirement fort is a condominium named appropriately SOMEWHERE IN TIME.

"There are only a few kids who ever run around the bay beach near the nun home, even with its inviting wraparound porch," Marion laments.

The home covers a whole block on the dune. There are over 50 bay-breeze windows facing the water. The windows are always open in the summer when the nuns are down convalescing.

"There are fewer nuns each summer," Marion explains. "Still, the kids pull on their mom's hands away from walking past the nun home.

"Perhaps their reluctance stems from the port-o-john placed by the town at the sandy pathway to the beach near the house."

Marion calls the home the "Hearst Castle of Cape May" when he stops to use the outdoor john. He doesn't piss in the head on his boat. He says the holding tank fills up too quick with Choker and Cresty on board now. Cresty is peeing a lot lately. Brennan still pisses out the bow hatch window facing the bay.

"Before I started the business of saving trees here, I started a blind cleaning business," Marion says while knocking on the truck door. "I knocked on the door at the nun home and a voice yells 'Who is it? I'm in the shower.' I yelled '*theeeee Blind Man*'..." after a minute a nude nun comes to the door dripping.

"She says, 'Oops, I thought you were a blind man and couldn't see.'"

"No way," Cresty says.

"Haha," Choker laughs. "What did you say to her?"

"I said, 'nice... nice abs... I'm here to clean the blinds.'"

"Ahhh, you got me," Cresty says.

"Old jokes," Marion says. "They never get old. They still work, like the lighthouse here. There is no shelf life to old jokes. They never end. Not like relationships, which always exit sad.... or they wouldn't end... or pregnancies."

Above, the mighty white Cape May lighthouse reigns over this cozy corner snugged into the southern-most tip of the state. Even the local's necks are sore by mid-day, gazing up to the top from the magnetic pull of the spiraling ivory lighthouse with the force of the Cern supercollider.

Looking up, Marion makes a loop in the lighthouse parking lot and drives around the circle at the center of The Pointe. He stops the truck on the side of the state park office, which also serves as a store. Choker struts over to a Frisbee lying in the street and wings it toward a dog and his master playing in the park before going into the store. Cresty sits on the porch, curling over her knees while holding the rabbits in each hand. Marion comes out with another pair of the old people sunglasses.

"Backups," he yells sliding into the truck while saluting the lighthouse. He turns and waves with a hearty "goodbye house of light" as he slashes a park trashcan making a right turn out of the driveway lot. He speeds to the backend of the Pointe.

"There is a fresh water lake around here somewhere. Lilly Lake," he claims. "Legend says Blackbeard holed up there. The lake is surrounded by old growth trees that cloaked the pirates with secrecy."

This section of Cape May Point farthest from the lighthouse is lined with sprawling low-profile new houses and is tucked up against the fringe of the bird conservatory. The homeowners let the milkweed grow wild to attract the Monarch butterflies.

The butterflies and birds swarm The Pointe, which for some reason has an 'e' at the end when just referred to as *The Pointe* and no 'e' when called *Cape May Point.*

"Howard Stern, the radio icon, visits here often," Marion says, placing his backup sunglasses above his other backups on his John Deere hat, looking like a jockey ready to race on a muddy track. "His sidekick Robin, the good-natured woman who laughs, owns a home tucked down one of the curvy streets at The Pointe.

"This bucolic, bird-watching cape community, however, isn't divided about having the controversial Stern visiting with hot young girls. People let each other live."

Swiveling his head, sending one of the backups flying, Marion looks both ways on Sunset before pulling out of the gated entrance of The Pointe. He is wearing one pair of large sunglasses, another landed on the dashboard and one with the tag still on, sit rests above the bill of his hat. He sweeps a sharp right and then a soft left on West Drive. At the 'Y' in the road, he hooks a right on a narrow street called Stevens. Farms flank each side.

"The latitude is the same and the climate is similar to Napa Valley in California, so grapes are grown at the wine vineyards down here," Marion explains.

The Willow Creek Winery, a burnt-orange plantation house with an accented red roof, is a private residence. In front and open to the public, rising with majestic grandeur is the wine tasting building with its spiral staircase to the second floor of the barn-looking house. An intoxicating sweet odor twists up the stairs.

Across the street, another barn with a lookout tower juts out like St. Agnes Church. Down the street is a Victorian house with an inviting wraparound porch and a sign on one pole reading "STEPHEN'S STREET BEACH CLUB" here on a street spelled Stevens.

Rea's Farm Market corners the junction of Bayshore Road. A white split rail fence surrounds a greenhouse at Rea's like a moat. Marion hops out of the truck and props on top of the fence. Twisting, he cuts his hand surveying the Napa-esque landscape.

"You're bleeding," Cresty points.

"Yes, I'm meant to be here," Marion nods. "Sometimes you got to get a bit bloody."

"What is this place?" Choker asks. "I mean, I know it's a farm."

"The air temp is the same here as Northern California. Reminds me of Altamont Motor Speedway."

"Huh? You sure, you better not be checking out for any leftover hippies," Choker says, grabbing his crotch sitting in the truck.

"In 1969, the Stones delivered a free concert at Altamont, remember? I told you," Marion says.

“Yeah, they hired the Hells Angels as body guards and paid them by giving them all the beer they could drink,” responds Choker. “Brilliant.”

“Yeah, the Stones always were… and still are ahead of their times, it wasn't their fault a fight broke out and a dude was stabbed. Half the Hells Angels were mixing in and partying with the crowd, the other half was fighting with the crowd.

“You see, you chose what side you want to be on. Do you want to live and sing Let It Bleed with the Stones or do you want to get bloody stabbing, killing someone? You pick your side of the fence.”

“You are preaching,” Cresty says.

“No, I do see it’s fitting then how you were stabbed here by this fence,” Choker says mockingly.

Marion stands on the middle rung of the split rails. He wraps his bleeding right hand inside the bottom of his sleeve and holds onto the top rung with his left hand. He is looking over the fields at Rea’s Farm wearing the two pairs of sunglasses. The early morning fog is higher now.

“Indeed, but these grounds are still giving off inspiration too,” Marion says. “Let's go, go, go.”

Marion swerves down the narrow sandy road winding between Willow Creek Winery and Rea’s Farm. The grape vines provide a gauntlet… a canal. The vines are tangled, but they are separated neatly on both sides of the road by posts. From above, the green fields make the landscape look like Ireland where the rolling grass is separated by white stone fences made from the rocks in the ground. Here, the wooden poles keep the vines in place and divide the fields evenly.

Marion chugs through the green tunnel of vine leaves, scrapping both sides of the truck. A white shed appears ahead.

"Yeah baby," Marion says. "I could see the shed from the top of the fence. Well hidden."

An older, slender man wearing baggy blue jeans and boots sips something from a cup on the shed porch. Over strong shoulders for a slight frame, drapes a Grateful Dead t-shirt that seems to stick to him as he scrapes his heavy feet a few feet from them. The holes in the sunbaked ashen shirt appear larger for Marion and his crew to see. He sticks his moppy head inside the driver-side truck window. His graying, half-inch groomed beard is streaked by ice cream under his mouth, separating his whiskers neatly into two sides.

"Welcome home man, I'm *The* Hunter."

"It is good to be back dude," Marion says.

The two hug through the window.

The Hunter draws an extended gaze at the truck. He taps the sides to the beat of "Not Fade Away" as he walks to the back.

"You know him?" Choker asks.

Marion lifts the large pair of sunglasses over his eyes with a "not that I know" and says, "Maybe, man, just maybe."

"I know we *gots* to eat," Cresty says. "No *maybes*, man."

The Hunter offers her the cup he is licking. There is a bit of ice cream in the middle where his tongue doesn't reach. Cresty shakes him off. He scrapes his boots with each stride until he reaches the inside the tilted shed.

"Maybe I do know him? Possibly from when I visited Woodstock back in 1993," Marion says. "When I went to Yasgur's Farm, it was 24 years to the month after the festival. I always wanted to visit Woodstock, so I drove myself one summer to Bethel to see where it all happened. Well, actually I went to the Baseball Hall of Fame first in Cooperstown.

"On the way weaving through the Catskills, I saw a sign for Woodstock Camp Ground and so I made a right. I knew I was on the right… path. I recognized a tree-lined road from the movie. Then I saw the field.

"The road split the field neatly in two. In one corner of Max Yasgur's farm was an American flag flying upside down."

The Hunter brings Cresty a carton of Jerry Vanilla. They all sit at the buckled wooden cedar picnic table with fresh pressure treated 2x4's supporting the worn legs and a statute of a man sitting on top.

"What's Buddha on a diet," Choker says picking up the statute. "Or is this you, *The* Hunter?"

"Imhotep," The Hunter says. "Builder of the pyramids."

"His name means 'the man who comes in peace,'" Marion says.

"Well, we come in peace," adds Cresty. "If you are going to chop our heads off and bury us in these fields, Sir, please do it now so my hunger pains go away."

The Hunter lifts his heavy boots on top of the table. He uses a finger to scoop some of Cresty's ice cream from the carton.

"I knew…I felt this was sacred ground here, too, and I was right with old Imhotep with us," Marion says. "Like at Woodstock, I needed a divine sign. "

Marion rubs the belly of Imhotep like he is making a wish.

"When I drove up to the other corner of Yasgur's farm, there was another American flag, but it had green and white stripes, not red and white. I pulled up to where there was a teepee, like the Indians used, and two leather tents that looked like they were from the Civil War.

"Sitting around a fire, and this was in 90-something degree heat in New York, which with the humidity was like 110 compared to my home in the mountains of Northern California, a man walks over to me with a dog. The pooch had a bandanna around its neck. I thought I was going to get my ass kicked for trespassing on holy ground.

"But the guy comes over to my convertible BMW and he is all peaceful. The roof was down. He stuck his head over the door and just said, 'welcome home, man.'"

"Yeah, welcome home, man, is what the guy said to me, just like The Hunter here."

"You know how sometimes words just come out of your mouth like a comet? Well they did for me, 'it is good to be back, dude,'" I replied to the man with the dog, not even trying to be cool.

"Was that you?" Marion asks The Hunter.

Without answering, The Hunter leaves the table and turning around says, "Maybe." Through the cracked window with a peace sign sticker, they see him studying the truck. His furry head pops out and he says, "People who know me can call me just Hunter."

"So, what is your point being here?" Choker asks the distracted Marion.

"You asked me if I knew Hunter. Well, it's the same guy from Woodstock. I know it… just as sure as I know every word from Hot Rocks."

"Cool," Cresty says. "That's righteous Rochambeau."

Hunter returns to the braced table with a clear bottle of dark syrup. A cherry smell livens the air as he pours the syrup on one finger and scoops some more of Cresty's ice cream. The syrup sticks to his finger.

"I dig the tongue hanging from your rear-view mirror." Hunter says in his gravelly voice. "I do art work myself. If you ever need any design, you know where to find me."

"I need a Fish Finder first."

"I know of a truck that has a Fish Finder too," Hunter smiles, showing a mouthful of teeth as crooked and shaky as the legs on the cedar picnic table.

"Do you want to try my wine?" he asks, pointing to a clear bottle on the outside sill, below the peace sign on the cracked window. "I make the Goethe wine here, all by meself with a little help from me friend, The Devil."

"Goethe?" Marion asks. "Like the German philosopher?"

"Right on," Hunter congratulates, "but Goethe also means grape."

"Goethe's last words were 'mehr licht,' "Marion says, "meaning more light."

"Ahh, he was seeing Heaven's light on his death bed, cool," Hunter says in warm agreement.

The four of them all squeeze into the cab of the truck.

Marion is driving out the one-way road they came when suddenly Hunter pulls the wheel to the right. Without even tapping the brakes, Marion continues down a sandy road that is strangled more by the vines than the entry road.

Hunter roars a mighty "harrumph" as Marion turns into an open space, an uncut field. The white garage, with the upstairs window half open and an old classic coke machine in front by the half-opened door, leans toward the bay breeze.

Although caked with seagull scat, the machine works as Hunter hands them all cans of coke.

"Sorry no Pepsi."

"Half the people like Pepsi and half the people like Coke in this country," Marion says.

"Something, isn't it? The country is divided over soda, too."

Pulling up his baggy jeans, Hunter reaches down to open the creaky garage door. With a *thwack* at the top, a nest of baby sea gulls flap for the first time before dipping into the grassy field a dozen feet from their home.

"Here are your wheels," he says. "Complete with a Fish Finder."

The vehicle is a gray hearse. Yeah, a coffin-carrying hearse.

"Is it a Chevy hearse?" Marion asks like it matters. "Looks like an early sixties model."

"Anyone in there?" Choker asks as they all wander over to the opening. Cresty peels off and checks on the squawking sea gulls.

Marion jumps right in the front seat as Choker steps back.

"The Fish Finder is here," Marion screams. "All she needs is a Stones live 8-track whistling to bring her to life."

"Is she the wheels Neil Young drove out to California when he started Buffalo Springfield?" Marion asks. "She is. Isn't she?"

Hunter sips his coke with a lengthy, approving draw.

"Yeah, Neil named the band after an old steamroller. I feel like I'm in Northern California again," Marion nods. "Will Neil mind if I have her, his ride for a bit?"

Hunter points to the bottom of the coke can.

"Nothing is made in America, dude," Hunter says. "The Hearse is a Jag."

"A jag?"

"Yeah, a Jaguar," Hunter says. "It came in undocumented to the country from England, but worked for years here, ran real fine. Now there are no parts to fix it. So, I keep my baby in storage …

"Just bring her back in one piece when you are done doing what you are doing. No charge. Leave your truck. I will search for a new Fish Finder and do some of my art magic to liven up your plain white wheels.

"The truck is grayer now from the Cape May sand," Marion says apologetically.

Behind the wooden wheel, Marion inches The Hearse out of the garage. The back doors swing open. Choker jumps back another two steps.

"They don't make these classics anymore," Marion boasts.

"They don't even make them," Hunter says. "They are Jag sedans that were cut in half with an extension body welded in the middle and new electrical harnesses installed."

"Anyway," Marion smiles, "for sure, we'll look cool down by the beach."

"I start her up every day," Hunter says.

"Start me up," Marion sings with silly glee.

"I'm not getting in it," Cresty says while kneeling near the sea gulls, their flapping wings stirring the two-foot high grass.

"Me foo-kin either, I'm too foo-kin young to ride in that. I thought we were just going to get a new Fish Finder and not the whole truck," Choker barks. "Not a foo-kin hearse.

"Really, how the foo-k do you nuts know each other?"

Marion pulls out an 8-track tape from a brown bag in his pocket and slips it in the slot. Jumpin Jack Flash blares and he sings: "It is a mask, mask, mask."

"This is going to need some gas to get you far, or home," Hunter says. "Use it until one of us find a Fish Finder for your truck. I'll do my artwork for a fee."

Edging closer to the driver's window, Choker says to Marion, "This is staged, right? Like your old jokes? You know him. Where did you really meet this guy?"

"Where do you meet anyone?" Marion responds.

Hunter points to a white rose painted on the side of the red door of The Hearse. Words border, serving as trim underneath the rose. They all trace the curvy letters with their eyes.

"I don't know what it reads," Cresty says. "I do know I want more ice cream."

"Me either, I mean I don't know what it reads either," Choker says,

"It's what you want it to read," Hunter says. "Some people think the letters on the Grateful Dead's American Beauty album cover says American Beauty. I see that it reads American Reality.

"What do *youse* think?"

"I always thought it read American Reality, too." Marion says confused.

"Reality and beauty, perhaps the same," Hunter says.

"Indeed," agrees Marion.

Hunter grabs another coke out of the machine and shuffles his heavy feet into the field, stirring the high grass like the flapping baby sea gulls behind him.

"Just find me when you get back." Hunter shouts, disappearing into the vines. "You'll have some fine art of a Stones tongue on your door. If I feel like… alive, you'll have a rose too."

"A black rose?" Cresty asks looking at Choker.

"As soon as we find a Fish Finder, we'll be back," Marion screams to the faint sounds a heavy, dragging boots in the sand.

For an hour, they unload all the tools, the saws and the bags like a surgeon's helper into The Hearse. They leave Cresty's motorcycle in the truck. Picking up Row and Way huddling under the dash where the Fish Finder used to hang, Marion seems as excited as Imhotep must have been when seeing the Great Pyramid complete. He leaves the back up to the back-up pair of oversized sunglasses on the dashboard.

"Fook, I can't believe you took this, you are stuck in time, you fooking freak," Choker unleashes. "Forget about the Fish foo-kin Finder, I'll buy you a CD player, then I can play my stuff too… and not just the *crawling* Stones."

"Just the Stones, all the soul needs," Marion says with Buddha peacefulness. "I'm stuck in time because I'm under the influence."

"So, what. A lot of the judo guys are big drinkers too and they move on," Choker says. "Pete did."

"No, fool, I'm under the influence of gravity. Gravity slows down time. You know, clocks on earth run slower than in outer space?" Marion recites in his preaching tone. "That's because there is more gravitational pull closer to earth."

The Hearse finds every bump through the grassy field and onto the sandy road strangled by vines. At the main entry road, heavy boots step out of the vines.

"Does this mean anything to you?" Hunter asks and without hesitation says, "There is a red Cadillac SUV parked next to the white split rail fence outside here…

"A squatty dude has a swab stick and he is poking around a patch of blood on the top rail."

Marion nods with a "maybe, just maybe brother," and Hunter points back to the entry road to the white shed, saying, "Take the Bat Cave road."

With Hunter plopping his heavy boots onto the back bumper and holding on to the top, Marion drives toward the shed. Hearing the Not Fade Away tap on the roof, Marion slows down and Hunter jumps off in front of the shed's crooked table.

"Welcome home," he says, pointing to a grass-covered opening in the vines.

At the end of the grassy, overgrown escape, Marion makes a hurried right and drives west on Sunset Boulevard. He is like the rising sun himself.

He waves to no one as he races past the sign for Higbees Beach.

"Poor West Cape May and The Pointe, all that money and they were divided by nudists, who are gone but the scars remain," Marion says. "We're all born nude… some of us were afforded the chance to make the eventual choice whether to be nudists or not."

Marion throws the oversized sunglasses he is wearing out his window as he sings to the Stones screaming on his new Fish Finder in the gray hearse with the curvy letters and wild rose. He follows a monarch butterfly flapping toward the bay on Sunset Beach Drive.

A wooden bird tower stands in the middle of a field mixed with sunlight and Whipporwills. Marion barely misses hitting the structure after making a left turn. On their right is a concrete World War II lookout tower with a wavy line of young families backed up at the steps for tours.

On the right is Sunset Beach Mini Golf. There are two hunched guys using walkers while putting around a small wooden lighthouse. The old men moan and bitch when they both get a hole-in-one and the bulb in the lighthouse doesn't light up. Behind the counter, a teenager playing an app game on his phone won't appease the old guys with free round of golf cards. The old men can't even win a *do over* in kiddie golf.

Beeping at the men with the walkers, asking if they "need a ride, two for the price of one" while pointing to the back of The Hearse, Marion parks between the Sunset Beach Gift Store and the Sunset Grill.

"The grill has an outdoor deck with a cabana facing the Sunken Ship," Marion says, "But the USS Atlantus can't be seen from the deck. The Sunken Ship has sunk so much it can only be seen standing on the beach here.

"Atlan*tis* and its hubris can't be seen either," he adds with unusual and awkward emphasis.

With patrons on the outside deck staring at The Hearse, the three of them each glance briefly at the Debris Decomposition Timeline board, sponsored by the Cape May Municipal Utilities Authority, before straight-lining toward the Sunken Ship. A young kid, wearing a Blake Griffin jersey, alone licking his melting ice cream cone with a basketball under his other arm, isn't tall enough to read the Sunken Ship sign. After first reaching to lift him up and then stopping, Marion reads aloud:

"The USS Atlantus at Sunset Beach… one of 12 concrete ships built during World War I… proved impractical after several transatlantic trips because of its weight… in 1926 the Atlantus was purchased by Col. Jesse Rosenfeld to be used as a ferry dock in Cape May… but on June 8th a storm hit and the ship broke free of her mornings and ran aground hundred 50 feet off the coast of Sunset Beach… several attempts were made to free the ship but none were successful…"

Inside the gift store, Cresty and Choker go to the back of the shop while Marion stops at the counter and waits for a man, older than him by a few years, who is wearing an olive gray army jacket with colorful patches, to stop talking on the phone that is mounted to the wall and still has a cord.

Standing out like a stranded school bus on the side of the road wearing his yellow rain hooded jacket with the wavy letters ALI inscribed in black ink, Mr. Hallward is alone in the back of the shop reading bookmarkers. Cresty and Choker flank each side of him. He looks at them both, turning twice, before saying, "Are you here to salvage the Sunken Ship too?"

Shaking hands, Marion engages in conversation with the army jacket dude at the counter, who tells him he "left Vietnam and *the war* behind" and "only wears the jacket to keep tourists from talking to me." Says he has been working in the gift shop since "you could see the top two-thirds of the Sunken Ship."

Marion picks up an address book on the counter and flips through the pages, starting near the middle.

"I lost so many old friends… I could probably name one for each letter of the alphabet in this book," Marion says. "And I wasn't even in a war like you."

"Don't think about it," the army jacket man says. "My thoughts are in the now… like how do we want to bring up the Sunken Ship?"

"You mean raise the Sunken Ship so the top two-thirds can be seen again?" Marion asks. "It looks like you can see the top third now."

"Only because it's low tide," the army jacket man says. "Look at the picture on the wall near the phone, it's from 1926. You could see the whole ship above the water line."

"I can see wanting to bring the concrete ship back up to its old level, but why not raise her above the water while you are at it… and build a pier to the Atlantus for tourists to walk around?

"Why not bring back the ship?"

"You mean raise it up?" the army jacket man asks.

"Why not? We could. Wouldn't it be wonderful, powerful to bring the past back to life?" Marion says with a surge of untapped excitement. "You know, you can't bring a broken marriage back, you can't rescue a friendship after *unfriending* someone on Facebook, you can't bring back a loved one, even an unborn one you didn't know, back from the dead … but maybe we can bring back the Sunken Ship."

Randomly pulling a yellow-paged, dog-eared paperback off the OLDIES BUT GOODIES RECOMMENDED bookshelf, Mr. Hallward says, "You can't *re-read* a book for the first time." He puts "The Great Gatsby" back on the shelf, but sideways on top of the other books.

"Indeed, raising the Ship from the dead would be Lazarusian," Mr. Hallward taunts. "Not even the great Jay Gatsby could raise Daisy from the past."

The army jacket man fixes the book, sliding Gatsby between "The Endurance" and "Field of Dreams."

"But why? Shouldn't the Atlantus, like people, be allowed to die in dignity?" Marion says to him.

"The great Ali shouldn't have fought his next-to-last bout against Larry Holmes… and then his last fight against Trevor Berbick… The Greatest ending with two losses…" Hallward laments and tapping the Ali letters on his slicker, says, "Just let her sink. That's how Ali should've gone out.

"That's what I would've done."

"And who are you?" Marion asks. "Only the chosen few die wrapped in dignity. The rest, are naked, some die before being born, and in despair."

Pointing to the letters on Hallward's jacket, Marion spells out A-L-I and says," You can't spell C*al*ifornia or *ali*ases without A-L-I … or re*ali*ty and ration*ali*ze without A-L-I… or even leg*ali*ze …or mor*ali*ty… or *ali*ve… without A-L-I.

"Can we spell *your* name without A-L-I?"

"No matter about me," Mr. Hallward snaps, but with an amused smile. "Just a thought, you know to let go… like I did, retiring from the Department of Corrections, letting go of the ones on Death Row who I never got to see serve justice, their just do.

"Let *her* go. Like yesterday and the day before, the ship is not coming back."

"But I need to hold on, to something, something I could, something I can, bring back," Marion stutters.

"Yeah, the Sunken Ship. *She* is worth saving," the army jacket man says, "like that hearse out there."

On the counter, Marion flips open a dusty writing pad with the Sunken Ship emblazed on each sheet. He writes "sign up for The Raising of The Sunken Ship" and puts the pad next to the cash register. He pays for the pad using his American Express card.

"We could argue about the worth of saving the Sunken Ship until the end of time," Mr. Hallward says. "And you know what, no one would be right and no one would be wrong. That's just the way life plays."

"Well, someone has to be right and someone has to be wrong," Marion snaps. "It's black and white."

"Yeah, like fishing on a rainy day, or not fishing on a rainy day," Choker says.

"No, it is just Perspectivism," Mr. Hallward says. "Plato introduced how truth comes from perspective in Protagoras."

Mr. Hallward extends his arms like the scales of justice. He levels his hands alternately up and down.

"Nietzsche wrote about it in God is Dead," Mr. Hallward continues with enjoyment. "Some say, he said, in the literal sense that the Christian idea of God was dead due to the death of moral principles. While others believe, from the death of morality that birth is given to freedom of thinking.

"You see, the raising of the Sunken Ship, the right and wrong of the resurrection, or the rebirth, or just the birth, is just perspective."

"Jack Nietzsche played studio guitar with the Rolling Stones," Marion says as if not to be outdone on archaic thought. "His solo The Last Race is a classic. Quentin Tarantino used the score in his movie Death Proof. The soundtrack was also used in The Exorcist and One Flew Over the Cuckoo's Nest."

"I feel we are living now in bits of each movie. Maybe, just maybe, all of the movies wrapped into one," Mr. Hallward says with an amused grin. "Cresty told me you were stranger than strange...

"Anyway, I looked you up, or my law enforcement connections did, and there is no Francis Marion that fits your description in any of the data bases. You must be clean. You don't have a rap sheet. You're not in Promis Gavel. Not in NCIC. Not in ACS. Not in FACTS, nothing juvenile.

"I had CJIS checked, you're not even registered with MVS, not even a driver's license with Motor Vehicles. You are like a ghost. Or like you were never born.

"You… Francis Marion… you are running from something."

Marion arches behind the counter and picks at his toenails. He peels the top of each toenail, trimming them with his thumb and forefinger. He cups the clippings in his right hand and says, "It's Marion Francis."

Cresty signs her name on The Raise the Sunken Ship pad. Choker gives the army jacket man a dollar and takes a Sunken Ship bookmarker.

They follow Marion to the water. He tosses his toenail clippings into the bay and watches the tide pull part of him toward the Sunken Ship.

"It's then like killing a dolphin. Isn't it?" Choker says to the stunned Mr. Hallward. "A dolphin that gets caught in a net would die anyway, so why not kill the dolphin before it gets caught in the fishing net?

"Right? Just Perspectivisim."

At sunset, the crowd gathered to see the reflection in the western sky over the bay, turn and circle the flagpole. The flag is lowered.

An elderly lady with a weathered face tells the vacationers how since 1973 the only flag to fly over the Sunken Ship has been the same one draped on a veteran's casket.

The Star-Spangled Banner is being sung by the hundred or so people as the flag of Larry Gene Bell of Alloway, New Jersey is lowered.

A distinguished man with white hair neatly parted on the side reads how Bell had blueish green eyes… enlisted in the Navy in 1966… attained the rank of Hospital Corpsman Third Class – HM3… was called "Doc" by the other medics… how on August 28, 1969, at age 22, while on combat patrol near Quang Nam in South Vietnam, after giving the last dose of penicillin to a wounded soldier, Doc died.

Chapter 10

Marion skids into a parking spot near the beach by the jetty, screeching like the brakes "the overnight rain made the surface slick." The gray hearse meshes in fine here at Devil's Reach at the end of the Promenade with all the older mud-caked jeeps and rusted four wheel-drives.

A teenage boy, wearing JFK-looking Ray Ban Wayfarer sunglasses and a red scarf with the white letters LIVERPOOL and white tassels on each end, carries a surfboard toward the ocean under one arm.

"Liverpool," huffs Marion, "the Rolling Stones never quit like the Beatles."

"You beat it," the kid snaps back. "Talking *fut-bol,* fool."

The early morning sun beats on the driver's side of The Hearse. Marion and Cresty examine the mural of flowers painted on the door.

"It reads Fish Finder," Cresty says after a few minutes studying the driver's side artwork.

"No, it reads Baby Saver," Marion says eating vanilla-chocolate ice cream out of a carton, like a cartoon, and drinking his favorite soda, cherry red. "We need Choker here to break the tie,"

Cresty climbs on the side riding board of The Hearse and looks out over the ocean.

"The surf is gnarly again today," Cresty says. "These overcast days spit out some angry seas. I heard yesterday the waves were washing over the rocks down past Pittsburgh Avenue on the east side of Cape May.

"We should drive there perhaps. Even the old-timers on the boards were calling it Freaky Friday."

Cresty slides through the open window. She removes her surfboard from the back of The Hearse as two kids on skateboards stop and stare in horror when the back doors fling open,

"Hunter had promised to do some artwork on the topside of the board," Cresty says to Marion. "He drew up a sketch he gave me yesterday of the Grateful Dead skull plastering the board in the center with the middle of the skull divided by a wave."

Marion doesn't seem to hear her. Instead he seems to be listening to two surfer guys, probably 40-something, talk about the shoals beyond Devils' Reach. They want to paddle out to Eph's Shoal, where the water depth dips from 19 feet to nine feet. A third guy walks by and says he paddles out to Prissy Wicks Shoal where the depth falls from 24 feet to nine feet. He says the breakers are better at Prissy Wicks, but it is not for the "prissy whipped" to paddle out for 45 minutes.

Cresty changed into a one-piece wet suit cut at the shoulders to show her ripped arms and at the top of her thigh, showing her athletic legs. She joins the three guys who Marion is studying. The one who paddled out to Prissy Wicks offers to carry her board. Cresty carries her own.

Coiled like a baby, or a snake, Marion is lying on top of The Hearse when after an hour or so, Cresty returns. She carries the board under each arm. The board is broken in half.

"You, OK? Must have been wicked, as you surfer types say. Catch any tubes today?" Marion says, appearing to act surfing cool instead of seeming concerned for her not being injured.

"No, I sucked so hard. It was way embarrassing. Since the surf was so rough, roaring, they posted some lifeguards out on jet skis, cramping us."

"It's for your protection. Even surfers need laws to live by."

"Well, I gots to get a new board," she says, wiping both knees that are scraped and seeping some blood. "Best time is now."

"I see. Indeed, sometimes you get bloodied-up doing what's right."

"I hope Hunter will still do his artwork on my new board. When I get it."

"Indeed. I will buy you a new board, but only if you'll understand that you can't do whatever you want on a wave, whenever you feel like in the ocean?" he says.

"Why not? It isn't like outer space with gravity and persuasion and all that. The waves rule. That's it."

"What do you think holds the water down? Gravity. If not, the ocean would be spilling into outer space, as you call it. People must live by laws as well. They can't do whatever they want, whenever they feel… even to their own bodies."

"I want to get a tattoo on my butt. Is that what you mean?"

"Get in, we have some tree tattooing to do."

With her knees still bleeding, Cresty picks up the two rabbits. The cage they are in fits better up front in the cab. There is more room in The Hearse.

Giving knuckle punches to the two transfixed kids on skateboards, Marion drives north toward the center of Cape May.

"We are hiding in plain sight," Marion says past the humungous columns of Congress Hall.

A pedestrian mall splits the middle of the downtown area. Three blocks of a former street were closed and blocked off decades ago. The mall separates stores on both sides of this trendy shopping district. Forty-year old trees cover the walkers, although the street vendors spread out to steal the shade. The butterflies in the trees entertain scores of old people with big sunglasses like Marion.

The Ugly Mug and Delaney's, two pubs with outdoor seating areas, command opposite corners of the mall on intersecting cross streets. A group of gray-haired Harley-Davidson bikers snap photos in front of the Ugly Mug. Young moms and dads with kids in strollers do the same in front of Delaney's.

Keeping his distance, as if she has leprosy, Marion follows a tattooed-up lady biker, who carries a parasol, into the Ugly Mug. She looks like she could be in Paris. The "Mug" is cut out of the French Quarter in New Orleans.

"I'm glad you stopped riding, Cresty," Marion says inside. "Now if you would only stop riding waves. You could've got hurt out there today."

"It wasn't raining when I was surfing, was it?" Cresty asks.

"Why?"

"The biker chick is carrying an umbrella," Cresty whispers as they take a seat in a booth with high wooden backs along the side of the bar.

"That's a parasol."

"Same thing."

"Actually, not at all."

"Sure, it is."

"No, an umbrella is to protect against the rain while a parasol protects from the sun," Marion says leaning over close to her.

"Who needs protection, anyway?" she answers.

The bar is filling up at mid-morning.

"We're celebrating, we'll both have a Guinness," Marion says to a dark-haired biker babe, who is their waitress. "And we would like our breakfast drink in one of the mugs hanging from the ceiling."

"Can't," she says.

"Sure, we can." Cresty says.

"No, you can't… you aren't a member and you aren't a dead member."

She points to the writing on the bottom of the menu as she walks away.

Lifting the oversized sunglasses and rubbing his eyes under the Aviator glasses, Marion tries reading the box in the menu with the old-time photo, but can't.

He hands the menu to Cresty.

"In the old days of vaudeville each member got a mug," she reads. "Deceased members of the club are honored by having their mugs hung facing the ocean."

"She's right, we aren't members and we aren't dead members," Marion laughs. "Yet."

A dozen dudes are seated at one elbow of the bar near the front door. The guys are split evenly at the bend. The biker babe pours them all a pint of beer in a Trappist mug. They all wait until the last beer is poured. She doesn't tilt the glass at all on the pour, so there is a layer of froth bubbling over the sides of each of the mugs.

Then, on a rapid count of "dix – neuf – huit – sept – six – cing – quatre" and a slower "trios… deux… un," they all blow the froth from the top of the glass. The smallest guy, who is sitting at the elbow facing the door, blows the froth halfway across the bar and onto the biker babe. She laughs and pours him another pint before she serves the Guinness to Marion and Cresty.

"What the foo-k was that?" Cresty asks.

The biker server points to another box on the menu with an old-time photo of guys wearing white dress shirts and dark ties, blowing the froth off their beers while women in fancy dresses and parasols cheer wildly.

Marion hands her the menu again. Cresty reads aloud: "On the first Saturday after Labor Day members and guests gather together…"

She takes a swing of her Guinness before continuing, "each receives a glass of beer and the one who blows the most froth out of the glass become the United States National Froth Blowing Champion."

"Man, that blows, wasting all that beer," Marion says.

"You blow," Cresty says laughing. "We should come back in two months for the froth blowing contest."

"Two months, I'm sure I will be blowing on the high seas, by then..."

Marion asks the biker bartender what type beer they use in the froth blowing. She tells him the beer is brewed at the Cape May Brewing Company, over in Rio Grande.

"It's Devil's Reach Belgian Strong Ale, served here only in a Trappist glass," she says hitting Marion on the ass with her parasol as he and Cresty leave the dark Ugly Mug.

He checks to make sure his backup sunglasses are on his hat as he steps into the sun and onto the mall, looking toward the closest end with the street running out of town and where Our Lady Star of the Sea Roman Catholic Church rises above the rest of the buildings. A white ticket booth leans a bit out front. Not under a tree. The wooden both, white as a life guard boat, stands crooked next to a white Mercedes.

Each summer a car is raffled off in the booth. Tickets are $2 - three for $5.

A ship's bell hangs near the ticket booth. On this peaceful day, no one dare rings the bell.

On the way, out of town on Route 109, Marion slows at each intersection before stopping at the railroad tracks. He puts the blinkers, or hazards on, as two kids on bikes pull up to the driver's side of The Hearse.

"Cool wheels," one says.

"Yeah, man, do you sell ice cream?"

Marion pats them both on their heads. He makes a K-turn in the street and double parks. He runs over to the ship bell and rings it hard once, then soft twice and then hard once.

An old man sitting on the closest bench spins his head so fast his wraparound sunglasses smash on the expensive pavers.

"I always wanted to ring the bell," Marion says as he gives him his backup sunglasses.

Cape Liquors on Route 9 is the last stop for alcohol after going over the high concrete bridge out of Cape May and getting on the New Jersey Parkway north toward Sea Isle.

"Should we pickup champagne for Choker, just in case he wins," Marion says making a proper U-turn at the start of Route 109, the only road into and out of Cape May.

"Let him win first," Cresty says.

Madame Palm's has moved to the space in back of the antique shop in the yellow house next to Cape Liquors, which is next to the Cape May Clinic.

"Are we going to Cape May Care, or Madame Palms?" Cresty asks.

"Only Madame Palm knows," Marion quips. "She doesn't miss anything, except her meth-head ex-husband's punch that hit her."

Marion seems connected on both sides of the liquor store, by Madame Palm's, now sharing the house with the antique shop, and the clinic. He parks in the lot behind the antique shop.

"I have a Japanese Flowering Cherry tree to plant, but it's too big to drop in the hole without Choker," Marion says. "He wanted to help, I know, but his tournament today takes precedence."

"Yes. What a change in him," Cresty boasts. "A few months ago, Choker didn't want to do anything but judo. He didn't want to work on the fishing boats, especially if it looked like rain, or then work with you even if it was sunny. Now he wants to work before the big tournament that he has been training for like the devil lurks inside him."

"I've changed too. In a lot of ways."

Cresty hugs Row and Way, taking them out of their cage in the cab as Marion paces in the back of Madame Palm's. He marks a spot for the tree, making an X with the heel of his foot.

"One benefit from having a reattached Achilles," he laughs. "My right foot is like a boot."

Marion looks toward the clinic. He looks like he is scouting the place out again.

"We got to dig a real wide bowl for this Prunus X Yedoensis. Madame Palm has a spot picked out in front. It's going to need a lot of water."

"You mean the Japanese Cherry tree," Cresty says.

"Good one. You will make a fine arbor woman someday. You are learning all the names. We'll just dig the hole for it. Looks like rain, huh? Awful gray out there."

"Sure does. Guess we'll have to hurry up and get this hole dug in the ground… or get us some parasols."

Cresty waits in the truck and plays with the rabbits as Marion digs. After two shovels, he looks up and sees the red Cadillac SUV pull up in the empty parking lot of the clinic.

"That's good, real plenty good… we'll get to the tournament early now," he says after scooping just another shovel of dirt.

The Hearse needs fuel to make the 40-minute drive up the Parkway to Pomona. The gas is cheaper on Route 109 than in town, so Marion pulls into the gas station across from the clinic where he sees the stocky rich man carry a small clear plastic lunch baggie with the swab stick. He knocks. Doc Hyde opens and shuts the door behind him

"Petro 109," Marion says with a nervous laugh.

"What's so funny, bro?"

"Get it, Petro 109?"

"No."

"Like PT 109."

"Still a no."

"JFK served on the PT 109."

"Oh."

"Kennedy protected our country. Our future president was on a small craft in the Solomon Islands when his boat was cut in half by a Japanese torpedo, like the head of a fetus during a late-termer."

"My dad told me it was a Jap destroyer that ripped apart the starboard aft side."

"We'll either way, the broken boat couldn't destroy the country," he says with defiance.

"Yeah, and now ironically we're planting Japanese cherry trees."

"Indeed, people… societies can change their hearts… and the great JKF went onto say: 'Let both sides seek to involve the wonders of science… let us explore the stars, conquer the deserts, eradicate disease, tap the ocean depths and encourage arts and commerce…"

"Let us do the same. One more, quick stop before the tournament. I'll be quicker than a comet in M87."

Flooring The Hearse, making the backend welds rattle, Marion hits 59 mph driving west toward the ferry on Lincoln Boulevard above the canal. He makes a left on Beach Avenue. There are only a few houses. He stops at this blue cottage with pink-trimmed windows. The house that faces the bay across from the dune above the ferry, perhaps a football field only away from the launch.

Marion seems to wait to see if there is any activity around the house. There is no car in a side driveway constructed of broken seashells. In front, on the same angle of the house facing the bay, a baby angel statue is laying on its side. He sits the cherub up before trimming the hedges and the bushes around the house. He finishes the job quickly while Cresty stays in the cab.

Cresty plays around with the rabbits. She cleans out the cage and takes the mess to the back of the house. She seems startled.

She stares at the hilly dune across the canal where they stood last month. The saplings can be seen above the grass.

"Let's go, let's rock and roll," Marion says, nudging her arm.

Marion throws the hedge shears into the back of The Hearse.

"Slow down, we'll still make the tournament. Let's enjoy the view for a moment."

"Can't… I want to take Choker out to dinner tonight at the Lobster House to celebrate his win. I'll work tomorrow while you two can go to church."

"You know I don't go to mass anymore and he isn't Catholic anymore either… not after Pete went away."

"You can restart tomorrow and so can he."

"I'm hungry," she says. "Hungry like a fasting Catholic on Good Friday."

Marion drives past the clinic with the red SUV still in the lot. He makes a slow right toward Cape May and turns in toward the yellow house's paved driveway of Madame Palm's, He slams the brakes to avoid hitting a woman riding a motorized bike crossing the two-lane highway. Without looking up or reacting to The Hearse's screeching breaks, she scoots toward the clinic. She knocks on the glass side door. The rich man lets her inside.

Taking both hands off the wheel, Marion folds them in prayer as he says, "I hope for continued growth. For Goethian growth."

"We didn't plant the tree, remember," Cresty says. "The Japanese cherry tree is still in the back of The Hearse. You are waiting for Choker to help, remember?"

"No, but I know. I do… I do, I do."

"You do?" she asks. "You do know what?"

Marion reaches across the rabbits and rubs her belly for his tacit answer and says, "About you."

The rich man leaves the clinic and puts the motorized bike in the back of the red SUV. The two ladies follow. Dr. Hyde sits in the back seat. The SUV spins out the side entrance onto Route 9.

Marion drives The Hearse over the grass at Madame Palm's lot onto the clinic's lot. He makes a left, too, and follows the SUV.

Chapter 11

The rich man's SUV pulls up to where his boat is docked at the end of the familiar nine-slip pier on the canal. The air smells again like a seagull burped out its morning clam.

Decelerating, Marion glides to a stop at the peak of the bridge crossing the canal. He mumbles how "the waterway was man-made" and laments how "the canal connects the ocean and the bay, but separates Cape May" as he watches from above as the three of them step onto the rich man's boat.

After a bald eagle swoops down, and majestically plucks a baby seagull from a flock on the bank of the canal and majestically sails back to its nest with the bird limp in its talons, Marion makes a U-turn on top of the bridge.

"Life," he announces in a resigned matter of fact while Leaving Cape May. "The survival of the fittest."

For some reason, Marion chooses the slower Route 9 North route instead of the fleet Parkway. When Cresty asks him why, he mumbles how construction on the ramps over the two cross roads with traffic lights into Stone Harbor will back up the late Saturday morning traffic of the renters leaving "delightful dodge," as he calls the shore. He adds how this July 4th weekend only "doubles the disasters' on the Parkway.

"You know, they should let nature be… the old ways work, like Charlie Watts with his basic drum kit," Marion says about the construction.

Marion slows down, seemingly admiring the old Corbin City Motel at the intersection of Route 109. He waves to no one while passing the red Swain Hardware Store.

"Leaving Cape May and the survival of the fittest behind," he yells out the window while beeping the horn of the gray hearse as bumper-to-bumper incoming traffic inches along Route 9 South.

A few miles outside of Cape May, Marion glows seeing signs for Historic Cold Spring Village. He crosses the railroad tracks, passes an empty two-story guard tower and enters the village and parks in the handicap spot next to the yellow train tower.

"I want to ring the Cold Spring bell," he says before Cresty can even ask why they are there.

"Going back in time," he says anyway.

A sign at the pathway tells them this is THE AGE OF HOMESPUN.

Marion explains to her the era was from the late 1780's to the early 1840's.

They stroll aimlessly down shady lanes, winding around the 26 restored buildings on the grounds of the village.

Out in front of the historic stores are various artisan's craft bowls, horseshoes and witch's brooms, aiding the tourist to imagine a different time. He thanks one woman, a 40-something-year-old, plain looking, peaceful sort with brownish-gray hair tied back in a ponytail, for sewing him the "pirate outfit."

"T'was the hit of the Halloween party last year," he says to her. "Still spooking some."

"I'd wish that pirate in you would stop the eagle at the canal from killing the sea gulls," she says. "The eagle needs to be executed."

Looking trapped in thought, Marion stops in front of the Husbandry.

"This is where the animal breeding was done," he says. "Someday, I predict, science will be able to breed the DNA from three people in one embryo."

With this proclamation, Marion rings the Cold Spring bell. Two ladies, as plain as the previous one, strut by spinning their parasols in apparent approval.

"I like it here," Cresty declares. "I like the simple life of the past… when there was no hurry to make more memories."

"Come on my dear *fellow* time traveler," Marion says pulling her arm while pushing his oversized sunglasses up on his nose higher. "You're living in the past… you know what they say …

"Yeah, yeah, yeah," she says shaking off his arm and her head. "You swim in the same pool and you tread yellow water every day."

"That's good, but the saying is 'if you live in the past, you die a little bit every day.' We *gots*, as you used to say, some living to do."

With the windows down, they motor past the empty football and baseball fields of Lower Cape May Regional High School on their left before passing the crowded parking lot of the Cape May National Golf course on the other side of the road.

With The Hearse keeping the 35-mile speed limit pace, Marion rides parallel with the empty railroad tracks on his left, crossing over the junction of Route 147 at Dias Creek where there is Cape Power Equipment. Up the road is Parkway Vet. Cresty lifts the rabbits triumphantly.

Marion passes a Halloween store with a rubber dolphin suit in the window, saying "Thanks Flipper for your assistance," and then passes Kelly Restaurant & Bar Supplies before turning onto the Parkway where Route 9 converges at Universal Supply Company.

On the Parkway, the ride to Pomona is uneventful, but sluggish. The traffic moves, though, as many of the weekly renters have already headed back to Philadelphia - and parts unknown - since it is after noon.

The parking lot guard at Richard Stockton University is wearing a gray turban on his head. He pokes at The Hearse door with his finger. The attendant, a man around Marion's age, scratches at the artwork.

"The cursive looks like American Beauty, my favorite of the Dead's albums. Well favorite studio album," the guard says. "My favorite live album is Europe '72, of course.

"The art work on the doors looks like the same artwork on the '72 album cover, you know the trucking boot stepping across the ocean and the fool smashing the ice cream on his forehead and LIVE being spelled out from the splashing ice cream, if you look real close.

"Hey, it does say Fish Finder around the Rose or the door," he says all excited. "What does Fish Finder mean? Sounds biblical."

"Just what it says," Marion says. "We find fish."

"Hey, my job sucks hard here. You need any help? I'll work cheap. And my gray turban matches your gray… vehicle."

"Do you have papers? What's your name, dude?"

"Whatever you want to call me. But, I've been going by Nivek Nahalac lately.

"Oh man," Cresty bursts. "You are that Irish guy who changed his name and became India's top surfer, or was. No one has seen him – you - since he went out in that typhoon last year. So, you are he."

"I believe you must be a surfer freak to know that," he says. "Believe what helps you through the day. What is your name, Mountain Girl?"

Cresty flashes the surfing pose with her arms extended.

"The inside cover of Europe '72 had a quote from Revelation," Marion says.

"Indeed," the freaky guard says. "Forget it exactly, but it was apocalyptic… perhaps about the Whore of Babylon."

"Indeed," Marion says smiling. "There was a reference by The Dead to the Feast of Fools as well."

"Indeed," the guard agrees. "Seems like we are living among the feasting fools now and the country is Babylon where a home-grown terrorist generation has sprouted from this legalized abortion generation.

"After they were born, killing was made acceptable and so these 40-something-year-olds know no other life… this is what they were born with, lived with all their lives… which is why I dropped out of life… taking a job here and there… pretending to be other people… will all be in my memoirs."

Glazing over The Hearse approvingly, the guard continues, "You must be the Gray Horseman of the Apocalypse."

Marion rubs the rose on the side of The Hearse.

"Did you know the Further Bus is making its 50th anniversary crossing of Atlantis, I mean America, as we speak," the guard says, unwrapping his turban. "The Further should be here in September."

"Indeed, I did know," Marion says, rubbing his hands in festive anticipation.

"See you there."

"Maybe… we won't tell anyone about you, my Merry Prankster friend," Marion says to him. "And, I'll keep you in mind if I need you . . .

"Hey, do you know the words to Fields of Athenry?"

"All of them. I even know to chant I-R-A during the chorus."

"Hardcore Irish, huh?" Marion asks. "Do you know… about B's?"

"B's? Big or little? I know B's need fertilizer… do you need some?"

"I'll let you know," Marion says.

"Park in the press section," the guard commands. "We never get as much press for this grappling as the men's hoop games... and the games are only Division 3."

"Right on, but D-3 rules," Cresty says while grinning, as if he has seen a revelation, Marion parks his *gray horse* in a remote section of the lot, shaking his head out the window and making what sounds like a horse sound.

The afternoon session of the tournament has already started. Choker had told them not to attend the morning rounds because he had a first-round bye and he would breeze by to the semifinals.

The crowd is sparse. Marion and Cresty sit in the first open seats in the front row. They hear a yell.

"Can I buy you a Guinness?" screams a waving Uwrenski, who has left his seat and scrambles toward them.

"How did you know what I drink?" Marion asks. "And we already had one for breakfast at the Ugly Mug."

"Choker told me you only drink Guinness because that's all Ronnie Woods drinks."

"That's right. If I only could play the guitar like Woody."

"Yeah, if you could play like the Woodman you would be on stage with Keith."

"You know your Stones."

"I saw them in '78 and '81 in Philly before I moved overseas to study judo at Tenri University in Japan. I saw the Stones at old JFK Stadium… before the city tore the brick stadium down.

"Anyway, your friend won his first two matches, easily. He looks great. Both wins were full ippons. He threw the first guy with a whomping osoto-gari and the next guy, who was leaning back to protect against the osoto, he tossed him with a beautiful ripping tai-otoshi, which is a front throw."

"Did he use any chokes?"

"Not yet, I'm surprised, chokes are all he used to use. He is much better rounded. Impressive. Someone has finally gotten to him."

"I'd like to choke some of the politicians on the hill in Washington. They're crazed and confused."

"Who isn't?"

"They're holding all the cards. Someone needs to get to them. But they've been out of touch for four decades. They aren't in tune like the parking attendant guy," Marion rambles. "Like, it must be 16 years ago now, I read where the governor of New Jersey signed a bill that would prosecute drunk drivers of double manslaughter if they killed an unborn baby and mother. But the governor is pro-choice. Can't have it both ways, can you?"

"Not logically," Uwrenski agrees while sitting on the floor nest to Marion. "Seems to me if a baby is not alive for an abortion, it can't be alive to be *man slaughtered.* You're right. Can't have it both ways. But that is government, always fuzzing things up."

"Laws should be black and white," Marion says. "No gray area for interpretation."

"Like judo. Throw, pin or choke."

"Yeah, that Governor also signed a bill into law preventing private golf clubs that rent facilities to the public from discriminating against women with regards to tee times. Signing bills so women can get better tee times like the men. It's fair of course, but what about priorities. That Gov. should've signed a bill banning partial birth abortions and not stress about tee times. And you know what, the governor was a woman, too, with man in her name - Whitman."

"She obviously didn't play judo," Uwrenski says. "If she did, she would respect all life, like Choker now. He is learning, which is why he is playing so much better. Judo is teaching him well. The coach of Stockton, the great Coach Bit, is impressed. I got to go talk to him before his last match."

Choker wins his next three matches all by pins, advancing to the championship as Marion and Uwrenski discuss Coach Bit's name. "Did he bite someone, or did he get bit." Marion had questioned. "Get bit?" Uwrenski had asked and then said, "There is no such word as bit… it's bitten."

Licking his lips, "This is his righting moment," Marion says, turning to Cresty.

Cresty, though, is somewhat asleep. Her head rests on Marion's shoulder.

"His what," she slurs. "Are you learning judo terms now?"

"No, but I hope to. The righting moment is, in sailing, the exhilarating moment when the boat is just about to tip over, but the weight of the keel rights the vessel upwards. I also like to think of the righting moment as that instant in life where you decide to do right in the face of a decision that will change lives.

"Right now, Choker can make things right for himself with a win."

After a takedown with a foot sweep in the first 30 seconds, Choker pounces on his opponent and wins the championship on a choke. A back choke that he tells Marion after the match is called okuriere-game.

"I want to learn that one," Marion pleads.

"I want to learn a lot, too," Cresty says as Choker gives her a knuckle-punch. "I want to learn to ride the killer tubes of bonzai. I want to learn the difference between a red oak and a willow oak. They both have green leaves. I want to learn why Mick Taylor left the Stones. I want to learn what is a particle accelerator, a super collider. I want to learn what a partial birth abortion is. I want to know if there is really a difference between an umbrella and parasol."

Marion smiles as he taps his head against Cresty's head. Shaking his head, Choker splits to pick up his medal.

"I can't help you on the surfing, but the red oak has bristled-tipped leaves, not willow-like leaves. They turn red in the fall while the willow oak's foliage turns yellow-brown in the fall. I don't know why Mick Taylor left the Stones either, crazy huh? But he did return to play Midnight Rambler and Can't You Hear Me Knocking on the '50 and Counting' tour last year.

"A partial accelerator is used in smashing atoms."

"Smashing atoms?" she asks, tapping his head with her skull. "*Osmosize* me."

"The largest in the world is back home, at Stanford, or is it CERN now in France, or Switzerland… anyway I know a bunch of physicist from many countries had been working for decades on smashing atoms to learn about the 'God particle,' which gives other particles a chance to grow, build mass… and I know three years ago, in 2012, scientist did discover the Biggs Boson particle, I mean Higgs Boson, which is called the 'God particle' and I know those scientist are now trying to recreate the Big Bang underground at CERN using the 'God particle'… I can't wait to hear the results."

"Big Bang?" Cresty pokes him, "You mean when you take a dump? Or the Stones' album?"

"It worked out that Taylor did leave the Stones, because that is when Woody joined. Well, he didn't actually join," Marion responds seamlessly. The Stones made him serve a 16-year apprenticeship before he got a full cut. He never complained though.

"What else did you say you want to know about?

"I think you know."

"Oh, the parasol…"

"I already know… tell me what I don't know."

"This will sound like a lecture, but it is what it is and a partial birth, technically called dilation and extraction, is when a fetus is killed by partly delivering the head through the birth canal and extracting the brains. It works also when a doctor partially extracting a fetus, feet first, then forcing scissors into its skull, inserting a suction tube and removing the brain, causing the skull to collapse.

Since it is done in the ninth month of a pregnancy. It's really… really, just stabbing a baby to death.

"It's no different from what that girl did in Central Jersey years ago when I lived in California, when she killed her baby at the prom in the bathroom and went back out and danced.

"The only difference is it's done at one of those clinics, like in Cape May. People wonder why our universe is so nuts. Since 1972 we've been allowed by our government to kill babies. No different from the old Romans, who left sick babies on the hills to be eaten by wolves. We're the wolves now. Kids have grown up thinking it's all right to kill their babies. They know no better.

"Just think if the Homespun folks of Cold Springs were allowed to kill their unborn babies in cold blood, well we might not be here… who is to say one of those Homespuners weren't in our family tree, or introduced our great, great grandparents, or took a wagon to California…"

"But the new Homespuners want to kill an eagle who kills sea gulls…"

"There is my lecture on life, there in black and white."

Marion begins to walk away when Cresty injects, "I still don't understand about abortions…

"When is a baby considered alive?"

Smiling like his shiny gold medal, Choker runs up to them. He gives her the medal. He turns to Marion and gives him a shy man hug.

"Thanks for your help. I wouldn't have won this tournament without you two."

"I didn't do anything, you did. You did all the work and training."

"No, I've been learning from you. And you gave me a job, place to live, a boat to piss in."

Cresty wanders away before Marion can answer her question.

Choker looks for her over his shoulder while posing for photos with his team. Cresty isn't around. She left the building.

Marion and Choker find her outside talking to the parking lot attendant.

Nivek is holding her.

"Are you, all right?" Choker asks. "You have that look… the look when Pete… before Pete passed."

"Tell them, Mountain Girl," the guard says. "You will feel better."

Cresty hands Choker the medal back and holds onto his hand.

"Sure," she whispers, "I'm just pregnant, no biggie."

Chapter 12

The Parkway and Route 9 also converge above the National Guard Amory between Stone Harbor and Avalon. Marion turns off of the Parkway and drives on Route 9 through Cape May Courthouse.

Cresty lifts up the rabbits triumphantly when passing the Cape May County Zoo on the right. Choker flashes his medal out the window when passing the Cape May Museum on the left. He then playfully tells Marion to check him into the Oceana Rehabilitation Center next to the museum, saying his "back hurts from pinning everyone for 30 seconds instead of choking them out in three."

Marion whistles out his window at two elderly women walking in the trailer park. The Fairview Cemetery conveniently rests between the trailer park and the Cape May Regional Hospital.

He points to Old Billy Bob's Car Wash outside Choker's window with old guys hand-washing their trucks. He then whistles at fit women doing yoga on the mats across the street at Curves.

Marion turns back on the Parkway where Route 9 converges at Universal Supply Company.

"Need any outfits?" he asks Choker, nodding at Cresty, while driving past the Halloween store. "How about a Fish Finder getup?"

The ride down to Cape May on the Parkway turned festive again before Cresty and Choker swapped turns telling Marion how she was born with internal testes and never thought she could have a baby. Playing with the rabbits, they told him how they never used protection. How she wasn't 'right.'

"I thought it was because you were Catholic," Marion, who was speechless otherwise, finally said.

"Hey, did you hear Pope Francis said animals can get to heaven?" he had added. "Pope Benedict said they couldn't, though, before Francis.

"How about that, the Catholic Church is divided over animals getting into heaven."

The Saturday night dinner traffic crawling into Cape May is as thick as the smell of the day's catch being cooked and cleaned at the marina ahead. Avoiding the back-up beyond the bridge, Marion makes a right on Route 109, waving to a young couple holding hands while sitting on one of the park benches outside the Cape May Clinic. He crosses over the railroad tracks. A thud. Another thud.

"Watch it, easy old man, Cresty is carrying cargo here," Choker says.

Marion hooks the left on 626 and crosses over the canal bridge back into Cape May, peeking to see the red SUV isn't parked in front of the rich man's boat, as Cresty and Choker just smile like never before and pet the rabbits. Suddenly, at the top of the concrete bridge, he stops The Hearse. He laughs at the green and yellow sign in the middle of the bridge with a line down the middle of the word Jersey and on either side of the line are the words "North" and "South" in big yellow letters.

"It's like the Mason-Dixon line, rhymes with Higgs Boson," Marion says. "Silly, huh? But fun, North Cape May divided here from South Cape May."

"I reckon it's the locals' way of saying anyone north of this line isn't local," Choker reasons.

"Yeah, but even the locals are divided," Cresty says. "The town folk who carry the parasols don't like the surfers who also do parasailing. And the Devil's Reachers hate the free divers, who share the same waves and water. And the gay guys not hurting anyone walking on the Promenade get 'the don't grow up like them looks' from the mommies pushing the strollers."

Marion throws his oversized sunglasses into the canal, leaving him just the smaller pair on his face, as a minivan filled with a fine-looking family pulls on the other side of the bridge to pass.

"I guess it is all your perspective," Choker says. "What did Nietzsche call it, Perspectivism?"

The three leave The Hearse and stand on the bridge by the sign. They stare down the canal. The dusk casts a dull light into the darkness where the canal opens-up to the bay.

"You know what old Friedich also said?" Marion asks softly as the open water breeze with the sun going down in front of them. "Nietzsche also said when 'when you look into the abyss, the abyss also looks into you.' "

Cresty kisses the North-South divide sign on the bridge.

"Truly, it is a wonder how anyone in this country can agree on anything," she says.

"That is why we're helping the ones who don't have a say, there're a lot of fish out there," Marion says, spreading his arms over the canal. "We're like the Army Corps of Engineers who dug out this canal during World War II. We're making openings to the world."

Choker helps Cresty into the front of The Hearse. He waves two more minivans around them.

"You know where the bend in the canal is? You should from when you worked on Mr. Hallward's boat?" Marion asks Choker, who doesn't seem to be paying attention while staring at Cresty. "Well that bend was put there to keep German U-Boats from coming into the canal.

"Kind of like an IUD," Marion says laughing.

The three of them appear haggard, too beat to laugh while waiting to be seated at the crowded Lobster House next to the main bridge going into Cape May. The Saturday night crowd is buzzing. Everyone is dressed in Sunday best white outfits.

Except the three of them… oops four…

They roam outside the Lobster house. Choker fakes throwing the table buzzer into the bay.

The popular Fisherman's Wharf swarms with vacationers and tourists from out of town. There is a long line at the outdoor takeout counter. A pregnant woman orders "Cape May brand sea scallops." Choker and Cresty can't peel their eyes away from her.

Their seating buzzer goes off and they return to the lobby next to a boat in a glass case that is filled with dollar bills for MED13L Syndrome. The hostess, wearing one white glove, tells them the wait will be longer than expected.

"Why did you buzz then?" Marion asks defiantly, turning towards her before suddenly stopping as the reflection off the glass with the boat reveals Dr. Hyde sitting at a table. He twists to see more of the reflection showing the girl with the motorized bike crying while eating scallops like popcorn. Twisting again, he sees the rich man opening a bottle of champagne.

"I'm starvin' like Marvin," Cresty says to the hostess, who raises her glove hand, pointing to a table for a distracted bus boy to clean. "I'll sit outside."

"Grabbing her elbow, Marion agrees, saying, "The air will be good for your luggage… your cargo."

Choker agrees with opting to take seats in the outdoor eating section on Fisherman's Wharf. The tables, surrounded by potted trees, buffer the view of the fishing boats down the end of the pier, as if protecting the patrons from seeing how what they eat is caught.

The old schooner "American" is dry docked next to their table. Flanking the "American" are the fishing boats "Wesley L." and "Alexandra L.," which are operational vessels.

Marion talks over the creaking ropes mooring the boats being pulled with the outgoing tide when the waitress comes up with "I like your bur oaks."

"My what?" says the waitress with the Fisherman's Wharf shirt spotted on the long sleeves with red tartar sauce.

"The potted tress, the bur oaks. They grow well in the city. They are splendid for shade because of their thick branches.

"I'll have a thick creamy Guinness. Two of them."

"What about one for me?" Cresty begs.

"You'll have just water, not even Guinness is healthy for the baby," Choker says.

"Baby, I hope your parents are better than mine," the waitress says.

"What did they do?" Marion inquires.

"They won't even pay for my college tuition."

"Evil. Why don't you sue their asses? Sue them good," Marion says.

"I think I will, thanks for the idea," she says scooping up a stack of bills left by the previous customers.

"I don't think I will have the baby. I don't want my kid growing up suing me, hating me. And I won't be able to surf all summer," Cresty suddenly says. "With El Nino, I'll be missing out the waves of the century. Plus, we don't have any money… and Choker is going to go off to college now that he is kicking ass in judo."

Listening to the squeaky ropes being pulled by the fishing vessels, Marion waits for the Guinness arrives. He takes a long sip, then a short one before a real long one.

"If you do kill the baby, you're missing a chance of a lifetime," Marion says. "That is much longer than going off to college. Some people only get one chance. You might too. This universe can be quite complex.

"This is your righting moment."

"Her what?" Choker asks. "Don't you mean Rochambeau?"

"No, righting moment," Cresty answers for Marion. "In sailing, it's the moment the keel rights the boat at the instant before tipping. In life, it is the moment to do the right thing, or the time you make things right, like you did in the tournament.

"But, I'm not going to have a baby in this universe if the father doesn't want it. I know he won't after the euphoria of the being a daddy thought, being like Pete, all wears off tomorrow."

Choker takes a long swig from the beer as one of the ropes mooring the schooner "American" snaps.

"Now this is life," Marion smiles. "We are living now. One person is celebrating the achievement of his young life by fighting for a judo title while another is simply choosing life or death. And a third person, yet unnamed, but every bit alive as us three, doesn't have any chance to fight for his, or her, rights and certainly doesn't have any choices. If he, or her did, we wouldn't even be having this conversation… and… and this is Independence Day weekend…

"Quite contradictory… hypocritical … unfair at the least, don't you say, this universe?' Marion rapid fires at them and adds, "But if life was fair, Brian Jones would've never have drowned in a swimming pool and still would be playing with the Stones… old schooners wouldn't be dry docked as floating restaurants… and parasols would protect from the rain like umbrellas."

Choker chews on the lip of his pint glass. He has no words or metaphors to add. Cresty chews on her fingernails.

"And, if the T-rex and stegosaurus were still here, we wouldn't have any choices either. We'd be dinner. We'd be getting our skulls smashed like the unborn," Marion says, spilling his wild thoughts into the clam-baked air.

"You know who is in the photo on the wall?" Marion points where the waitresses all gather waiting for drinks.

Barely, they both shake their heads no.

"Me neither, probably some ship captain from back during the pirate days," Marion says.

"That is the great Captain Arne Jensen," a bus boy, wearing the t-shirt of the schooner "American" with spotless long sleeves, says triumphantly while clearing the table next to them. "Old Arne caught a 37 and ¼ pound Lobster back on July 3rd in 1985 on the 'Courageous.'"

"Well, old Arne looks like the great Clint Eastwood in the Outlaw of Josey Wales with that bad-ass beard."

Marion takes a knife from the bus boy's bin. He turns the sharp side facing him and swipes the palm of his left hand. He then swipes the palm of his right hand. He puts his hands together like he is making a blood oath.

"Never saw it," the boy says, being careful not to splash any of the tartar sauce from the plates on his sleeves.

"Me neither," Choker says, "but Uwrenski talks about the movie a lot, like its religion."

"I like U-man more," Marion says.

"Yeah, he said it was about fighting back. That's important in judo. He said sometimes if you think about how tough the fight is, you will never fight it. Like in judo, if you think about how tough your opponent is, you will never try to throw him, or choke him," Choker explains.

"He said Josey *reckoned* in times like those, when you might just get your ass kicked royally, you just have to `plum fight like a junk yard dog.'

"That's what I did today. I thought about that. I fought like a junk yard foo-kin dog."

"But, you fought with respect too," Marion praises. "And, you used other moves than chokes."

"Yeah, I'm proud of you," Cresty says between bites of her fingertips. "So is Uwrenski. He is going to talk to the Stockton coach, what is his name - Swan or something? – Again."

"No, Bit," Marion says in a scolding tone.

"So, I bit my fingernails," Cresty says, "I'm starving…"

"Bit? It's bitten," Marion says while he orders another Guinness.

"Who trims your trees here?" Marion interrogates the waitress, pointing to the picture of old Arne."

"Clint does, himself," she says. "I heard you talking about him in the picture, so why not?"

"She probably says that to all the guys," Cresty says. "You guys get so worked up about Clint."

"That's because Clint, in his movies, fights for what is right. You know, Uwrenski was right too, at least in the beginning. But at the end of the movie, Josey had a choice between fighting and walking, between life and death. Like we all do."

Gazing over the weathered bow of the schooner "American" with a shiny sign NIGHTLY GHOST

TOURS, Marion doesn't look at Cresty or Choker as he continues sipping and talking.

"He, Josey, was living in some Comanche land, territory, with some Kansas-ians, or Missourians, who went west. The Comanche was going to kill all of them because the white man betrayed them with 'double tongue.'

"So, Josey rode into the Comanche camp and spoke. The Indians were war-painted up. He rode up right to Chief Ten Bears. Josey told him he came here to `live with him or die with him right here."

Standing on his chair, Marion says dramatically, "Wales said… 'life is in my words and death in my pistol… you make the choice.'"

Sitting, and raising his Aviator sunglasses, Marion squints his eyes, turns his head to one side, spits into a tree holder next to the table, lowers his voice: "Josey said, 'dying ain't so hard, it's living that's hard when all you cared about has been raped or butchered.'"

Marion turns his head to the other side. He speaks in an even deeper voice as he holds the front tip of his tongue.

"Ten Bears said, 'It's good warriors like me and you get together in the struggle of life and death.'"

The bus boy comes back around to listen. Marion orders another Guinness from the waitress. He spits again in the tree holder, but the shorter spray splats on the left sleeve of the bus boy.

"Well, what happened?" Cresty asks. "Did they live or die?"

"They made the hard choice," Marion says oblivious to the bus boy using a wet towel to try and clean the Guinness splat above his wrist.

"They chose to fight?" Cresty and Choker say at once, startling the bus boy. "Right?"

"No, they chose to live."

Another spit from Marion sends the bus boy to another table. Marion turns his knife over and swipes his palms again. He clasps his hands.

"They made a blood oath. From all they've been through in life, they both knew living would be harder than dying. These two great warriors chose to live."

"Like the ballad by Clannad?" Choker asks.

"Yeah, their song from Harry's Game," Cresty says. "Pete taught us. He said the Gaelic words mean 'in war no one wins.'"

"Indeed," Marion says. "Josey Wales and Ten Bears seen all that was important was life. Not money, not land, not whiskey… not the Rolling Stones."

"Man, if Mick ever heard you say that," Choker says with another enjoyable swig of the dark stuff.

"Never met him, but I would say that to him too. Mick knows. His long-time girlfriend, the former model, took her life in New York over the winter."

"Dude, what would you really say to Mick if you ever met him?"

"Let's stop talking about life and death," Cresty suggests, banging her right fist on the table like a judge's gavel.

"That's easy, I would ask him if he would like to go out to the F150, put on Fish Finder and listen to a few songs from Hot Rocks. Then I would ask him where they shot the cover for Hot Rocks because I'd like to be buried there."

The waitress is back with more tartar spots on her sleeves. They order another round of Guinness.

"I have to take a squirt," Marion says standing up.

"Just climb one of the trees out here," Choker bursts, "and go."

Holding her belly, Cresty laughs. It is good to see her laugh. Her laugh sounds alive… again, like at the Avalon basketball courts.

"No, I'm going the conventional way, anyway, I thought I saw someone I know go into the john."

Marion goes to the bathroom. He leaves them alone. Cresty steals a quick swig of Marion's beer.

"Whoa, there Smellie. So, who is the father?" Choker pokes her. "Marion?"

She spits out the beer, spraying the potted tree.

"Do you really think the old captain caught a 37-pound lobster?" Cresty asks.

"No."

"You don't either, huh?"

"The lobster was 37 and ¼ pounds," Choker says.

The outdoor bathroom is tight with only two standup urinals. A stocky man at the first stall takes up space in front of the second one. Marion slides in anyway. Rubbing elbows with the man, he looks over and says, "Sorry sailor." The man grunts before looking up and saying, "Who are you?"

Confirming he is the rich man from the boat, Marion sings, "Who are you?"

Wiping his hands-on Marion's sleeve, the rich man says, "You better flush or I will take your urine, for a DNA sample."

"Another one?" Marion responds,

"Why don't I just piss on you so you can have a souvenir," he adds as he slides past the stocky man, leaves the outdoor bathroom and goes into the gift shot.

Wearing a pirate eye patch from the gift shop over his left eye and slightly laughing, Marion loops inside and walks past Dr. Hyde's table with the girl and the rich man.

"Join us outside for a night cap," Marion says to Dr. Hyde with a pirate, or Keith Richards' "errrr" at the end, which doesn't amuse any of them.

"Are you the pirate Blackbeard or The Fish Finder," the rich man asks, injecting tension into the cheerful room of vacationers.

"Do you fish, too?" Marion asks.

"I do."

"Bait fish?"

"No, seine fishing… you should know what that is? Pirate."

"I do… cheat fishing." Marion lashes at him. "Using a dragnet, a weighted net, holding the bottom down while floats keep the top above water… like fishing in a barrel… might as well use a gun… or stabbing the little fishes caught in the webbing with scissors."

Outside, they eat lobster Panini sandwiches. Marion leaves money and takes the dinner knife. He spits one more time in the tree bin. They leave the outdoor wharf, stopping inside to put a dollar in the boat for MED13L Syndrome. The reflection from the glass shows Dr. Hyde's table is empty.

They walk fast, arm-in-arm, to The Hearse.

"Let's go to the beach by the lighthouse and see the sunset," Marion says twirling the dinner knife in his fingers like a drumstick. Maybe we can see M87 galaxy. You should be able to see it this time of year."

Chapter 13

The black-gated fence guarding the driveway entrance to the lighthouse and the small white shack at its base is open even though the hanging sign says CLOSED. Still wearing the pirate patch and with his Aviator sunglasses perched on his head, Marion scrapes the knife on each rung of the metal gate with an outstretched arm as Cresty drives The Hearse into the parking lot. She parks near the pavilion bordering the dune at Cape May Point State Park.

"Good driving," Marion applauds. "Hard for me to see out of one eye, so thanks for taking over the controls."

Marion weaves up the ramp toward the pavilion where the Interpretation Center is closed. The screen door is padlocked. Cresty and Choker sit on the two rusted ship anchors, which must be 12-feet long, outside of the bathroom as Marion makes another deposit.

Walking down to the beach, they cross a platform used by the birders. Then they cross the dunes, which are as high as the floor of the pavilion. The walk is downhill to where the ocean meets the bay. Migrating birds mix in flight above. The people who are leaving the beach and the ones walking down to the beach cross paths without even a nod.

The beach is particularly beautiful in the illuminating moments before sunset. The glow spreads over the sand, which is now as wide as a football field with the tide low. A dune where kids roll down is not nearly as steep as the sandy hill overlooking the canal up from the ferry.

Cresty stops and watches the kids play. Wonder if she is thinking like I am now how it was just yesterday, a blink in time, when she was jumping off dunes and we had our whole lives ahead of us, even without her mother with us. She had gone back to Turkey, where we met one summer night like this one under the stars while crossing the Bosphorous from Europe to Asia. We were young. We were drinking. The other side of the river dividing Istanbul and separating the two continents looked inviting. The Asian side was. We created Andie, or Cresty, on a boat lying in the hull.

Clutching Choker's shoulders with both hands, Marion says, "Show me the judo choke. I need to know, bro."

"You can choke from in front and behind your opponent," Choker explains. "Both work. It's the angle and pressure that matters."

"I want to learn the one from behind."

"It's called the Okuri-eri-game. Now say it."

"Why do I have to learn the name? Just show me."

"You must know the name, just like you tell us we must know how the universe works."

"Okuri-eri-game," Marion says deliberately pronouncing each vowel like a first grader with a nun staring him down. "Okuri-eri-game… Okuri-eri-game… Okuri-eri-game."

Choker positions his body behind Marion and kicks him gently in the back of both knees. Marion buckles a bit.

"With your right hand, you grab the opposite collar. With the left hand, you come under the chin and encircle the neck while gripping the opposite collar with your left thumb inside. Now, pull in and down with the right arm and around with your left while pulling up."

Marion starts gagging. Choker lets him go.

"Simple. Man, it works," he says between gulps of air. "That's foo-kin great. Now I have to learn it."

"You already learned it, now you have to practice it and practice it and practice it and practice it. And when you are done practicing it, then you have to practice it some more."

"How do you think the great De-rek Je-ter learned to hit to right field?" Cresty asks, coming up from behind with her hands outstretched like she wants to learn the choke move.

"That's the only way to do the grip. When you get someone in that choke, you don't want to let him out. Match must be over. I know."

Marion and Choker proceed to spar, to grapple for a good half hour, although I'm not good with time. Cresty crouches next to them both. She observes. Her stillness is strange.

She is watching the kids play on the dune as the sky turns darker with each piece of sand sliding down the hourglass.

"Hey, what is the hunking structure over there?" she asks, snapping out of her trance.

Gasping to catch his breath, Marion says, "It's an old concrete World War II bunker. The bunker was built by the Army in the early 1940's and manned through the Korean War by the Navy.

"Now, the once majestic structure that protected us, is being allowed to slowly die and undignified death. Our government should assist the once-proud military fortress and support the ones, the groups who want to help bury the bunker, give it a noble goodbye."

"I'm going to give you a noble goodbye," Choker snarls, grabbing him around the neck.

Marion and Choker continue practicing chokes, holding each other in the same position for minutes at a time. They roll on the dune like little kids playing violently without their mom watching. Marion is really into learning the grips and holds… and mostly the chokes.

"Dude, you got really strong hands," Choker says. "Really, you're going to be an Okuri-eri-game master in no time. You won't know any other chokes, but that's fine for now. How did your hands get so strong?"

"In my old job… I used them a lot. I needed strong hands… and a stronger stomach. I already had the weak mind."

"What was your old job? You never told us. Where are you from?" Cresty rattles. "You keep saying back in California…"

Flopping on his back in the sand. Marion studies his hands as if he is making an invisible choke. He is intense. He doesn't seem to hear her.

They both plop down next to him. They look up to see darkness. The stars can't be seen yet, but they are out there, next to me.

Standing abruptly, Cresty brushes the sand from Choker. The dinner knife falls from Marion's back pocket as he stands and says, "Since we missed the sunset, we should look for the M87 galaxy. You know the M87 Galaxy is traveling away from the earth at 700 miles per second. The whole galaxy is moving at 700 miles a second."

"How do you think that happened?" Cresty asks. "I'm dumber than a stick."

"There was an explosion, but it wasn't a fart. It was a bang, a big bang. That's how God created all this. With a bang."

Holding her belly, Cresty laughs. Marion hugs her. Choker playfully tosses sand at them both.

"You know when you asked me when life of a baby starts?"

"Yeah, I would like to know the answer."

"I don't know," Marion says softly, looking up into the darkness as if he will see the answer.

"You have to, you know how the universe started with a big bang, you have an answer for everything. You know all this about the world and how the Stones started, but you don't know something simple like when life starts for a baby.

"You got to know for me."

"No one knows, not even Einstein or Goethe. Not Jagger or Je-ter… just God of course," Marion says.

"I think the parking attendant might know. Under his turban is the answer," Cresty says. "He knew everything."

"The way I figure, He wants to keep it that way too?" Marion says.

"Who is he, the parking guard freak?" Choker asks.

"I think that is His, God's plan," Marion continues. "To weed out the good from the bad. He doesn't leave gray area. Either you are for life or against it, meaning either you believe in Him or you don't. You can't be in the middle. Man, does He know what he is doing or what?

"There's no Rochambeau and not Gott würfelt nicht neither. Just the Righting Moment."

They sit again on the beach and look skyward for at M87. The kids are gone from the dunes.

"You know what JK said?" Marion asks. "The parking guru reminded me of JK and the sky reminds me of his quote.

"You mean JFK?" Cresty asks. "JFK from the PT 109, right?"

"No, he means JK Rowling," Choker says with an embarrassed grin.

"No JK, the great Jack Kerouac!" Marion spits out like an excited kid. "JK said, 'there was nowhere to go but everywhere, so just keep rolling under the stars.'"

"Indeed," Choker says. "We are rolling under the stars, but without the Stones."

"Indeed, we are going no fook-in where but everywhere," Cresty says, rolling her hand over her belly. Marion rubs her stomach, too, with his right hand. With his free hand, he reaches for Choker's hands that just crushed his windpipes and place them on her belly also and says, "And this is the answer to when life starts, what we feel now, the feeling of your unborn baby's breathe is nowhere but everywhere."

Marion picks up the knife sticking into the sand and turns the sharp side down. He swipes his left palm and draws blood. Choker sticks out his left hand. Marion swipes the palm slightly. There is blood.

They clasp hands.

"We will protect Cresty and her unborn baby," Choker says.

"We will protect all the unborn," Marion says.

The rain starts as they fall asleep under the pavilion used by the bird watchers. A blanket, which must have been left under a bench, now wraps around them.

Chapter 14

Cresty wakes first. The rainstorm makes the morning air feel like a warm blanket. A Monarch Butterfly, a female with the thick black stripes like veins on her yellow wings, stirs her, flying around her belly. The waves are crashing so frequently beyond the dunes below the pavilion, the ocean sounds like a waterfall.

"I thought it would be warmer sleeping near the beach here at The Pointe since it is closer to the equator at the tip of Cape May than on your boat," she says to Marion, pulling the blanket around her and away from Choker. She points toward the ocean. "I'm going out for a ride, maybe that dude already out there surfing will let me borrow his board."

Like someone shook the pavilion, Choker and Marion shoot right up in the cold, fresh dawn air.

"No way," Choker says.

"No, no, we should go crabbing," Marion argues with gravitational force. "A good day for crabbing today. Unless you want to go to church first?"

Walking with a purpose, but still sleepy, Marion waddles to the back of The Hearse while Choker and Cresty go in the front and free the rabbits from the cage. They sit on the bumper, next to a northern bayberry shrub well over six feet in height. Choker picks at the pale green berries.

"The berries are an important winter food source for the yellow rump warbler's and tree swallows," Marion yells from the back of The Hearse. "You should leave them, unless you wait until September when they turn blue gray and are covered with wax coating, which they are then used to make bayberry candles.

"Problem is, it takes nearly five gallons of berries to make one candle... the wax is also used in making soap.

"I need a bath," Cresty screams out. "I feel dirty inside and out.

Sitting snug in the front seat, the blanket from the pavilion now covers them completely, except for Choker's one hand that is wrapped in a rag from The Hearse, a cloth Marion handed him to cover his seeping wound from the blood bonding. Marion wraps his hand, too.

Choker starts to pet Way. Choker strokes Row gently.

"I didn't think you liked animals," Cresty pokes while throwing fresh poop pellets from the cage into the smaller bayberry shrubs on the dune. "Fertilizer."

"I can't decide if I do or not," Choker shrugs. "Just like I can't make up my mind what to do with… but since the Pope says animals can now go to heaven…"

"What do you mean? I thought you already decided. You know back on the dock that morning, back on the Fishing Boat with the butterfly," she demands. "No gray area."

"That's only with the weather."

"I knew it last night," she says with the acceptance of fate.

Marion looks into his slashed hand, which he unwrapped. He pulls out his Galaxy phone. He has the letters set extra big, so he reads slowly. He rarely even uses his phone.

"How about this," he says. "In the worst tragedy in the history of the Philadelphia Zoo, 13 primates were killed in a fire in the Monkey House on Saturday night. Says here it left the zoo officials 'devastated.' The cause of the fire remains under investigation."

Holding the phone closer, Marion continues: "Overwhelming outpouring of grief has come from all over the world and the Monkey House, one of the most popular exhibits at the famed zoo, has been replaced with beds of flowers."

“At least the poor monks can go to heaven now,” Choker says.

Marion tosses the Galaxy phone on the dashboard. It bounces off the windshield and lands on the rabbit cage.

“How many babies were killed on Saturday night in Philadelphia?” He groans. “There are no stories on newspaper articles about them. No one is laying beds of flowers for them. Why is that?”

Cresty reaches on top of the cage and grabs the phone. She scrolls.

“The headline next to the zoo story says government OK's stem cell experiments from aborted babies. What does this mean?”

Marion reads the phone again. He twirls his watch.

“Now the government is playing God. We have to work quickly.”

“I thought we were crabbing?” Choker says as Cresty quickly adds, “Yeah.”

“Oh yeah,” Marion says looking over to the pavilion where a girl gets off her motorized bike. Instantly, Marion scurries over to her, holding his Aviator sunglasses so they don’t fall in his haste.

“Where’s your eye patch,” she asks, locking her bike.

"Only wear at work," Marion answers. "Are you OK?"

"Yes, now… now after talking to Dr. Hyde and Mr. Rich," she says.

"That's his name. Rich?" Marion asks before adding, "What lies did they tell you?"

"They encouraged me to have my baby and told me how they could help me find an adopting family I like," she says. "I'm relieved…"

Marion speeds through the empty parking lot and drives the back way out. The lighthouse marks the exit. He must see the path, seemingly following the rising sunlight. There are two swans in the lake doing nothing, but looking spiritual, as The Hearse rips by them and out of Cape May Park.

The lifeguard boat in the middle of the boulevard leading into, or out of the park, is painted with the black letters CAPE MAY POINT. The nun house towers in front of The Hearse. A birder with binoculars up to his eyes strolls toward the nun house.

They ride into the sun on Sunset Boulevard. Marion bangs an awkward left on Broadway. He misjudges the turn and has to back up into the intersection before taking Route 162 over the Cape May Canal.

Marion makes a left on Route 9, going west. Before the road ends at the ferry, Marion turns north on Bayshore Road, as if he is going back to see Hunter. But he continues north, driving past the Ponderlodge Golf Course. He speeds by the Cape May County Airport before connecting above The Villas onto Delsea Drive.

"Delsea Drive used to be the main drive from Philadelphia to Cape May before the Atlantic City Expressway and the Garden State Parkway," Marion tells them. "Now only the locals use the single lane road."

The former main drag curves and weaves with the shoreline along the bay.

Under the blanket, Choker and Cresty sleep as Marion drives past Leesburg State Prison on the banks of Dividing Creek, which runs from Union Lake in Millville to the bay.

"Something how Dividing Creeks spurs from Union Lake?" Marion says, waking the sleepers. "Where did the creek go wrong?"

Choker and Cresty aren't awake enough to catch the paradox.

The ride to Port Norris weaves through glorious green wetlands before depositing here into the Delaware Bay. They might as well be in Antarctica. There is nothing around them but wetlands

After crossing over a one-lane wooden bridge, they stand on the dock of Dividing Creek Boat Rental. They have a whole day ahead of them for crabbing, if they chose. There aren't butterflies here like in Cape May.

"The Monarchs must have been eaten by these killer greenheads," Choker says, swatting at flies.

"The sun is stronger here without the ocean breeze," Marion says, "making perfect breeding grounds for greenheads."

This is one of those really sunny days when you don't take your eyes off the ground until after dinner. They might be pulling in crabs like pennies out of a wishing pond at the mall, but the sun is screaming already at 9 in the morning like high noon in Tombstone.

Cresty looks into the rising sun over the water. She does a double take. Edging close to Marion she whispers. "The red boat." A dockhand is loading a red metallic cooler on the boat with ice from the dock store.

Turning quickly, Marion asks a teenage boy for a crabbing boat with a canopy. The kid loading crabbing baskets said no one else uses the "roofed vessels."

"The poles of the canopy tend to get in the way when pulling up lines tight with a crab at the end," the boy with a jagged three-inch scar between his thumb and forefinger says. “And, scooping the little blue clawed beasts is even more dicey with needing to dodge the canopy.”

“Listen, it’s either the canopy or covering myself with layers of bay mud, kind of like how the Lewis and Clark Expedition caked themselves in mud to protect from the mosquitoes on the Missouri River,” Marion says.

Choker and Cresty put the baskets in the canopy boat.

“I feel really good about the future of our expedition on The River Queen,” Marion says, choosing a name for the double-benched, four-seater.

“You should feel great,” Cresty says. “The kid, Billy, saved us because we didn’t bring our own baskets.”

“Let’s pull in some blue claws,” Marion says moving the two wooden baskets with metal handles to the front of the boat. “Let’s see who is on the red boat.

“Think just two baskets will be good enough for our catch?”

Marion laughs at his joke and adds, “A quick lesson. When you feel a bite, pull hard to get the crab good, then soft to make sure, then hard to get the blue claw devil into the boat."

They drop anchor not far from yelling distance to Billy on the deck of another boat without a canopy, filling up with college kids and a cooler.

They crab in the middle of the 20 to 30-yard wide banks of the river. It's too deep. The boat is drifting. The anchor doesn't hit bottom. They are being pulled by the current.

"Let's sail closer to a bank," Marion says like the captain, like he is Shackleton himself. "It's low tide, the best time for crabbing, but the water level is so high here…"

He drops anchor again. This time they drift closer to the far shore. They move out of the current.

"Excellent seamanship," Marion congratulates himself.

"The anchor pulls us around perfect," Marion says. "The brackish water off the bank is just right… although it's still high here."

Marion cuts the heads off the bunk. He hooks the meat on the end of the string. They don't use hooks, but triangle vice grips.

"When you feel them pull slowly pull up the string," Marion says like an expert. "They grab on and won't let go."

Choker and Cresty both pull up without any crabs.

"They key is to keep in shallow water, 7-10 feet is excellent," Marion advises, "but I can't find any low spots.

"They stay in holes, if you get in a hole or next to one, you will be pulling in one after another," Marion the crabbing captain adds.

"Who are you, the King Crabber?" Choker mocks.

"You won't be able to get the bait on quick enough," the captain says.

Before Choker and Cresty pull one crab, Marion already has bagged a good half dozen keepers in the basket. He threw at least as many back since they weren't the four and a half inches needed to keep.

"We can't crab either," Choker says. "I can't fish, I can't foo-kin crab, I can't play basketball. I can't even play chess."

"You might want to keep the bottom of the boat quieter," Marion says reeling in another blue claw.

"We might want to get rid of the canopy," Choker says.

Cresty points. She is reaching dangerously over the side of the boat with her arm.

"No foo-kin way, boys."

Chokers flashes a disbelieving grin when seeing the crab in her net.

She points to the top of a signpost in the high

water reading “hot spot” with a sea gull on top. Even the wildlife points to this spot.

“Marion found the spot,” Choker says. “He is like Dr. Doolittle, communicating with the birds.”

They worked the hole until there were no more hits for 15 minutes or so. They probably have bagged a dozen crabs, all of them the minimum size.

“They are so big this boat will sink,” Choker says laughing.

“Big like Choker,” Cresty laughs

They move on. The captain anchors near the sign reading “Devils Triangle.”

“What are the chances?” Cresty says. “Total Rochambeau, bros. I was going to surf at Devil’s Reach this morn and now me ass at the Devil’s Triangle.”

“Perhaps Satan himself is following, I mean pushing you,” Choker says.

“Indeed,” Marion responds. “You might have too much sympathy for the devil, or your thoughts do. Perhaps Lucifer is pulling you like gravity.”

The boat rocks side to side. They almost tip when a speeding boater creates a wake.

“That’s not right,” Marion says shaking his head and pulling up a line. “The fooker pushed us into the bank.”

Looking up, Marion sees a lady at the helm of

the familiar, the unfriendly red boat closing in on their canopy boat.

"Sorry mate, didn't see you in the weeds," says a lady with long black jeans over her wide hips from the bow.

"No worries, mate," Marion mumbles.

"Watch out for the pirates down here, mate," the lady says laughing as she slips the engine in reverse to stay even with the crabbers. "Do you need a tug getting out of the weeds?"

"Maybe in a bit," Marion says.

"Well, I apologize, can't wait, have to get ice home," she explains, "with the rising water levels in the Delaware Bay due to climate change, the electric lines running to our house up the bay, in the town of Money, short out.

"Our son has special needs, and he needs cold drinks, so I have to return with coolers of ice."

"No worries, mate," Marion says. "Hey, I think I've seen the boat in Cape May, the red is… the color is unique."

"Yes, my husband does business in town," she says. "But he spends as much time as he can with our two teenage sons, who both have developmental delays so severe that they have to be supervised at all times, they would walk off the boat and drown… we don't know how long they will… make it…

unless stem cell research finds a cure for this rare genetic disease, MED13L syndrome, there are only 15 known cases in the world and we hit the exacta with two of them."

"So sorry, miss," Marion says. "We'll pray for them."

"Yes, we will," Cresty and Choker both say as they dip their lines into the water.

"Thanks," she says, "but like sailors say, pray to God, but tie up your boat at night."

"I understand," Marion says, "pray but also take care of business yourself, don't rely on government to protect you."

"I wouldn't eat those crabs, not with the water this high," she adds. "The government doesn't tell you and neither does the shellfish industry, but many homes in Downe Township here have their septic tanks compromised with the water levels this high. Just saying."

She waves and says, "Save the Bayshore… no retreat" as the red boat pushes down river, leaving the crabbers in Devils Triangle.

Cresty pulls up the first crab there, but it is a half-inch short. She lets it go and pulls up another line, pulling what has to be a keeper.

"This is heavy," Cresty says. "This is really heavy."

Marion helps her while Choker watches the red boat peel away. Marion yanks the rope hard, then soft and real hard again. Up come two big crabs – both in a rusted metal crab trap.

"I thought we had a bushel," Marion laughs.

He expertly handles the two crabs, tossing them into the basket with their tasty friends. The two crabs are connected like Siamese twins.

"Hey, look at them," Choker says. "They are conjoined alright."

"Hope we don't have twins."

"Their mother didn't kill them because they were connected," Marion says. "They weren't perfect, but they survived. Nature rules."

Marion reaches in the basket and tosses the connected crabs back into the bay, shaking his hand when he is clawed between the thumb and forefinger.

"I hate when foo-kin bit," he says.

"You mean bitten," Cresty smirks.

"The bit will hurt for days," Marion complains. "But sometimes doing right hurts."

Marion soon pulls up another crab with one hand. This time without any rusted hardware around the crab or without the blue claws being connected. He asks Chesty to bring over the net.

She comes in too close.

"You scared baby blue away," he snarls and then explains how "if you come from behind with the net and scoop from the side" you won't lose the catch.

"They will swim right into the net," he says.

Soon, Choker nets one with one claw.

"They grow back," Marion says about the claws. "But babies don't once they get cut out."

Cresty makes a surfing pose in the boat. She rubs her belly.

"I should be surfing, not crabbing."

"Do you think she still should be surfing?" Choker asks. "You know, with you being, you know. We have to be careful, don't we?"

"Gravity will slow her down when it's time to slow down," Marion says.

"What do you mean by that?" Choker asks.

"When she gets bigger, she will slow down. It's really very simple. The more mass, the more pull by gravity. At least here on earth."

"So, if she was surfing in the middle of the earth with the Hobbits, she could be nine months pregnant and not feel any pull?"

"Except," Choker says, "from you."

"Wouldn't there be more pull at the center of the earth?" Cresty asks holding her pose and not rocking the boat.

Marion throws the one-clawed crab back. The brackish water swallows up the crab without a splash.

"What would happen if she was surfing up in old M87?" Choker asks.

"First, she would have to catch a mighty big bad tube to get there, bigger than any of the wimpy 20-foot El Nino swells last winter at The Pointe, or between the lighthouse and Devil's Reach," Marion says.

Choker argues: "Come on man, M87 is traveling away from earth at the speed of 700 miles per second. It's still exploding away from the Big Bang.

"And, she would be surfing a lot shorter than nine months before she would have to stop for a few days to have the baby," Marion rambles. "That's if she's going to have the baby."

"What do you mean?" Cresty says.

"Why would it be shorter?" asks Choker.

"It's easy to explain. Much easier than learning that okuri-eri-game choke. Here let me practice on you."

Standing in the boat, Marion gets behind Choker and puts the chokehold on him. He applies pressure and Choker starts to cough. He taps him on the arm to stop the choke.

Choker coughs. The boat rocks. Cresty holds her surfing pose.

"You got the choke down. All you need now is to be able to put the choke on someone."

The marina owner, a man wearing a red, white and blue American flag skullcap, throws Marion a line. Marion misses the rope as he is adjusting his Aviator sunglasses high on his nose while snugging his hat tight with his left hand.

"You have a nice catch," the man says as Cresty hands him the two baskets, both half-filled and Marion ties the boat to the dock.

"You have a nice business here," Cresty says to him.

"Thanks, but it's more of a hobby for me," the man says.

"What's your business, then?" Cresty asks.

"Well, it's complicated."

"Try us."

"Well, procurement. I procure for myself and for friends with controversial taste," the man says.

"What do you mean?" she asks.

"It's different."

"Try me."

You won't tell anyone?"

"No."

"So, I practice Pescetarianism," the man says.

"Pesticide business?" she asks. "You do have killer greenheads here."

He laughs.

"Pescetarianism? My friends and I eat fish and seafood, but not the flesh of other animals. We don't believe in killing animals."

"Oh."

"Yeah, eating animal meat, well it's inhumane."

"Is that it?"

"Well, I'm also a practitioner of Aestheticism. Actually, I'm a collector."

"Collect what?"

"Well, Aestheticism is artwork that focuses on beauty rather than meaning," the man says. "I collect art from the Decadent Movement of the late 19th century, it's an attractive artistic style favoring unbridled beauty rather than the silly Romanticism's depiction of life."

"That's it? That's all you collect? Just art?"

"Well, no. The Aestheticism movement includes literature. I collect rare Gothic novels, original printings of Edgar Allan Poe's The Raven, and Mary Shelley's Frankenstein and Bram Stoker's Dracula."

"You're an original. What's your name?" she demands.

"Henry Hatton," he says casually. "My friends and family call me Harry."

"Lord,'' she says. "Man, that's a wild name.

"Suppose," he says, "I look at, or view the world… differently."

With one arm out the window, Marion zips past the Hawk Haven Vine Yard and Wineries, which is filling up with the lunch crowd, and makes a wild right on Breakwater Road as he breaks wind.

Still laughing, Marion turns into the Cape May County Airport. The famed Naval Air Station Wildwood was deactivated after World War II and bestowed to the county.

The large sign on NASW Hanger No. 1 screams CAPE MAY AIRPORT MUSEUM in big bold letters.

Hunter, who tips his cap to the three stunned crabbers, is giving a tour to a half dozen older folks. A grandfather-type is wearing a Yankees' 2009 World Championship jacket with the words on the back "27 and counting." He is holding hands with a young girl, maybe his granddaughter.

Cloaked in an over-sized torn Grateful Dead long-sleeve t-shirt, Hunter tells the crowd how the TBM Avenger has three machine guns for protection and a 1,600-pound bomb in its belly that "drops like a torpedo" for destruction.

"The Grumman Eastern Avenger was the most widely produced naval strike aircraft of all time,"

Hunter says. "Nearly 10,000 Avengers were produced by the parent company, Eastern Division of General Motors, between 1942 and 1945."

Hunter spots Marion in the back of the crowd standing between Cresty and Choker. He tips his cap again.

"Although the Avengers was designed primarily as a torpedo bomber, but problems forced it being modified to apply glide bombing technique," Hunter added.

The grandfather inches to the front with his granddaughter's hand squeezed tight.

"I was a turret gunner, near the end in 1945," the grandfather said proudly, pointing toward the glass bubble on the bottom of the tail. "I manned the 50-caliber machine gun, we called it the 'stinger position'"

"The stinger had the highest rate of casualties," Hunter says.

"I know it, I did it so my granddaughter, Lilly, here could be free like I was at her age, watching the great Babe Ruth play for the Yankees at old Shibe Park against the A's in Philadelphia, not worrying about a German bomb falling on my lap and spilling my Cracker Jacks.

"I was also responsible for monitoring the radio and radar equipment and tending to the bombs, or torpedoes as we called them, on board," he continues, holding everyone's attention as if he is going to tell them next he planned the Invasion of Normandy with Ike, General Eisenhower himself, and arm-wrestled with Dugout Doug, General MacArthur, on an aircraft carrier in the Pacific.

The grandfather hesitates, seemingly waiting for someone else to speak before adding, "I also hand held the camera to record the attack damage."

Everyone in the group waits for him to tell more. He seems embarrassed by the attention. Marion senses his hesitation. He moves up next to the frail man with the bouncy girl in hand.

"It says here the Avenger was the first US Navy aircraft to be fitted with under-wing rocket rails for either 3.5-inch or 5-inch rockets," he says reading the placard. "Please tell us more."

The grandfather sits on the bench under the propeller of the Avenger. His granddaughter sits on his side. The group circles tight.

"The good people of Trenton were the real heroes, they took the fight to the Nazis," he said with teeth slightly clenched. "The children went to school, but they still spent time collecting aluminum cans, old tires and newspapers to be recycled. They also worked in the family 'Victory Gardens" after school, growing veggies for the family so the farmer's food could be sent to us overseas.

"Really, for me to fight was nothing," he says. "I'm a Ward, we come from the Fighting Ward clan in Galway. I'm told there is a documentary movie out now on the bare-knuckle Fighting Wards. You can look me family up, my great grandfather, Patrick, the Trenton Terror, is buried in St. Mary's Cemetery in Trenton.

"So, I fought."

He pulls his granddaughter closer.

"But so, did Trenton, fighting 24 hours a day, seven days a week back home," he says. "Women and residents recycled and rationed food and gas and shoes and typewriters.

"You name it and it was recycled. Did you know Trenton was the national capital from 1783 to 1785?' he adds, seemingly forgetting what else to say about the war effort.

"Oh yeah," the old man quickly adds, "the Homasote Company In Trenton provided prefabricated building materials back in the 1920's and even for Admiral Byrd's expedition to the South Pole."

Cresty pokes Choker in the side as she sits on the bench next to the little girl.

"But during World War II, Homasote manufactured building products for military bases and housing throughout Europe and in the Pacific."

"Knock 'em down then build 'em up," Marion says, helping the grandfather to his feet.

Hunter resumes the tour. Marion and Choker join the walking line, but Cresty stays seated on the bench with the grandfather and little girl.

"Thanks for sitting with us," the old man says. "They will be turning my drinking glass at the Ugly Mug the other way soon. I wanted my granddaughter to see, to learn… to grow up and know she isn't here just because of me, others made tough choices for her to be here… for her to not fear to make the tough choice… for her to always chose to protect life… like others did for her."

Lagging behind the tour walkers, Marion marvels at the old warplanes. Choker urges him to keep pace, telling him the cold, damp hanger isn't healthy for Cresty. When Marion remains alone, staring at the turret of the Avenger, Choker clamps a chokehold on him from behind.

"You glowingly talk about the War and killing, but what is the difference between dropping bombs on innocent civilians in Germany and aborting innocent babies in America?" Choker asks.

"There's a difference," Marion says. "I just don't know what the difference is. But there must be one...

"Maybe the German guy Nietzsche provided the answer… Perspectivism… maybe the ancient Greeks nailed it with the Apollonian and Dionysian concepts, you know Zeus' two sons contrasting each other, with Apollo being the god of reason and rationale and Dionysus being the god of irrational thought and chaos.

"Sorry I don't know the answer to what makes killing different if all life is sacred, but I do know people have been thinking about what you're asking for a long time, back before the know-it-all Greeks.

"Maybe I'm just like the Dividing Creek marina man, Harry the Hat, just viewing America differently."

A college kid, who is sturdy like a linebacker, tells Hunter to finish up the tour, saying "the old guy talks too much… he's cutting into my Happy Hour time at the Ugly Mug." Marion creeps behind the obnoxious lout and slaps a chokehold on him.

Marion squeezes his neck and pulls down on the linebacker-like shoulders. Within seconds, the college kid is passed out on the floor. Marion lets go, saying, "Damn disrespectful kid… I'm ready.

"Don't remember the name of the choke hold, but damn, I'm ready."

With his tour duties over, and the pissed-off college kid off to his Happy Hour, Hunter joins their discussion. He tells them he has been helping out at the museum to restore the paint on the old planes.

"I re-painted the teeth on the nose of the Avenger," he says.

"That's cool," Marion says. "I see where you hone your painting skills."

"Yeah, I come here most week days," Hunter says, picking dried paint from his beard. "It's quiet, not like back in the day when the Wildwood Naval air station was built, back in 1943.

"No, not like during its peak in '44 when this training facility was home to 200 planes and 3,000 personnel, both military and civilian. There were 17,000 takeoffs and landings a month.

"Now we get like 17 visitors a month."

Marion picks a chunk of dried paint from Hunter's beard.

"I read where 41 men died in crashes during training exercises here and around the air grounds," Marion says. "I read where Harry Groome died in '45 when his plane crash on a training mission at the Sunken Ship.

"We can't bring back Harry, but we can raise the Atlantus. At least, we should try to resurrect the Sunken Ship."

"Are you trying to save the past? You are," Hunter says. "Perhaps you should allow the past to just die gracefully like the old man telling his granddaughter stories of back in the day, but not climbing back into the turret."

Before pulling out of the old air station, Marion stops The Hearse at the Vietnam Forgotten Warriors monument near the front game.

"Wonder how our Vietnam vet friend is doing at the Sunken Ship," Marion says. "We need to talk with him and see how many signed up to resurrect the Sunken Ship."

Chapter 15

The red traffic light at the foot of the bridge backs up the SUVs. There are groves of pine trees on both sides of the Parkway, making the road look like a nursery. On the right, in between two bushy trees, is a CAPE MAY WHALE AND DOLPHIN RESEARCH CENTER sign, On the other side of the road, a metal sign on a metal post tells drivers how CAPE MAY IS THE LAST TOWN TO THE SOUTH ON THE NEW JERSEY COASTAL HERITAGE TRAIL.

Most of the fishing fleet is already out this morning. Still enough fishing boats mix with the luxury boats, sprinkling the harbor water on both sides, to make this South Jersey port a twin of a New England marina, worthy of a post card.

Just past the line of trendy old shacks on Fisherman's Wharf is where Route 109 turns into Lafayette Street.

French General Lafayette, a Napoleon contemporary in France's fight for freedom, fought alongside George Washington during the Revolutionary War. He is known, well known by the seemingly few people nowadays who care about providing freedom for the ones who can't fight for liberty as "The Hero of Two Worlds."

Really, Cape May is two worlds within itself. There is the slumping Vance's Bar section on the way into town and the elegant Victorian architectural splendor in town proper. There is the workingman's harbor with fishing boats juxtaposed with the wining and dining man's luxury liners. There is Madame Palm reading futures next to Cape Care where there are no futures.

From The Hearse, "Sympathy For the Devil" blares. Jagger's voice is pumping from the Fish Finder as if he is standing on the rabbit's cage. Cresty rests her head on the shoulder of Choker, who pets the rabbits.

With unusual urgency, Marion pulls into the parking lot of Lucky Bones Grill.

"Did you see the newspaper clipping on the exhibit board back at the airplane museum? The clipping of Geraldine Doyle?" Marion asks, turning down the music.

Cresty doesn't budge her head from Choker's shoulder and he keeps petting the rabbits.

"You see Geraldine Doyle was believed to be the unwitting model for the WE CAN DO IT poster of the woman flexing her biceps in a factory doing World War II," Marion says. "The newspaper said the image of her later became a symbol for the American feminist movement.

"Incredibly, she was unaware of the posters existence until 1982 when she was going through a magazine and saw the photograph. She recognized herself. She was 5 foot 10 and slender then and just 17 in '42 when Geraldine took a job as a metal presser at a factory near her home in Inkster, Michigan to aid the war effort. A United Press photographer shot pictures of her working.

"She quit the factory job about two weeks later when another woman had smashed her hand while using the metal press. Geraldine Doyle played the cello and didn't want both her hands smashed, so she quit.

"We can't quit... our war effort."

Marion turns The Hearse around. He drives back across the bridge, pausing at the top to stare toward the clinic briefly before he parks in the liquor store lot. He nods to the owner, Skip, a short but powerfully built man with blonde hair, who listens right in on their conversation as he restrings his fishing rod.

"I'm more interested in knowing why it would take longer to surf in M87 than in Missy Doyle posing for a picture that she didn't want," Cresty says.

They sit on the hood of The Hearse as Skip offers them a six-pack of beer, but Marion declines. "It's not only 5 o'clock somewhere, it's 5 o'clock here," Skip says.

"There was an experiment in the '70s, about the time of the Stones' Exile on Main Street album, which was their only double-album in a studio," Marion says. "This experiment was really as simple as Charlie Watt's drum kit and what it proved is simple to understand.

"What happened was the Navy did this experiment with three atomic cesium clocks.

"Remember, I think I told you that the atoms of cesium radiate a continuous and an exact wave of frequency.

Choker and Cresty nod slightly. "You sure you don't want some beer?" Skip asks running both hands through his thick yellow hair. "Sounds like you will need some suds to understand."

"So, the two clocks were set precisely the same and couldn't be altered. They kept one clock at the Naval Observatory in Washington. The genius types sent one in an eastbound jet and one in a westbound jet. It took the dueling jets three days to circle the earth. When they got back, the eastbound clock had lost 59 nanoseconds and the westbound jet gained 273 nanoseconds compared to the Washington clock.

“Big deal… the rock clock lost less than a second in three days. Our digital clock at the dojo always loses time,” Choker says.

“They used cesium, it beats forever on earth without losing time. What caused the atoms to lose time one way and gained time the other way above the earth?

“The Rolling Stones!” Choker declares, opening one of Skip’s Bass Ales.

“Yeah, you sing time is on their side,” Cresty says.

“They could've if the Stones wanted, but the answer is gravity. What this experiment proved is clocks run faster at high altitude where gravity isn't as great and clocks are affected by traveling with the earth's rotation or against it.

“Gravity rules.”

“So why… how then why wouldn't I be surfing as long in space?” Cresty asks.

“Yeah?” Skip says. “Explain.”

“Time flies faster at higher altitudes. Now if she were on the edge of the universe, time would be speeding by, compared to earth that is. Listen, in 1976, the year of the Stones' only double live album, 8-track, `Love You Live,' there was the Chesapeake Bay Experiment where the geniuses used an atomic cesium clock, protected the timepiece from temperature, vibrations, magnet fields, and synchronized it with a cesium clock on earth.

"They sent the clock on a jet at 30,000 feet and monitored the two clocks." Marion says spinning the dial on his watch. "The cesium clock in the air gained three billionths of a second every hour. Then, they shot a rocket, 6,000 miles above the earth, same deal with the clocks.

"This time the clocks ran faster by one billionth of a second. So, the higher up, the faster time goes by. Or. Mick wouldn't be singing `Time is *not* on My Side' up in space.

"So, what… what does it mean?" Choker asks, downing the beer.

"Yeah, we will all have our drinking glasses hanging from the rafters at the Ugly Mug turned around someday no matter how fast or slow time goes by," Cresty says.

"Your Perspectivism is precise," Marion says. "The meaning is how we live, that's all … what we do to protect others, like the old man flying in the Avenger."

Taking his fishing rod and leaving the beer, Skip goes into the liquor store as a girl, with a bulging belly, wearing pink pants and a blue blouse, with her hair tied back, waddles into the front door of the clinic.

“This is my time now,” Marion says. “This is my Righting Moment.”

Marion points to Choker to slide behind the wheel of The Hearse.

“I'll be back,” he says in the Arnold the Terminator voice. “I’ll foo-kin be back with a pink or blue bag. When you see me, start up The Hearse.”

Cresty and Choker sit and talk about finishing the last four beers in the six-pack. They discuss the pros and cons of drinking the rest of the bottles. They talk about drinking one of them each. They talk about every variable of drinking the beer until they see Marion running out the side door. He is spinning one hand in the air like a tank commander to start the engine. In the other hand is a bag, a blue bag.

Starting the engine, Choker opens the door with his left hand while being pushed by Marion, who casually places the blue bag in his lap, into the middle seat. Marion sits and turns the wheel in one motion.

The Hearse speeds out of the lot. He hops over the curb.

“You can't blame rolling that bump on your eyes, this time you got an excuse for hitting the curb, you're driving on two wheels,” Choker says.

“Thanks for the understanding. Thanks for the judo hold too. It worked well.”

The Hearse tilts to Marion's side, almost flipping. He is going faster than ever before. Marion's hands are sliding on the steering wheel. They are bloody. At the first light, he turns on Route 109. He hits the gas and thump, thumps over the railroad tracks. He then turns sharp right onto a sandy road. He pulls to the side by high weeds.

He quickly opens the bag. There is more blood, massive blood. Then he pulls. There is a little head… arms… legs.

Marion turns the body over and slaps the ass.

The baby cries.

Cresty screams.

"Oh my God."

"Foo-k," Choker gags. "Foo-k. Foo-k. Foo-kin foo-k."

With one arm on the wheel, Marion pulls off his shirt and wraps the screaming baby in the bloody shirt. He kisses the baby's bloody forehead. He hits the Fish Finder and it roars Street Fighting Man: "What can an unaborted boy do except fight in the streets now."

The gray hearse speeds up the sandy path alongside the railroad tracks as if it is driving itself. The Hearse goes faster on the straight patches. The Hearse makes a hard left on a dirt path.

The Hearse stops at a creek. Historic Cold Spring Village sits beyond the trees. Marion washes the baby in the creek. He also does some doctoring to the baby with medicine and stuff from a black bag he pulled from behind the seat. Choker and Cresty kneel on the dirt road, holding each other.

The baby is wrapped in a clean white towel from the back of The Hearse. Marion's hands are clean. He crosses over the creek, handing the baby to Cresty, who puts down the rabbits.

The Hearse drives up the dirt road into a parking lot where a wedding reception is taking place at the Cold Spring Restaurant and Caterers. The bride walking up the steps is pregnant.

The Hearse makes a quick left and a quick right onto Fishing Creek road. The baby is quiet. They all are quiet until passing the Cape May Brewery as Marion whispers, "I could sure use a fookin Devil's Reach Ale now… to celebrate…"

The Hearse creeps along Fishing Creek Road until a dead end at the rusty guardrail. There is a chain at the dead end blocking the entrance at 1011, a golf-looking, one-story bungalow house overlooking the dune and into the bay.

Down the road, a new plastic bench sits behind and old wooden bench. Down a few blocks is a sign for historic Town Bank, established in 1635.

There are two white benches with white flowerpots behind them across from Harpoon Henry's Restaurant and Deck. The windows are boarded up at Harpoon Henry's. The abandoned palm trees on the deck are plastic.

Roslyn Avenue runs into Beach Ave. where there is a one-story white house on the corner with a small wooden boat now used as flower pot on the side lawn.

The Hearse stops across from the one-story pink house with blue shutters on the corner of Beach Avenue.

It's the house that sits on a diagonal facing the bay.

It is the same house Marion and Cresty went to the day of the judo tournament when no one was home when he had just cut the bushes there on Saturday. This time, they drove in the back way.

There is a minivan in the driveway. Marion parks across from the house. Staring at the bay, he takes the crying baby's head out of the shirt. He kisses the roaring baby's cheek.

"She still has the minivan, huh?"

Marion flips his Aviator sunglasses up on the bill of his hat and runs up toward the front door with the wrapped baby in his arms.

He stops as if shot. He stares at the small white statue ornament at the point of the front lawn. He puts his John Deere hat on top of the little baby angel's ceramic head.

Marion slowly turns and walks back to The Hearse. He slides the sunglasses over his eyes. He staggers back to the shaking hearse. Choker and Cresty are shaking. Marion drives past the ferry and makes a right on Bayshore Road.

He slows down driving past Turdo vineyard and waves to the kids in the playground where the road curves. The park, with new tennis courts and basketball courts on Hoffman Road, is empty. He slows down and looks at the house with the water well in the front yard before making a right on Route 626.

He crosses the canal, passing the North-South divide sign without a peek and makes a wild right onto New England Road.

The old rusted tow truck still sits rusting. The brown alpaca seems to nod his head in approval as The Hearse passes the house with wooden sleigh.

He speeds up the dirt path cut out in the wildlife area and past the concrete ramp used for a bird watch with the landfill looming behind.

The three of them hold each other walking up the muddy white seashell path with overgrown

Whippoorwills or whatever they are called at the bottom of the landfill. On top of the trash hill overlooking the bay and the canal, Marion pats the heads of Choker and Cresty. He rubs her belly. Marion goes over and stands in the middle of the dandelions. He fixes the flowers and the tree saplings.

Holding his phone close to his eyes, he dials.

A lady's voice.

Choker and Cresty nudge close to hear her as Marion says, "Go to the small wooden boat now used as flower pot on the side lawn and wait for me."

They see the lady. She is wearing a tight white tennis one-piece outfit, step out of the front door. She looks over at the flowerpot. She sticks her arm in the air and turns her phone off so anyone nearby can see as Marion reaches to say something. He asks Choker to hit redial. There is no answer.

There is no answer again as she steps inside and turns off the lights. He redials three more times. No answer.

Marion redials again. "Seven tries… seven a biblical number, right?" he says looking at Choker and Cresty. "Seven… seven tries."

He drives The Hearse back over the canal bridge. There is no answer when Marion stops at the fork in the road where a left takes him back to the house. He makes a right as he hits redial again.

"Life can be like a sunken concrete ship," Marion says. "Sometimes relationships just can't be salvaged either."

The ride along side of the canal is quiet. Even the baby is silent. Once back on board the boat, Marion unhooks the dinghy on the stern. Brennan jumps on board.

Cresty puts the baby in Marion's lap. He rows across the canal toward the house with the swimming pool in the front yard.

"She better get a car seat for that minivan, for you," Marion says to the baby, wrapped in his white pirate shirt with the thick collar and the V-neck black string tied around the boy's wrist, on the other side.

Marion runs up to the front door. He knocks. He leaves the baby in the pool house, placing the boy inside the aqua green and gray rubber raft with his head placed on the blue-gray rubber tail of the dolphin outfit Cresty wore that first night.

He quickly rows across the canal. He pulls up on the side of the boat. He goes and sits in The Hearse.

Cresty and Choker dash over as he dials his cell phone. They can see the house with the swimming pool in the front yard.

Marion puts his hand over the cell phone.

"It's your baby now. Go to the pool house. Don't ask any questions. No one will come asking for the boy. The mother tried to kill him. She thinks the baby is good and dead. The doctor won't say anything either, she knows she has already broken the law and won't want the attention. No one else knows the boy is alive… well, maybe one rich man, but he can't say anything either."

The lady looks around as she walks to the pool house. With the baby wrapped in her arms, she gets on her knees and blesses herself.

In the parking lot of Utsch's, the three of them sit on top of the dumpster with the dead tree saplings, watching the reflection of the setting sun off the canal to the east. The ferry whistle blows in the distance down the canal to the west.

"The ferry says mercy," Marion says.

"Why did you leave your hat at the other house, the one facing the bay?" Choker asks.

"You know, back at the air station, while you two were helping the old guy and his granddaughter into the taxi, I was reading about Kilroy at the entrance to the exhibit," Marion says.

"You see old 'Kilroy was here' is an American cultural expression that became popular during World War II. It said the mysterious origin and simple graphic of Kilroy quickly spread to the GIs across the globe."

"What does Kilroy have to do with your hat?" Cresty asks.

"You see Kilroy was depicted as a baldheaded man with a prominent nose peeking out over a wall. It was viewed by some as graffiti, however American servicemen saw 'Kilroy was here' scratched on beachheads and walls of abandoned buildings as a sign on the Western Front of the war. They knew they were not far from other servicemen.

"And old Hitler was paranoid, as was Stalin, of Kilroy. When German intelligence found Kilroy on their own artillery, it led Hitler to believe that Kilroy was a high-level allied spy.'

"That's cool," says Choker.

"Where did Kilroy come from," asks Cresty.

"You see, Kilroy's origins are debated," Marion says. "But some historians suggest the illustration was first drawn by shipyard inspector James Kilroy and he used his character to mark the rivets he had checked.

"Just like I left my hat on the cherub to let her… my… to let her know, to know I was here.

"That I would be back."

Back inside The Hearse, Marion turns on the

Fish Finder and he sings As Tears go By: “It is the evening of my stay, I sit and watch the unborn playing, smiling faces I can see, if not for me, I sit and watch mom’s fears go by, my riches can't buy the real thing, I want to hear the unborn sing, all I hear is the sound of pain falling on the ground, I sit and watch as fears go bye, it is the evening of my stay, I sit and watch the unborn play, doing things I used to do, they think are new, I sit and watch as fears go by.”

Chapter 16

The Hearse parks by the recycle sign near the old shack down by the Sunken Ship. Plenty of spots are open across from the big out-of-place billboard called the Marine Debris Timeline, which lists a bunch of consumer products, and shows how long each one needs to decompose, since the July 4th week is over.

"A paper towel - 2 weeks, an apple core - 2 months, an aluminum can - 200 years," the army jacket vet from the gift shop reads aloud to them. "Yeah, a plastic - bottle 450 years, almost as long as it will take for Vietnam to decompose from my system."

So, let's drink out of some glass bottles," Marion says.

The old shack's outside bar is open. The porch with the overhead roof facing the bay is empty, even with its inviting reggae music floating out to the bay. The four of them command a table at the Sunset Bar and Grille, located between The Pointe and the ferry, at the end of Sunset Boulevard where the sunken concrete ship, the S.S. Atlantus, sinks with each of their sips.

Sitting on the side outside deck, Marion and the Vietnam vet face Choker and Cresty, with the two towers behind them, a football field or so from the end of Sunset. Both are decrepit but in better shape than the Sunken Ship. The towers once overlooked a factory of some sorts during the war years.

"The Atlantus was built in 1919 and was in service for about a year," the vet says. "During World War I, steel was in such mad short supply, so the federal government came up with the brilliant idea to build concrete-hulled ships. The Atlantus, this once 3,000 ton, 250-foot ship, was the second concrete freighter built. Only 12 were ever built.

"Following the war, the ship was scrapped and towed to Cape May from Norfolk, Va. by an investor. The ship was sunk as a slip for the ferry to Lewes, Delaware."

"Now the Cape May-Lewes Delaware Ferry launches on the Cape May Canal at the entrance to the bay to the north, between the high dunes and the blue cottage with pink-trimmed windows." Marion says.

"Back to the Atlantus," interrupts the vet. "In 1936, a storm ripped the ship from its moorings. She sank in 10 feet of water. How fitting, Plato's fictional island Atlantis, a utopian state envisioned by the Greek philosopher, also sank in the Atlantic Ocean.

"The Atlantus, named after another lost civilization, is steadily sinking."

"Sinking not only under its own weight but with the confluence of the rising water levels in the bay due to climate change," Marion injects.

Nodding, the vet adds, "With Atlantus' death, so dying are the popular diving and fishing spot drowning. If only the Navy knew. Not even the Pillars of Hercules could keep the USS Atlantus afloat."

"We should raise the ship," Marion says. "We can raise the money. We can put an old beggar's can by the recycle sign and tourists can drop in their one dollar instead of buying Sunken Ship book markers in your store."

"I've been thinking about your idea to raise the ship," the army jacket man says. "The Sunset Bar and Grille is a popular food shack. The owners sell bait to fish for the surfcasters as well as tuna fish to eat. You can buy a plastic container of squid for $4.27 to eat raw or bait hooks.

"The shack, though, is out of business without the Sunken Ship. So is the gift shop…."

Marion picks up a newspaper at the empty outside table next to them. "Who reads newspapers?" Marion smirks, lifting his Aviator sunglasses.

Cresty points to the board and says, "Newspaper - six weeks."

"I'll wipe with it, don't worry," Marion says.

Marion opens the paper and sits low behind the entertainment section headlines. He slumps like he doesn't want to be seen.

The vet goes back into the kitchen of the shack. He walks out with an empty large food can and rips off the red bell peppers label. He places the can under the debris timeline and leans against the pole.

"I haven't felt this good since my first Stones concert," Marion says. "We're going to save the ship."

"Why, tell us why, tell us everything about the hill, the dune," Cresty says, "the house, with the pool, the blue and pink cottage with the baby statue, the baby, the boy, the lady, the lady now with the baby, the boy…"

"Who are the ladies?" Choker demands. "What the foo-kin foo-k? Forget the dead sunken ship."

"Not now. When the time is right. We just had one Righting Moment. There will be others. God willing. It's time to order a drink."

"Does God approve of you stealing a baby, even though it was going to be aborted? Aren't you now playing God?" Cresty whispers, holding up the newspaper. “You think you are the God particle now?”

Marion points to the newspaper article, which is the lead story above the fold in the Entertainment Section.

“A British model had an abortion so she could still model,” he says through the other side of the paper.

He shows the photo of this beautiful girl in a tight red dress. She can’t be thicker than the ketchup bottle on the table.

He rolls up the paper and throws it toward the beach.

“Our society has sunk as the concrete ship. We are as sunk as the island of Atlantis,” Marion says. “There is no way to bring back what is right… think… where did these homegrown U.S. terrorists come from?

“But we can bring back babies.”

“How can you generalize about society?” Choker asks. “And Atlantis was a fictional island.”

“Well, listen when Bill Clinton was the president, he and Hillary used to refer to unborn babies as fetuses.” Marion says. “Now that their own kid, Chelsea, is pregnant, they refer to their unborn grandchild as a baby.

"You see when it comes to the unborn, it's all about convenience, both for politicians and parents. Believe me I know."

"Do you? Or is it just your Perspectivism playing out?" Choker asks.

"Maybe it is just Rochambeau?" Cresty says rising from the table, picking up the rolled-up newspaper.

"No, God has a plan for everything. Gravity holds everything in place for Him while He works with us."

The waitress delivers three waters.

"Are you suing your parents for college tuition?" Marion asks her.

She spins around and then turns her head to see if anyone is behind her. Walking away, she says, "I hopes you tip nicely so I don't have to sue them."

Not amused, Choker asks, "If that is it, why doesn't God use gravity to make us make the right decisions?

"I mean, why are there a-holes in the world? Why doesn't God just use his gravity to make people do the right thing? Make people make the right choices. The world, at least to me, would seem a lot better. And easier."

"I think God's gravity is working on you, Choke," Cresty says.

From his pocket, Choker pulls out a folded-up envelope, pulls out a letter and spreads out the paper on the table. It is a scholarship offer to Stockton State.

"Uwrenski got this fax from the Stockton coach, after the tournament. I won't be around you anymore. After today, I think I'm getting out just about the right moment. But, I have to say, and I never thought I would, I will miss you, dude."

Marion tilts his water in salute. "This calls for a special tribute," he says.

Marion goes up on the music stage. He takes off his work boots. He sits behind the drums and grabs a guitar. He starts to play. Both at the same time. It sounds like... just sounds before it starts to sound like music. Marion begins to sing.

"Jiving Sister Nunny's hidden stain was big like a dinosaur," Marion screeches.

He plays the whole song with his feet banging the drums and playing the guitar and singing. When he is done, he falls backwards. The army jacket man claps for him and then helps him up before going outside.

Marion sits back down at the outdoor table with the rolled-up newspaper in the middle.

"How did you do it?" Cresty asks.

"I used to play the drums in college out west on University Avenue and I've been practicing the guitar, it's not much harder than the sitar."

"No, how did you get the baby?" Cresty says. "How did you get the baby alive? I don't care about the foo-kin sitar. How was the baby, the boy still alive?"

Marion takes a long drink. He looks prouder than when he got the applause for his music playing.

"God, I can only imagine how the Stones feel on stage."

"The baby," Cresty presses. "How'd you, do it?"

"I used the choke hold, uri-jame-whatever. Like the college kid at the airplane museum, I choked out the abortion doctor. She'll never admit to what happened because Dr. Hyde was doing a late termer and the baby was being born alive when she reached to stab the little boy with a scissor. I'm sure she'll never report it. That would be her ass doing a later termer and obviously that is all she cares about if she is making money killing babies.

"Unless, of course, she was going to sell the baby body parts for stem cells."

"How about the young girl?" Cresty asks.

"She was sedated, she didn't know a thing. How else would she let sweet, smiling Dr. Hyde deliver her baby and kill her boy? She had to be on drugs to let them do that to her baby boy this late."

"How about nurses?" Choker says.

"None. The doctor didn't want any witnesses. I knew that. She knows, too, as well as she knows her rack rules."

"Who was the lady, the lady you gave the baby to by the hill?" Cresty says. "The shed lady?"

"Not now, this isn't the moment for that."

"We got time," Choker says. "We aren't working anyway. I don't hear any sirens dopplering."

"Is she someone you did it with?" Cresty blurts. "Did you do it in her shed by the pool?"

"Well, then… well she is from the double-big bang."

"The what?" Cresty says.

"I got to hear this one." Choker says.

"Later," Marion says, suddenly leaving the table. He taps the decomposition sign. One post cracks. The sign tilts. The word apple from apple core falls to the ground.

A middle-aged woman, with a parasol in one hand and an ice cream cone in the other, argues with the Vietnam vet in front of the recycle sign and the "Save the Sunken Ship" can.

"Saving the ship would kill the fish hatching there," she yells between licks of her ice cream cone.

Choker and Cresty walk holding hands past the Sunken Ship and a fenced in area of new growth plants surrounded by dead Christmas trees being used as wind breaks. They stroll toward Cape May Point, stepping over a jetty with rusty metal jutting between the boulders. Marion walks a dozen steps behind them. He looks as low as Atlantus as he passes The Bunker and declares how "the water at the beach looks higher than the horizon."

They all join up around the Nun Home. Then, walking together, they turn at The Pointe and walk east toward the ocean waves crashing into the bay at Devil's Reach.

They stop at The Bunker. The army jacket man is feeding the seagulls with scraps from the outdoor grill.

"Back in the bunker's day, back when German U-boats were so far up the Cape May bay that the Nazis ate fresh striper daily, it was called the Gun Emplacement," the vet says.

"The concrete bunker was built in 1942 as part of the Harbor Defense Program initiated two years earlier. Gun blocks, round turrets, flank each side with six-millimeter guns."

"The Panama Mounts, horseshoe shaped gun mounts out front, once held 155 mm coast Artillery cannons. The guns are as quiet as Atlantus, now.

"Inside the bunker are mazes of rows. Here, inside the bunker, our boys stored the ammo."

"The bunkers were built to protect the ones who couldn't protect themselves," Choker says.

"A sister bunker stands across the Bay in Lewes Delaware," the army jacket man continues. "The bay divides the two defense systems."

Cresty traces the letters on the army jacket with her right hand on her belly and her free hand's finger – VANE.

"Your name?" Cresty asks.

"Vietnam Always Never Ends," he spells out as he walks north, back toward the Sunken Ship.

Marion sits inside the bunker, on a row where the ammo was once stored. Choker and Cresty sit opposite of him on another row.

"The double big bang doesn't have anything to do with the creation of the universe," Marion says unprompted. "It happened the first time I ever ate Mexican Food when I went to Cal-Berkeley. It was also our first foo-kin date."

"I see, to that lady you gave the baby to?" Choker asks.

"No, she is a different lady. Do you want to hear the story or not?"

"Sorry. Tell us. Now," Cresty demands.

"Well, it started when I was talked out by this girl into going out to eat. She was real hip on Mexican food, and since I was trying to impress her for the obvious reasons, I dug into the spicy stuff too. I went back for thirds. I was coming down the home stretch too when the gas suddenly metamorphosis into solid waste.

"I figured I'd put the squeeze on and asked her to go. I figured I could make it back to her place even with the squeeze on. So that is what I did."

"Why didn't you just climb a f-in tree outside?" Choker asks.

"I wasn't a climber back then. I thought I could make it. We made it to her apartment all right. But I didn't have time to even lock the bathroom door when I could feel the levee breaking. The Squeeze wasn't foolproof. It came out, actually exploded like a quasar, all over the place. I cleaned up and jumped in the shower, she soon joined me. Then, the other Big bang for the daily double came.

"Unlike the toilet shot, this was a bull's eye."

"She got pregnant?" Cresty asks.

"Just like that. If I didn't shit my pants, it probably would've never had happened. That's life, I guess."

"That's Rochambeau."

What happened to the baby?

“We both said it wasn't the right time… so we killed it.”

Chapter 17

The crispness of the ocean air adds to the buzz of downtown, with joggers higher on their toes and mommy's pushing strollers with a bounce. Cresty is humming, making just cheerful sounds sitting beside Marion and Choker. They watch the clattering trolley pass and a Monarch butterfly flutter with equal attention and amusement amid Cape May's cacophony.

Trolleys run on Ocean Street, which intersects Lafayette Street and Beach Avenue like the main cross bar in the letter 'A' - connecting the road out of town with those living in downtown of this historic section wrapped forever by the Atlantic Ocean.

"It's good to celebrate Bastille Day on Lafayette Street," Marion says. "July 14th is the French Independence Day, when the people of Paris, the Parisians stormed the prison, the Bastille.

"That's what we need to do, storm the prison and free the unjustly doomed."

"But what about the justly doomed… the deserving prisoners?" Cresty asks, stopping from humming to question.

The streets in the middle of Cape May don't run north south or east west. Rather the streets offer a confusing combination of both, since the beach and ocean curve. The downtown is a web. You can't traverse on car or bike out of town without weaving through the streets here, reaching like the black veins on the wings of a Monarch butterfly.

"Sir," a lady with a newspaper stops Marion in front of the Chalfonte Hotel, an1876 National Historic Monument Landmark, "are you looking for the estate sale?"

A kid on his bike with training wheels turns to his mother and says, "I wish we had that house," while admiring the Chalfonte.

The charm of historic Cape May mixes with the confusion. Charm and confusion live together and work as one, in unison like the Monarch's wings. People are lost and enjoy not knowing what the next block brings, just admiring the colorful homes and enjoying the enriching air. Even the locals don't curse the puzzling streets. They flow with the curves, making decisions at the end of each street which way is fastest out of town, or for many, which way is the slowest so more of the soothing sea air can be sucked and stored into their cluttered heads.

"The proper people of downtown actually feel the curvy streets keep more *N'ortherners* from crossing the canal," Marion says as another trolley runs straight in front of them on Ocean Street.

"This is the umbilical cord connecting the dreams of people sitting on the beach hoping for a better life when their vacation starts on a splendid Saturday afternoon with the reality of driving out of town the next week, stuck in traffic on a stinking Saturday morning," Marion says, stretching his hands out in both directions, mimicking the width of Ocean Street.

Watching the trolley this morning, Cresty puts an arm around both Choker and Marion. With each exaggerated inhale, the sea air intoxicates her… before Marion irritates again.

"We should roll, like the Stones," he says, ruining the bliss of just being, adding "gas, gas, gas" as Cresty holds both of them down.

Surreys are rented at the end of Ocean Ave across from the Promenade. Families pedal these four-seat monoliths going nowhere but bringing them closer together.

Walking and sitting keeps Cape Mayers busy. No one is reading at the Mall in the middle of mid-town. There is just too much to see, too much air to breathe, too much of the past to seize.

A ghost tour stops in front of a house on Columbia Avenue and a man on the porch goes inside and comes out with a white sheet over his head and yells, "boo."

Another trolley passes, blocking the view of the girl from the clinic speeding by on her motorized bike. The girl turns toward the library downtown.

Cresty releases her grip and the three of them pop up. They speed walk like the mommy's in yoga pants pushing strollers, not slowing down until they reach the Cape May Public Library, a block from the mall on Ocean, across the street from where Marion parked after they watched the sunrise on the jetty at Devils' Reach.

A green park bench, like the Forrest Gump bench, sits out front flanked by the rusting green metal book return box and the motorized bike.

Cresty and her boys sit on the bench, watching readers take books and give them back. Take and give. Give and take.

"Butterflies can fly out of town but trolleys can't," she says sitting.

The one-story yellow concrete library building rises out of place among the quaint Bed and Breakfast houses lining both sides of the street.

The gray hearse parked across from the green bench doesn't fit in either here. Kids peek in the back while their moms pull their hands away.

"Bet the surf is up today," Cresty says. "Good day for riding pipes, I bet, down by the jetty. The Devils' Reach should be grabbing."

"The Devil is always grabbing, always reaching," Marion says. "But never catching the butterfly."

Marion reaches to snatch an elusive butterfly near The Hearse. He lunges again, knocking off his Aviator sunglasses, but the Monarch is too lively. The top metal bridge of the glasses is cracked. Marion collapses to his knees. Holding his eyes, he shakes with each sob.

Cresty and Choker pull hard, then soft, before pulling hard again to lift him to his feet. They slump arm-in-arm to The Hearse, looking back in unison when they hear the motorized bike start and the girl zoom off with a book under her arm.

Slumping into the passenger side seat, Marion turns on his weather machine and listens. Outside the window, he is poking for the Monarch a few more times, grabbing just air. Choker lies down with his head on the curb. Cresty curls next to him.

"It's gray up there in M87 land. Choke, you don't work when it's gray."

"Old rules," Choker rolls his head. "Plus, we, I think, need some quick extra money."

"Let's eat first," Cresty says.

Choker drives off to a pancake place near the beach, across from Devil's Reach. Cresty orders three burrito breakfast sandwiches at the Cove

Restaurant. She looks out the window and watches the surfer chicks sitting with their men on the brick façade of the Jetty Motel. The sun is just reaching the window as they spread out and watch the waves crash onto the beach.

"There is something spiritual about this," Cresty says. "About surfing."

"About the sun… rising," Marion says, "Indeed."

"No, about surfing, I said. Are you losing your hearing with your sight?"

"Back in the early 16th century, people got real freaked out about the sunrise."

"Can't we just, just freaking work today?" Choker asks. "No lessons."

Pressing the sides of his Aviator sunglasses so the broken bridge isn't bent, Marion studies the sun.

"Between 1519 and 1522, Ferdinand Magellan circled the world going westward. He counted the days by the sunrises."

"I even could do that," Cresty says, pouring sugar onto the table and making a circle in the white pile. "So, what's the big deal?"

"When he got back to Portugal, and saw what day it was there, he noticed he lost a day."

"How'd that happen?" she asks.

"Maybe it was gray out one day and he couldn't see the sun," Choker offers. "I've had those days. Maybe he was hung over one day. I've endured those days, too."

"I know. I know. I know! The sun rises in the east, right, of course." Cresty says. "If you go west around the earth, you will see one less sun rise than if you were going east."

"Right, you win another burrito."

"I'll eat it on the road."

Insisting he is ok to drive, on the short ride from the beach joint at Devil's Reach back to the Byrd boat, Marion hesitates crossing Jackson and Decatur Streets intersecting through the mall. All pedestrian traffic has the right of way, of course. Meaning, it takes many minutes for Marion to cross.

He stops and goes. Goes and stops. Marion almost hits as many cars as walkers. He isn't seeing well today.

He stops in front of the Physick Estate on Washington Avenue, the road the locals use on the way out of town. The Physick Estate is Cape May's lone Victorian House museum.

"The estate was once the home of Philip Syng Physick," Marion explains. "He was a doctor.

"A doctor named Phy-sick?' Choker huffs. "Who the foo-k would go to a doctor name Physick? Sounds like he doesn't know if he helps his patients get physically better of stay sick."

"He is considered the Father of American Surgery," Marion says with odd defiance. "He invented countless, well numerous medical instruments and surgical procedures still in use today."

"How do you know?" Cresty asks. "Did he invent your pirate sword?"

"I had to know," he says. "Like his schizoid name, all the tools weren't used for good, to save lives."

"Please tell us, I need to know," Cresty says. "How did you kill your baby?"

"Easy. She… we had an abortion."

Driving up Washington Ave., the street named after the Father of America, the girl on the motorized bike cuts right in front of them. Marion overreacts and slams the brakes, sending his Aviator sunglasses smashing into the dashboard. Both bridges are now cracked as he fiddles to put the unattached flaps on his ears before giving up. "Where is she?" he asks as The Hearse makes a right on West and then a quick left on Massachusetts… where the girl sits sideways on her motorized bike while leaning against an oak tree with a low, sprawling leafy canopy draped by hanging ivy. Marion edges diagonally across from her where they are close enough to read the cover "Midnight in the Garden of Good and Evil" and see the tombstone photo of a young girl with her arms spread like the scale of justice.

"I saw the movie," Cresty says.

"Ironic, huh?" Marion responds and innocuously adds, "On Mass Ave. now and this week Massachusetts Governor Deval Patrick signed a bill tightening security regulations with regards to protestors and demonstrators at state abortion clinics."

Holding his broken specs to his eyes and looking at the girl, who is immersed in her book, Marion says. "The bill ensures safe access for women seeking reproductive health care services.

"The baby beating bill went into effect immediately. The women have safe access, but who protects their babies if they won't?"

"Why now?" Cresty asks.

"The righting moment," Marion responds tersely.

"No. Why are you waiting to talk, to speak to the girl?"

"This is Mass' response to the United States Supreme Court decision last month ruling against the buffer zone law enacted in 2007 by Mass, which banned protestors within a 35-foot radius of the abortion clinics," Marion continues, ignoring Cresty's question.

"Our high court unanimously spiked the McCullen v. Coakley ruling saying it rightly violated our First Amendment right to free speech and expression.

"I guess they won't have to paint over the yellow arc lines at 35 feet."

"That's is a long 3-pointer," Choker cracks, breaking the terse talk.

"Leave her be," Cresty turns to Marion, poking her index and middle finger into his broken Aviator glasses he is holding on his nose. "She is giving her baby up for adoption, remember…

"And look, she is sleeping… she needs her sleep… I know."

"I just wanted to tell her the ivy, the ivy handing from the tree is poison oak," he says while starting The Hearse. "I don't want her to get tangled in the ivy that looks so inviting."

At the intersection, Marion stops in front of the Massachusetts streets sign. He flips the middle finger to the sign.

"No Rochambeau," Cresty says looking at the sign.

The condos on the left of Texas Avenue need a side parking lot for just the baby strollers used by mommies taking a run and now buying coffee and donuts at the Wawa. He almost hits a surrey filled with a family crossing from the condo's parking lot to the harbor. The dad drops the bag of donuts. He chucks his coffee at The Hearse. The cup explodes on the windshield.

"There isn't an hour that goes by that I don't think of what I did," Marion says. "I can't believe I allowed myself to get to the point where I didn't know what was right and wrong. My whole view of life was a big gray spot. I rationalized that it wasn't alive, or it wasn't wanted.

"I played God. Einstein and Goethe all in one. No one can play God… or be the God particle."

Marion flicks on the windshield and in a few swipes the dripping brown coffee blotch is streaked in smeared lines across the glass.

"My thinking became so complicated I didn't know what was basic right from wrong. At least, that's what I want to think now. I don't want to think that I was so unbelievably shortsighted and selfish to think my career was more important than a life," Marion whispers as if he is in a confessional box with a priest.

"I try to keep life simple now, like Charlie Watts' drum kit."

With her arms outstretched over the steering wheel, Cresty makes Marion stop. “I got to go,” She says getting out of the truck. She goes into the Wawa with a pained face.

“I needed to put on the big squeeze to make it to the bathroom,” Cresty says getting back into The Hearse as Marion tries to wipe the caked coffee smears with his hand off the windshield.

“I didn’t even know Wawa has bathrooms,” Marion says.

“This one doesn’t, I went by the big garbage containers on the side,” she says.

She slides in the middle seat, wiping her hands clean with a Wawa brown recycled napkin. She wipes Marion’s coffee-caked hands, but the smear streaks into the lines of his palms.

“Your wife had a say in it too, it can't be all your fault,” Cresty says soothingly. “Even if you wanted the baby, she still could've done it.”

“She wanted the baby. I talked her out of it. We spent hours and hours talking. The more we talked, the more it seemed the right thing to do, the more tangled the choice became. That’s why you can't trust yourself. You can't talk about things that matter. You have to have a game plan before situations like that even come up.

"The more you talk, the more the Devil reaches. If you have to talk, the Devil can reach."

"What do you mean?" Choker asks, wrapping his arm around Cresty, who is petting Row and Way.

"I mean you need a philosophy," Marion continues speaking… and rubbing the palms of his hands. "I look at it like this, the Stones have a million of great songs. They can't play them all in the same night, and if they could I'd want to be there."

"If they couldn't," Cresty says, "you'd still want to be there."

"Good point. But my point is, they have a set list. They stick to their set list. The only improvising they will do is if Keith plays an extended solo somewhere, which he should do more often, but he improvises in the structure of the song… only inside the Charlie's beat."

"Or," Choker says, "if he forgets what he is playing."

"Hey, watch yourself now, you are talking about Keith. Anyway, the beat of the band still goes on while the great Keith Richards goes off. His mates don't let him stray too far.

"I shouldn't have allowed my wife to sway. I needed to provide the beat."

"C'mon, what do you mean by a set list?" Cresty demands, handing Row to Choker as she holds Way.

"I mean, you know, well we all need a set list for life. We need our own set rules, a philosophy, a game plan, a list of songs we play by. You can't make how to live up on the run. Even the Stones can't just wing classic songs on stage. As people, we need to develop our set list before we step on stage.

"Shakespeare wrote `life is a stage.' He was right. But he didn't tell us we needed a set list. Mick shows us that. I see that now."

"Bro, you haven't been seeing clearly for a while," Choker says, tapping the broken bridge of the Aviator sunglasses with his free hand. "You've been weaving onto the shoulder for a couple of blocks now. You better drive straight across the bridge or we will be beat.

"Why don't you let me drive?"

"Can't, I told our Hunter friend I'd return his hearse in one piece and you were shaky behind the wheel earlier. You can't swim, how are you going to drive?"

"That's why I don't want to fly off the bridge."

Cresty reaches over to Choker and hugs Row while squeezing Way.

"So, you are saying that every person needs a set list," Cresty says. "That set list is your beliefs and morals and stuff. I believe in surfing, so I should stay with it, right?"

"Sort of, but that is like the encore of the set list. You need the core first. The songs that set the mood. Back then, when I got on stage, meaning when I had decisions to make with my career and the baby, I didn't have a set list to get me through. I got stage fright, I guess. I let the moment mess up everything. I should've developed my set list. I should've started with life. If I put life first, I could've never had… encouraged an abortion, not with my baby."

Marion crosses the concrete bridge out of Cape May. He is headed toward the wavy and faceless Parkway where every mile looks the same.

"But, I don't know where I had life listed," Marion continues. "In the set list of life, the No. 1 song of the set is like gravity pulling everything together, you know what path to follow. Just think if the country thought that way?

"You can't leave personal choices up to Perspectivism."

"Well, that is exactly what Perspectivism is," Choker says. "Isn't it?"

"Yeah but Perspectivisim changes in different parts of your life."

Marion makes a sharp left over the illegal path on the median strip toward… well, where gravity must be pulling him… and he stops.

"We wouldn't endure Dionysus debates over legalizing doctor-assisted suicides like in Oregon, because life rules… we wouldn't argue for or against the death penalty, because again, life takes priority over everything else. Life rules."

"We wouldn't have embryos being created just so their stem cells can be used for experiments.

"We wouldn't have abortion.

"We wouldn't have laws allowing yellow lines to be painted on asphalt around clinics except for kids to shoot 3-pointers with their mommies."

The Hearse pulls into the newly paved lot at Madame Palm's behind the antique store.

"We need to plant two Southern Magnolias."

"Southern, will they grow here?" Choker asks.

"Sure will, they are great in northern climates. They will grow to 80 feet with white leaves that bloom in late spring.

"Cresty, you can water them if you feel all right."

She puts Row and Way in their cage, petting the black stripe going down Row's face and fluffing the fur behind Way's ears.

"I feel like talking to Madame Palm. I'm going inside. I hear her calling me."

Marion and Choker push back the branches of the overhanging second growth before digging. They both dig. The five-foot trees are planted. Marion backfills the holes. Choker waters.

They are packing up the tools when Cresty comes out, smiling like when she is in a trance petting Row and Way.

"She told me to go to the clinic today," Cresty says. "Madame Palm did."

"To go in?" Marion asks.

"No… just to go."

Wiping dirt on each other, Marion and Choker walk behind Cresty over the clinic. There is a half dozen or so enraged people outside with signs again. Dr. Hyde comes up to the three. She wears a scarf or smock, or something girls wear, around her neck.

"How are you today?" Marion asks childishly, balancing his broken-bridge Aviator sunglasses on his nose. "How do you feel?"

"Just fine, my love," Dr. Hyde says, rubbing the back of her shoulders with both hands. "My neck is a little sore. Where is your hat?"

Choker hugs her, faking to kiss her on her neck as he tugs on the scarf. She stops him mostly, but he still gets a peek at the back of her neck. He sees the bruise and smiles, saying, "Yeah, he wants to take you on a date."

"I think that man, the rich man makes him jealous," she says. "I think we would get along well. He would have to clean up a bit.

"Perhaps purchase shiny new wheels, too."

"I would clean up for you, but we don't agree on our set list," he says. "How choice is a lie. Babies never choose to die."

"Sure, we should talk about it. I think you will see why I do what I do. Many, like myself feel this world isn't safe for babies. It sure as hell wasn't for mine… or my mom's baby."

Dr. Hyde starts to cry, turns and runs back to the clinic.

Cresty stares at the door, as if waiting for someone to come back.

"Less ladies are agreeing with Dr. Hyde," Marion says.

"Why did, didn't you stop her?" Cresty says as the protesters listen too.

"Because the statistics made the babies just sound like a number. The numbers took away their face," Marion says. "And besides, just one is too many."

The Hearse drives through the protestors, who politely part in the middle, and stops at the traffic light at Route 9.

Cresty picks up Row and Way. She hands Row to Choker as Marion putts slowly across the bridge back into Cape May. A sunburned man and a boy caked in sunblock fish off the bridge. A little girl sits between them bouncing a basketball with one hand and playing with the minnows in a bucket with her free hand.

"You know the earth and moon circle the sun, the sun circles the core of the galaxy at 175 miles per second and the Milky Way galaxy is hurling around other galaxies," Marion rattles as quick as the girl pounds the ball on the concrete bridge. "What makes this planet different? Life, that's all.

"Perhaps we all end up like Mars if Babylon here keeps killing babies. All that will be left is methane gas."

Weaving around the potholes, Marion drives down Sunset Boulevard. He stops at the Sunken Ship. The young kid wearing his Blake Griffin jersey fishes from a kayak around the Atlantus.

Handing Row back to Cresty, Choker hustles out of the truck. He picks up the kids' basketball sitting in the sand. He tosses the ball out to the kid and with the splash next to the kayak, Choker yells, "Always keep your basketball with you… it always bounces back… not like life." Choker skips a shell off the bay water before picking up a discarded plastic coke bottle.

"Saving the planet," he says shooting the bottle like a basketball into a plastic blue can. The bottle rims out. He heaves the bottle toward the Sunken Ship, turning before it lands short of the water and in the wet sand.

Marion drops the first dollar into the "Save the Sunken Ship" can that the army jacket man made.

Looking at the Sunken Ship, with Row and Way wrapped in one arm, Cresty whispers into a half clam shell she picks up next to the bottle thrown by Choker. She kisses the shell and skims it off the water. On the third skip, the shell hits the concrete ship… and flips, splashing into the water on its back, the curve side… and floats.

Back in The Hearse, Marion takes a different route into dormant Cape May Point. He doesn't take Lighthouse Avenue into The Pointe where "the gate offers fake protection of the private community, where the towering lighthouse kept mariners safe for a century."

"But that was a different century," Marion adds, "and in ways a different country."

The Hearse chugs down Cape Avenue. Marion makes a left onto Oak. Then a sloping right down a hidden road with a lake. The lake is fresh water.

"The stories, the tales… lore says Blackbeard buried treasure here when hiding from the law, having his way with women and generally living the good pirate life," Marion says with an envious twitch. "The pirates aren't all gone from The Pointe.

"Now only ducks protect the hidden booty, if there is any loot under the lake."

Looking intently at the lake, Marion must not see a line of little ducks crossing the road behind their mother. Choker reaches with his leg over Cresty and stabs the brake. Choker leaps out of The Hearse. He runs to the front of the line. He helps the ducks cross the road, making like a schoolyard crossing guard.

Marion smiles with both hands on the wheel and his head looking back. He is looking like he saved a duck.

A Range Rover beeps behind the idling hearse. The horn makes the sound of a duck quack. They must be bird lovers. Or hunters. Choker doesn't seem to care for their inconvenience. He returns to The Hearse only after all the ducks are safely under bayberry shrub on the other side.

Choker rips open the driver side door of the truck. He lunges over Marion and hugs Cresty.

"I want our baby."

"You'll be a great father," Cresty says. "God already answered my prayer… the one I sent in the clam shell."

"Let's go back and get that coke bottle I threw at the Sunken Ship," he says, "my spirits were down. I need to put the bottle in the recycle can."

"I already did," Cresty says. I already did."

Chapter 18

The late July sun reclines high in the hollow sky already by mid-morning as Cresty lounges around the deck of The Byrd. She plays catch with Brennan. The old dog limps on his back right-leg back to her with the ball in his mouth.

Marion lets Row and Way hop about the boat now. The wild rabbits don't run away and Brennan doesn't bark at the rabbits anymore. The other boat owners here at Utsch's don't stop on their way to drink at Lucky Bones and make small talk about the rabbits. No one seems to care about them, like the tree saplings.

The bunnies bounce around in safety. Dr. Hyde wants to adopt them. She said since she doesn't have any children of her own, she "needed something, somebody to love." She said her empty house needs some filling. Choker, though, wants to keep the rabbits.

Marion said he would talk to her about adopting them because "they soon would need a home." So, he made a surprise visit and poked her about her empty "New York Avenue Mansion" next to the Coast Guard base. He said he drove to her house two days ago to plant a free dogwood tree, but couldn't unhook the chain protecting the private road with the half dozen houses as "big as The Sea Mist."

Dr. Hyde told him the chain was only there because of the endangered birds nesting on the beach where the Coast Guard Base juts out past the jetty at the most northeast point of Cape May.

"The birds need protection from humans," she had said.

Drifting back to the bunnies, she said she would change the rabbit's names to Siegfried and Roy. She said she needed a bit of magic in her life, adding she didn't particularly like the name Row, claiming the name conjured violence, accusing that 'row' also means a fight. And, she explained how she associated the word with death row, pontificating how she was against the death penalty, railing that our country's penal system was "barbarically inhumane" and "no more civilized than the guillotine dropping in Mid *evil* Europe."

Marion fired back, accusing her of not liking the name Row because her "life is a row, submerged in a moral rut." He said she could only change the rabbit's names to Sigmund and Freud, "close enough to Siegfried and Roy" but only if she promised to change her "stinking *way* of thinking" and "*row* with the flow of the living."

Yesterday, while stirring his coke with a snickers bar and telling Dr. Hyde he is changing her name to "Bam Bam," he told her Sigmund believed in the "death drive," which he explained is the opposite of Eros and the fight to survive and reproduce. He said Freud called the death drive Thanatos, named after the Greek god who was born with a sword. He told her she needed to put down her sword, dramatically putting down his snickers bar before showing her where he stashed his "pirate sword" from the night on the raft at the rich man's boat in the back of The Hearse.

Holding onto the rail decking, Cresty inches to the ladder going below deck. Choker gives her a pat on the stomach as she walks by him. She leaves the door open to the head. The door taps the jam as the docked boat rolls a bit from a wake.

Marion hops off The Byrd and zips over to the end of the pier and into a patch of trees. He still doesn't piss on the boat.

He drains himself a bit until he hears, "Oh fook" from The Byrd. He is fixing himself and halfway out of the tree patch when he hears a thud.... and then a scream.

On board, he sees Choker laughing and through the hatch door he sees Cresty spread on the floor below deck.

"What, you forgot to do *The Squeeze*?" Choker mocks pointing to the bathroom below as if the stunned Marion doesn't see her. "You got to tighten those cheeks."

"Only veteran *Squeezers* know how to do pinch right," Marion says looking relieved.

"Fook," she moans again, "fook, fook, fook."

With their smiles gone, Marion and Choker initially look at each other while she squirms below. They drop below. They both peek into the bathroom. Blood. A red smear on the mirror. Cresty is wailing. Her pants are down.

"What the fook… there is blood," Choker says. 'I thought you couldn't have your…"

"Let's go," Marion screams. "Help. Get her up!"

Marion staggers up the steps. He kicks the built-in bench on the starboard side.

"We got to take her to the hospital? Right?" Choker yells as he carries her up on deck.

Marion wraps the blanket they found at the pavilion around her waist. He covers her entire lower body as a Monarch butterfly flies away from behind her.

"This doesn't mean anything, not necessarily," Marion says, barely audible over the roar of a kid jet skiing through the canal. "You just rest here for a moment."

He makes a call on his Galaxy phone while putting Row and Way back in their cage. A limping Brennan pushes a ball toward Cresty. Marion kicks the ball into the bay.

"We got to take her to the hospital," Choker says again.

Cresty sobs - I never even seen her cry as a kid, not even when the ball I shot came off the rim hard in the backyard and broke her nose.

Choker leaps off The Byrd and sprints like he is back on the courts, running the wing on a fast break. He grinds the ignition starting up The Hearse.

"We got to take her to the hospital," Choker screams over the roar of the engine of the jet skier playing in the wake he makes.

Holding her up, Marion walks Cresty to The Hearse. His right arm slings around her. The other reaches across his body and supports her elbow. She rests her head on his shoulder.

I should be there. My baby needs my help. So, does my grandkid.

The Hearse flies across the Cape May Bridge, drawing the finger from a man fishing with his kid and causing a girl to stop dribbling her basketball. For the first time, Marion zooms past the Cape May Clinic without stopping, speeding by the pristine white building on his left, he doesn't slow down and look.

"Let's go up to Stone Harbor…" Marion says, "I know a good doctor there."

He runs both red lights on the ride up the Parkway. The Stones' song on the Fish Finder is the little-known Lantern: "We in our present strife, know the stars are light, that if you are the first to go, you'll send a butterfly to let me know, tell me so, please carry the lantern right," Marion sings.

At Exit 10, Marion makes a wild left, away from the ocean and inland toward the hospital. He glides to a stop in front of the emergency room.

Blocking their path to the check-in counter are a lot of annoying people - kids crying with only a bump or bruise, moms looking disinterested into their ringing cell phone, dads in golf clothes looking at their watches.

Marion barges to the front desk. A doctor with some white in his hair to match his uniform comes right out. The two exchange some sort of fraternity handshake and then Marion and the doc do a whacky high five.

"Nanker the Banker," the doctor says to him. "How the hell are you? Where the hell are you? Are you touring with the Stones down in Australia? You got the gray beard thing going good. I thought none of the Stones had beards?

Marion's face is blank. He nods toward Cresty.

"Or did you buy into the Stones like you said you were," the annoying doc continues. "You know, Marion had so much money he used to wipe his butt with $2 bills before the Fed pulled them from circulation… he'd wipe right on Thomas Jefferson's face… right on the Father of Independence…"

Looking at Marion, who is holding Cresty. He says, "You're not laughing."

"Sorry. This is Dr. Weed everyone."

The doc smiles reassuringly at Cresty, ignoring a mom who bugs him to see her kid, with an abrasion cut on his hand, first.

"Listen, Cresty here needs an ultrasound," Marion says. "Like I said on the phone, she is probably early second trimester… and she had a little spotting. Can you take her right in? I'll take care of the paperwork with the nurses."

"For you… and Cresty, sure can. Come on back, you all can sit in the waiting room by the ultrasound room. Can I get anyone a drink?"

"Yeah, a Guinness."

"Make that two," Choker says.

"Three," Cresty groans.

"I got some in my locker," the doc says to his old buddy, "you know where it is."

"I just downed a few myself."

The tube TV blinks in the ultrasound waiting room. In between rapid flashings can be seen a local commercial for "Weddings by the Sea" showing the St. Agnes church at The Pointe and below it on the screen is a crawl add for the Cape May Clinic.

Unwrapping the blanket from her waist, Chesty rests her head on Choker's shoulder again, asking Marion, "How do you know this doctor and why did he come right out?"

"He was my roommate from college. We had a falling out. Wish I could change the past. But he answered the bell for us."

"I know what an ultra sound is but how does it work?" Cresty asks. "Does it hurt? Will it hurt her?"

"They bounce sound waves through the mothers' belly to see the shape of the baby and how big it is. Remember how I told you how the Doppler effect works with sound? You know… how a train's whistle makes a different sound coming than going."

"Yeah, because when the waves get closer they get smaller and the pitch gets higher," Choker says. "It reverses when it is leaving."

"Excellent, you'll be a great teacher to your baby… soon… someday."

Choker pats Cresty's stomach proudly with “will I see the baby in the ultra sound?”

“Yeah, it’s like an x-ray looks. You can see… a lot after only three months. You'll be able to see the head and appendages developing… we should just wait until we hear what the doctor says.”

Cresty adjusts her head on Choker's shoulder.

“What type of doctor is named Weed?” she asks.

“Great name, isn't it? He was the only one in college at Cal-Berkley who didn't smoke any grass, none, so we called him weed.”

“He must have been boring for you?” Choker says casually, like asking questions at the Ugly Mug.

“No, he could out power drink all of us.”

“Did he say he just had a few this morning? I'm worried if he did, if he needs to… work on me I could end up turning my empty drinking glass around at the Ugly Mug.”

“No worries… you don’t even have a drinking glass at the Ugly Mug,” Marion says. “Not yet.”

Two sleepy nurses help Cresty through a door into a private waiting room. Choker leans his ear up to the closed door.

“I’m worried,” Choker says. “More than I was for even my judo tournament… I know you were just talking about me being a good dad…”

With her feet crossed, Cresty is snoring on the table when they enter the room. Leaning on each side of her, Marion and Choker gently try to wake Cresty, alternating poking her with light, playful punches to her belly.

"The ultrasound technician said they are reviewing the results," Marion says to her. "No worry, cherry."

During the wait, Marion and Choker each hold one of Cresty's hands. She falls back to sleep.

"How do they know what to look for?" Choker asks.

"Just because they are doctors don't mean they know jack," Marion says nervously. "I know. Did you know that Ronnie Woods doesn't even know some words to a lot of Stones songs?"

Marion paces the room. He fakes strumming a guitar with a nervous concern. His Aviator sunglasses slide over his eyes, held together with white medical tape he snatched from the bottom drawer of the desk in the room. Choker paces opposite of him.

"Woodie had his glasses on during r-r-rehearsal once and was r-r-reading the lyrics," Marion stutters, "and he said he finally could read the TelePrompTer and before that he never knew what some of Mick's famous words were."

"No wonder you like him, he can't see like you. At least he has glasses."

"I don't need to see. I got all my radars to do the seeing for me."

"When we get F150 back," Choker says with urgency, "I want you to show me how they work, the radars."

"The Doppler radar works like the Doppler effect," Marion rattles nervously. "Instead of sound, the radar uses light rays. Light is bounced off clouds to measure weather systems."

"Why don't they use sound?"

"Light is faster than sound."

"And, they use light because it is not affected by the crack of lightning like sound would be, right?"

Their senseless sophisticated chatter continues over Cresty as they both stopped pacing. Their anxious strides are replaced by nervous words, but only passing minutes advance them closer to the answer.

"You know now how gravity can affect time with the clock experiment," Marion tells him. "Intense gravity can create a black hole too. In a black hole, light can't even escape. So, light is affected by gravity too, just like you are. If you were crossing a black hole, your body would never be found."

"No one would miss me."

"Your baby would. And, you'll understand why it happens too."

"Go on."

"I told you how gravity affects light and you know how it affects time. At the edge of a black hole, light isn't moving. It isn't going anywhere."

Marion strums, with fake satisfaction, on his air guitar.

"Not backwards or frontwards," Marion keeps rambling. "Now, this is where it gets really cool and this is why I won't miss you. Like light, time doesn't go anywhere at the edge of a black hole. It's just there. That means time stands still at the edge of a black hole.

"Through the black holes, God is showing us there *is* a heaven. There is a black hole out there that *is* heaven. The ones who live their lives with a belief in God, asking for His forgiveness, for redemption, are going to stand timeless in heaven, someday."

"Right," Choker says with disdain.

"Right it is," Marion says. "I believe William Faulkner had it right when the American author wrote about some old town, 'where the past is never dead, it's not even the past' about somewhere. I believe he could've been describing heaven… we'll see…"

"If we do the right thing, of course," Marion spits out quickly. "If we make the right choices. That is why we have to do the right thing."

"You're telling me this now for a reason, right?" Choker asks, as if he is sitting on the stone steps of the Parthenon and waiting for an answer from Socrates.

"Right, I mean hell could not be worse than all the worrying here," Marion grimaces like the devil just sent him a text message. "The Inferno itself, all of Dante's nine rings of hell, couldn't be worse than all the worries here on earth."

With a brief knock of warning, not asking for permission, Dr. Weed enters the philosophical waiting room without any jokes or one-liners. He is alone, without the two nurses. He sharply nudges Cresty, waking her up. She turns on her side. There is more blood on her hospital gown.

The doc turns on the ultrasound monitor by the bed and then rubs a gooey jell over her bare, uncovered belly bump. He moves the wand of the machine over her belly.

"I just want to double check," he says, now very serious, as if a weather person announcing an approaching hurricane.

"I see the baby," Choker exalts, exciting Cresty and leaning closer to the screen. "There is the tiny head. You can see the arms and legs. This little guy looks like a judo man already."

Dr. Weed grabs his arm, handing him a stethoscope that is connected to the machine.

"Listen close, the heart-beat... there's a… there… there might be a problem."

With arms over each other's shoulders, Marion and Choker pace outside the hospital, making mindless loops around a dead tree.

Walking out of the hospital is the waitress from the Lobster Shack, the one with the long white sleeves spotted with tartar sauce. Marion sways over to her and asks, "Hey there, you OK? You served us the other night…"

"OK? What do you mean?" she answers.

"Well, you *are* leaving a hospital," Choker adds.

"Oh, yeah," she says. "Just a check-up."

She rolls up her sleeves on both arms. There are scars on both wrists.

"My stitches were seeping… still," she says as nonchalantly as taking an order of lobster. "I had to wear long sleeves because of the blood the other night. Now I wear the long sleeves to protect from the sun."

"What happened," Choker asks.

"I was bummed out that my boyfriend broke up with me."

Crossing a driveway, Marion and Choker slump under a live tree across the parking lot from the dead one. Marion picks at one of the leaves. The leaf is white. Most of the other leaves are dark purple.

"This is a Washington Hawthorne, isn't it?" Choker asks mindlessly. "This one is a beauty."

"You know your trees now… a crataegus phaenopyrum."

A songbird begins to whistle somewhere inside the tree. A Monarch butterfly circles the songbird on the branch of the Washington Hawthorne. Marion shakes. He starts to sob.

"Are you, all right? Why are you so upset, it was my baby fighting for life in there?"

"Yes and no. The baby is your baby, but the baby is all of ours really. I mean mankind's baby, too. When one star burns out in the Milky Way galaxy, light is lost."

"I'm not ready to get too deep on this. This is between Cresty and me. I mean how can you say that? Really how would you know?"

"I do know. My wife had one… a miscarriage."

Choker, as if reflexively, takes a step back.

"Oh, I'm sorry, I didn't know."

"Don't be sorry, how could you know? I never told you."

"Tell me now. What happened?"

Marion points up to the tree.

"You know in a couple of months there will be small, red fruit on this crataegus phaenopyrum. God willing, you and Cresty will be back for another ultrasound with some good news.

"When that happens, I want you to sit under this tree so I can be with you in spirit."

"Cool out a little," Choker says. "If we are back here, you'll be driving us. The Fish Finder will be fixed or a new one found for your F150. If you can still see, you will drive. If not, you can play the Fish Finder and I will drive.

"But just tell me first about your miscarriage."

Biting the side of his lip, Marion says, "It all started… or ended when I talked my wife into having, having an abortion.

Marion licks the dryness from his lips.

"I told her with my new practice, I wasn't ready financially yet. She didn't want to do it. But, I talked her into it…

"So, we killed the baby, as I told you. I didn't do it, my partner did. He also went to school with Dr. Weed and me. We called him Sprout, because he only needed to smoke a little grass to get really high."

Choker lies in the grass next to a paper wrapper blowing in the light breeze.

"We're you there? For the abortion?"

"No way, I wasn't even there for her. I went out and played golf because I felt so relieved. Plus, I was invited to play Pebble Beach. Can't pass off Pebble Beach. I had never played there. Never thought I would get another chance to play there. So, I played.

"But every time I hit the ball, all I could think of was the baby getting hit on the head and killed. That is what happens in abortions. But, I shook it off as well that's life.

"She called to see if I really wanted to go through with it. She left a message at the clubhouse for me to call if there was a change in plans. This was before cell phones of course. I never got the message. At Pebble Beach, the 9th hole and 1Oth holes don't end and start at the clubhouse because the designer wanted as many holes on the ocean. So, it is a figure-8 design, like the loops on a noose...

"Anyway, I never stopped at the turn to go in the clubhouse. So, I never got the foo-kin message… I let the baby… go… so I could hit a golf… that day, I hit the famous cypress tree in the middle of the 18th fairway.

"Neither my wife and I ever talked about the missed phone call."

Marion leaps up and grabs a branch and hangs from the bending limb.

"We didn't even do it for the next couple of months. It seemed longer. But it wasn't, because nine months to the day she had the abortion… she had a miscarriage… end of first trimester."

"Sorry."

"I was out playing Pebble Beach again, when I got the call at the turn. I got a second chance to play there. I even hit the famous cypress tree again in the middle of the 18th fairway."

"But we didn't get a second chance with the baby. This time we wanted the baby so bad. The timing was right for us. We went out and bought all the toys, the furniture, Barney blanket…"

"But it wasn't that we had all this stuff and couldn't use it, we wanted a baby. Both of us did. The sad thing was, I wasn't any more financially secure then as I was when we had the abortion. Nothing changed, except we wanted the baby."

"Perspectivism, huh? Choker says.

"We never got another chance…

"How did it happen?"

"The same as Cresty… not saying she had a miscarriage… it was right around three months. I remember when she came out of the bathroom after she saw a trace of blood. I knew what was happening, I told my wife to lie down and when she fell asleep I tried to find the heartbeat. I couldn't. Just the night before I could hear it with my bare ear. But now I couldn't hear it with a stethoscope. I knew at least one out of every five pregnancies end in a miscarriage."

"I guess," Choker barely says, "it's like Rochambeau."

"Yes, that is nature's lovely way of aborting the baby. It is God's way of doing it. And the number of miscarriages is definitely much higher than 20 percent. That is all that are reported or treated. Many women will just have their period in the third month and just think they missed the first two for whatever reason, but really they were pregnant and lost the baby."

Marion pulls his sunken soul up and sits in the tree. His words filter through the leaves.

"I was hoping the baby just moved and that was why I couldn't hear it, or the baby slowed down the beat by itself. I kept telling myself that. I kept thinking Keith Richards could slow down his heart, so my kid could too."

"Yeah, but Keith was using drugs."

"Not entirely, he also listens to Rastafarian music because the constant drum beat is one half beat below the heart rate. He calls it a necessary trance to relax you. He even plays with a band called the 'Wingless Angels' that use that beat."

“Maybe that is where my baby is now, a wingless angel,” Choker says. “Both of our babies.”

“That is what I was thinking too because I didn't take her to her gyno until the next day,” Marion says, swinging his hanging legs. “That night, I remember watching her lay asleep there in bed, all I could think of the poor dead baby was inside her. I loved my wife.”

“All I could think of how much I would've loved this baby. What it would've been like. What college it would've gone… went too. I thought if he or she would've been a doctor? I wondered if my baby would help others. I couldn't wait to take her to a Stones concert. I tried to convince myself the baby was alive, but the lovely baby was dead.”

“She, my wife, was lying there so peacefully, but there was a dead baby in her stomach. That was the first time I was ever around death, I felt, not like any of the hundreds of abortions I did.”

Marion drops down from the tree, knocking some leaves on the ground.

“Time, for some reason, just stopped for the baby. A doctor didn't kill the baby. I wondered where the baby's soul went. Did it just float in to outer space and be nothing? I hated to think that my kid was lost in space.”

Choker pats Marion on the back. He jumps up and hangs from the tree branch.

"Maybe it went to a black hole, like you told me, time stops there right."

"I hope, that is when I started reading more, not about philosophy and all that, but how the universe worked. I wanted to know where my baby went."

"What do you think? Where are our babies… your baby?" Choker asks, catching himself, acting positive while swinging his legs. "Is it all just Rochambeau? Is there a reason for all this? Is there a reason to live? Am I here just by chance or by luck or for a reason? Where's my baby?"

"All I can figure is they are either on the edge of a black hole, or traveling at the speed of light around the universe. Time stops at the speed of light too. Someone traveling at the speed of light crosses the universe in no time."

"I don't know if I get it, I feel like I'm speeding across the universe. Slow down. Tell me what happened after the miscarriage?"

"For the next three years we tried to have a baby. Never could. We tried everything. We went for all the tests. I even had to go to a doctor and get checked. My equipment was working, so was hers, but we just couldn't get it done."

"We tried the medicine and all that. I knew, golfed with the best reproductive docs. Nothing. Finally, she just left me. She moved to Cape May here. She loved butterflies. She loves how they migrate. She loved how they could just leave."

"She never said good-bye. She didn't have too. I killed her baby first and then nature killed our baby second."

Marion leaps up and grabs the tree branch again. They both hang from the branch.

"How did you meet her?" asks Choker, trying to lighten Marion's spirit.

"Hanging from a tree, I guess."

"Tell me the story."

"Another time."

"Tell me then about your wife, you know, her now."

"That is why I got the sail boat, to sail back into the past," Marion says easily. "I knew nothing about sailing, but Cape May is meant for boats.

"So, I figured I would learn to sail. Go north and anchor off the shore… try to slide back into her life…"

"We had bought a little cottage near the bay here, made the sale over the internet a year earlier. She wanted to study the migratory habits of the

Monarchs in the summer. She was a biology major at Cal-Berkley."

"I herded mega money, so I bought the house without even seeing it. For me, it was one of our toys. We, well I had every toy you could imagine. I thought who ever had the most toys at the end won. Man, was me foo-kin wrong or foo-kin what?

Walking toward them, Dr. Weed stops and smokes a cigarette while waving to Marion and Choker to come join him. Back in the room with Cresty, he turns up the sound on the ultrasound to level 10. Choker peels off the stethoscope. From the monitor's speaker, a beat, beat can be heard... faintly.

"I hear it, the baby," Cresty rejoices.

They all tilt closer to the machine, like offensive lineman in a huddle, trying to hear the quarterback in an opponent's raucous stadium.

Silence.

Marion bangs the top of the machine as if to restart it, like all it needs to send the beating sound is a swift boot. He leaves his right arm on top of the monitor as if a threat of another whack to come…

A beat.

They listen.

The beat they hear is just the tick of Marion's watch.

There is no beat to hear.

Marion pulls Choker out the door. They leave the hospital and convene near the tree again. "Sorry," he says as he climbs up the tree.

"Yeah, me too," a stoic Choker says. "Sorry for you, too. And your wife."

Choker swings up and sits next to Marion.

"What did you do after this, the miscarriage," Choker asks. "What did you do for her?"

"I knew she needed her mind to stay busy… I didn't want her to do anything stupid to herself," Marion says. "I agreed the change of scenery would be best…"

"My wife was the one who taught me about trees and plants when we lived together in Santa Cruz."

"She taught me about the Monarch butterflies, too. She loves the yellow Monarch and she loves yellow forsythias. She loves the color, yellow."

"I was just yellow."

"You're tough now," Choker says. "You know how to choke someone out."

"I see a Monarch and I think of our baby," Marion says. "I see a forsythia, I think of our baby."

"I can't escape my thoughts. The Monarchs migrate at the end of each summer to Mexico, but I can't... let my guilt go."

"The dark winter goes by and the forsythias are the first ones to bloom in spring. Each spring, I stay on the boat a week watching the forsythias grow. I wondered what it would be like if we had a baby playing near them. She has never seen me here in Cape May. I called her… I watch her with binoculars from a hill."

"I can see her gardening. I wish she could feel my guilt."

"You never talked to her about the baby? Maybe it would've eased your guilt."

"It was more," Marion says. "It was not just about our baby I killed, but my guilt grew like the forsythias. I started to think back to the chicks at concerts I used to bop. I didn't even know their names. We always were stoned."

"But I wonder if they ever had my kid. I mean think of that, there could be my kid out there and I don't know it. Now that kid or kids would have their own teenagers. A teen with no grandfather. I wish I knew. It's killing me. I would want to help them. It would be my kid."

Choker drops down from the tree.

"Come on, let's go get my kid."

Marion leads Choker back into the room where Dr. Weed swiftly works the stethoscope on her stomach. He furiously tries to find a heartbeat.

Nothing. He stops and stares at the screen. Using the computer mouse, he zooms in on the fetus.

He stares closer, until his nose is pressed on the screen, as he reaches and rests his right hand on her belly.

Making the sign of the cross, he walks away. Marion follows.

"Stay with Cresty," Marion says with his head down to Choker.

After fidgeting with the door, they step out of the room.

"Weed, after the D & C, I want the fetus, the baby."

"You know… we keep it."

"I'm not letting you use the stem cells, to sell them. That baby is a real person. Can't you see what is happening? Soon, people will be killing babies just to harvest body parts."

"We've been through this debate a million, billion times way before the public even heard about stem cells when we were drinking beers and you were playing the drums with your feet on University Ave. in Berkley, amusing the freaks and geeks.

"Let's not get in a row over this again," Marion whispers.

"Now everyone knows the promise of stem cell research," Doc Weed whispers back. "You can't hide it. You must know now even though you don't listen to the radio… just the Stones… I bet Mick and Keith know."

"I know. It still doesn't make it right."

"It doesn't make it wrong either. We aren't here to play God, just to help people."

"Who's going to help the unborn? Who's going to help the defenseless, the least of God's children?"

"The *born* have more political power than the unborn. Their votes count."

"I'm taking the fetus, the baby, and burying him… her… like the others," Marion says shaking, holding his broken Aviator sunglasses up on his nose."

"Listen, again, the stem cells could help you and your condition. There's great research going on and someday could cure ALS, Parkinson, and Alzheimer's and maybe could help you… and then you could help others, I mean help more."

"What about MED13L?" Marion asks before quickly adding, "I would still have to answer to God. The promise of doing right doesn't bend the righting moment further into the future."

"But, the baby is already dead. We're not taking stem cells from a frozen embryo or one that was created just for stem cells."

"Right… I wish it was black and white, like knowing to go out fishing or stay ashore when gray clouds hover… but that's not the way it is…"

"I'm done playing God. I'm taking the baby."

"Well, you have to leave Cresty here for a couple hours. We need to do the Discharge & Cleaning now. She is a special case… did you know?"

"Yes, I only recently learned. She didn't think she could get pregnant."

"Well as you know only a small percentage can… she was one of the lucky ones with internal testes that could."

"Rochambeau, she would say."

Marion and Choker walk slowly to The Hearse. From the back, Marion hands him a pink and blue bag. They return to the hospital and take the elevator up to the surgery floor. They wait for Cresty's discharge and cleansing to be done.

Marion talks to Dr. Weed.

"We need the blue bag," he tells Choker.

With the pink bag dangling from his back pocket, standing in the middle of them, Choker holds both elbows of Cresty and Marion as they walk out of the Stone Harbor hospital. Marion is in a trance like he is stoned. Cresty tucks the blue bag in one arm tight against her like carrying a football. With her other hand, she reaches… and holds onto Choker's hand.

Choker stops and turns to Marion. "How did you get started doing… to doing this?"

"Over last winter, in December, the famed cypress tree in the middle of the 18th fairway at Pebble Beach toppled in a storm," Marion says. "That is precisely when it hit me I had to do something. I had to make it right.

"I'm making my life right."

Crossing over the Garden State Parkway, The Hearse glides to a stop in front of Our Lady of Lost Angels Roman Catholic Church on 99th Street.

"You missed the funeral already," a kid says throwing a tennis ball against the sign saying the church is part of St. Paul's Parish.

"We are on *our* road to Damascus," Cresty says.

"We should walk then like Paul," Choker says. "Maybe we can save… save babies."

They walk back toward the bay on 99th. They cross Corinthians Drive.

"Paul actually wrote to the Corinthians from Ephesus," Marion says.

"In Turkey," Cresty nods," where my mom lives."

"In his first letter to the Corinthians," Marion says, placing his arms around both of them, "For no one can lay any foundation other than the one already laid, which is Jesus Christ."

Chapter 19

Shoulder to shoulder, the Three Horsemen of the Apocalypse ride The Hearse with my deceased grandson from the Stone Harbor hospital to the Parkway with an unexpected peacefulness. Swerving on a construction truck only ramp. The broken Aviator sunglasses can't shield Marion's ashen-face as he merges onto the Parkway. Cresty, with her white face blushed red, holds the blue bag in her lap. Her baby. With his light-skinned, black face calm, Choker pets Row and Way while crawling in the middle of the heavy traffic. Riding alongside them on the outside lane of the Parkway is the rich man cruising in his red Cadillac SUV.

With a yank of the wheel, Marion peels off at Route 109, leaving the rich man going straight into Cape May. Marion makes a left into the line for the ferry. He pulls up below the long, green glass walkway leading to the ferry from the massive white terminal with a bright blue roof. There is a modern plastic playground with swings and fake palm trees facing the ferry, but there are no kids are enjoying the built-in fun. Marion studies the cars in the ferry line before saying, "No followers."

Walking back, saying with sudden certainty, "today isn't the day to cross the bay," Marion turns around The Hearse. "We know," Choker says as Cresty squeezes her baby. He exits the lot with the cars coming off the ferry from the Lewes, Delaware side.

With an anguished scream, he slams the brakes and slides in the sandy lot at the bottom of the landfill.

A sudden warm breeze off the bay lifts the Whipporwills, tilting them upward as the dandelions seem to reach skyward for the fuzzy plants.

With his trembling hands, Choker reaches for a shovel out of the back of The Hearse. Cresty carries the blue bag to the top of the hill.

Thud.

Marion turns back to see standing in the sand upright is the shovel.

With his hands, Marion digs at the end of the dandelions.

Choker carries the shovel back to The Hearse. He carries Row and Way back with him. He walks to Cresty, who is looking out over the bay.

She peels back the blue bag. Through the yellow fluid of the clear bag, they see their son's eyes. The eyes look open.

Choker collapses. Row and Way hop away. Cresty kisses the clear bag over her son's eyes.

Walking backwards as she continues to gaze over the bay, she stops when Marion says, "Now… the Righting Moment.

With a kiss over the blue bag, Cresty places her son in the hole.

With Row and Way hopping around his heels, Choker bends over and kisses his son lying in the hole.

They all kneel.

From his breast pocket, Marion pulls out a seed. He backfills some sand, places the seed in the hole and spread the remaining pile of sand over the seed. He pats down firmly, saying to them, "All we're asked to do by Jesus is have faith the size of a mustard seed and we can uproot a mulberry tree."

Standing up, Choker and helping Cresty to her feet, he asks Marion, "Why does God allow so much misery? We lost Pete too soon and now our baby before even soon started..."

Kicking the sand to spread over their footprints and where they kneeled, Marion replies, "The prophet Habakkuk asked the same question and said, 'The Lord answered me and said write down the vision… for the vision has its time… if it delays, wait for it, it will surely come… the rash one has no integrity, but the just one, because of his, shall live.'"

"Well, then," Choker says, "We must hoist a Guinness to the lofty wisdom of Habukkuk."

Back at The Hearse, Marion flips on Fish Finder. He says, "The Stones remind us life is a blink with As Tears go By…"

He sings along sadly, "It is the evening of my stay, I sit and watch the unborn playing, smiling faces I can see, if not for me, I sit and watch mom's fears go by, my riches can't buy the real thing, I want to hear the unborn sing, all I hear is the sound of pain falling on the ground, I sit and watch as fears go bye, it is the evening of my stay, I sit and watch the unborn play, doing things I used to do, they think are new, I sit and watch as fears go by."

When the piercingly sad song ends, Marion abruptly starts running. He weaves through the second growth of trees on the backside of the dune. Choker and Cresty try to follow, passing the twisted drift tree on the beach, but he is gone. They go back and sit on the two dead tree trunks coming out of the sand, marking the entrance to the path back to the parking lot. They toss broken seashells at the rusted drainpipe pile.

"Don't you do that whisper thing anymore, into the shell?" Choker asks.

"Not anymore," Cresty says, "I guess I'm not just as patient… as holy as Habukkuk."

In the distance, the ferry whistle blows and, as if he appears with the sound, they see Marion running farther up the beach toward The Pointe.

With no more shell around them to flip, they wait on the dead tree stumps. They sit and wait without words.

They wait for hours as Row and Way hop around the dead tree stumps.

Marion is gone. He doesn't return.

Choker and Cresty drive The Hearse slowly with only the Fish Finder clicking from track to track on the way back to Marion's boat where smoke hovers in the air.

On the deck, Brennan limps to them, not putting any weight now on back right leg. The guy, who cooks burgers on his boat, offers Cresty a burnt one as he fans the smoke away from his grill.

Inside, they find Marion sleeping in his wet, sandy clothes and partially wrapped with a Barney blanket.

“It’s the one left over from wife's baby shower he talked about it when you were in the hospital,” Choker says about the tattered purple blanket.

Cresty and Choker plop on the bed before leaning back, looking at the clouds through the skylight as the boat sways in boater’s wakes, rocking them to sleep.

With the sun sneaking into the corner of the skylight, they both reach out and pat Marion like he is Row or Way. Brennan cuddles in the bottom corner of the bed with the two rabbits.

"Let's go fishing." Cresty says.

"Again?" Choker asks. "Yeah, really, isn't it a bit early to do it again?"

"We should go fishing for fishes," she smiles. "Not babies… not yet."

They walk with their arms around each other over to the gray hearse in somber solace and without the fishing rod. They drive to Cape May Point State Park "to now kill time," says Choker and "let Marion revive," adds Cresty.

Cape May Point State Park was originally a military base built to protect the coast here, but it was abandoned after the 1962 Nor'easter, the same slamming storm that devastated Strathmere and Sea Isle to the north.

There was once 900 feet of land before the bay, but now with unrelenting erosion, only a few feet, perhaps yards, remain of beach in front of the bunker.

"There's a lot to do here, hiking trails, nature trails," Cresty says, sounding like she is trying to lift Choker's spirit, reminding him that even though he can't fish, he can still walk.

They stroll without hurry in front of the old, abandoned concrete World War II bunker on the beach.

"They were built to defend those who can't defend themselves. Now they are antiquated," Choker says. "Now the Navy employs laser weapons on ships in the Persian Gulf."

Cresty feigns being impressed with "who the fook are you, Mr. Jeopardy?"

"The Navy's 30-kilowatt laser is sold-state and is being fired in operational action on board the USS Ponce," Choker continues. "We now have our first deployment of a sea-based, directed energy weaponry to protect ships who already can protect its own ironsides.

"Listen to you, you college dropout," Cresty says.

"Who protects those who can't protect themselves?" Choker wonders.

The bunker is dying an indignant, ugly death, not used to protect anyone anymore, just the fish that swim around the concrete pilings to hide from the larger fish.

Choker fishes with just a line and a hook he pulled from his back pocket. There is no bait on the line. He stands inside a concrete circle in front of the bunker so "not to get his kicks soaked." Cresty sits where once 155 mm Coast Artillery guns fired in the air, aiming for unknown enemies.

"I need a weapon to blow the fish out of the water," he says.

Choker casts the line with an underhand motion. Quickly, he attracts the angry lifeguard, who points and waves from down the beach like a cop at Times Square on New Year's Eve.

"It's like I just breached national security," he fusses.

Unbothered, Choker mopes to the other side of the bunker where the lifeguard can't see him. No bites. They leave.

They wander into The Pointe museum inside the park. Under glass, they see a skull of a loggerhead turtle. The placard says the turtle had died from ingesting plastic.

"At least the Pope says the turtle goes to heaven," Choker teases, poking Cresty in her belly.

"Will our baby?"

"He is with Pete."

"Should we name him Pete?"

"We should."

With heavy and hurried footsteps, Marion surprises from behind, saying, "The loggerhead's main food is jelly fish and it had mistaken the plastic for the fish."

"Hey, at least, I saved a turtle by throwing away my plastic soda bottle," Choker says, wrapping his right arm around Marion and poking Cresty again with his free hand. "And, I did save at least one fish today by not catching it."

"How'd you get here," Cresty asks, squeezing Marion.

"The burger guy," Marion says cheerfully, "he burnt his grill up and I told him he could recycle down by the Sunken Ship… he gave me a lift."

Outside, where the clouds are dark, the three walked past three pyramid shaped antenna towers. They march with a quick pace down to the jetty in front of the lighthouse, about 75 yards from the lifeguard stand.

Climbing onto the jetty, Marion's face turns as dark as his mood. He paces up the jetty, almost falling between the rocks with each step. Back near Choker and Cresty, Marion sits crossed leg. A wave splashes over his legs.

He slides in the rock crevice as he hands Choker his broken Aviator sunglasses. He dips his whole head into an incoming wave.

"During one partial birth abortion procedure I was doing, the baby was alive," he says.

"The lady wanted the baby… but she was afraid."

Marion dives into the ocean.

He pops his head up and screams, "I killed it."

Choker and Cresty pull him on the jetty like a flounder.

Wrapping the blanket, they brought and their arms around him, Marion says, "She came back, weeks later, and told me she wanted to kill the baby herself. But instead of feeling relieved that I killed the baby for her, I knew then I had to fix… that was my last abortion."

"She was the lady you gave the baby to across the bay, huh?" Cresty asks knowingly.

Marion nods.

"What are the chances she was from West Cape May and was going to college out West?" Marion says shaking and scratching his head.

"Rochambeau," Cresty says.

"I quit my job. I realized money killed me. I started reading about, you know, the universe and stuff, and I learned how the Snake River Canyon in Utah was once a part of Alaska. How scientists found the identical components of rocks in Alaska and in Utah and concluded they were once together. I couldn't read enough about the universe. I realized, too much embarrassment, life was bigger and older than me for the first time."

"Choker told me about your wife. Did you talk to her, try to fix your marriage?"

"Maybe life is, really just Rochambeau," Marion says. "Wasn't meant to be, a second chance was as likely as raising the Sunken Ship."

"Come on, the Stones didn't come together by chance."

"It doesn't matter now," Marion says, not looking at her. "I'll soon be as dead as the babies I used to kill. I don't have to worry about them kicking my ass in heaven because I'm not going there."

Cresty reaches, hesitates and then touches his arm… forgivingly.

"You're not going to, uh, kill yourself, are you?"

"I'm dying."

He dives back into the ocean. Choker and Cresty pull him back out. They sit on the rocks wrapped in the blanket around themselves again.

"When I had those blood tests to see if we could have a baby, the results showed my prolactin level was low," Marion says. "I had to get an MRI, which showed a tumor on my pituitary. It was inoperable, but it wasn't growing. Well, it started growing. That is why I'm losing my sight."

"Isn't something… isn't there anything the doctors can do?" she asks, shaking his arm as if to stir his fight for life instinct.

"Yeah, what was Dr. Weed talking about at the hospital?" Choker asks. "It sounded like there was some way to help."

"He was talking about taking the stem cells from your baby and other miscarriages and abortions and using them fetus for tests, studies to develop drugs for cancer treatments as well as other cruel, unfair diseases making the innocent helpless.

"That's what makes the rich guy in the red boat, Daddy Starbucks richer."

"How do you know his name?" Marion asks.

"I've been doing my own checking," Choker says. "You got to keep checking your options."

"But, the problem is even more morally challenging, they are now talking about creating embryo's just to take the stem cells. Now they want to kill babies when they are only a couple of hours old. I'm not going to be a part of that."

"I would've given you the stem cells from our baby," Cresty says, "if it would save your life."

"What is the foo-kin point?' Marion slams his fist against the rocks. "The world is going to end soon any way."

"What the hell you mean by that?" she asks.

"It is simple, it is the Big Bang and Big Crunch."

Choker and Cresty hold each other on the rocks. Marion pops up, does a surfing pose and then sits again with legs crossed.

"Big crunch, is this another scat story?" Choker asks.

"The universe consists of billions of galaxies flying apart from when the Big Bang took place. A guy named Hubble invented a way to estimate the distance of galaxies. He used the Doppler effect to judge their speeds. Hubble, which the telescope is named after, reasoned everything started with the Big Bang.

"Creationist don't agree, but that is another story."

"What is the disagreement?" Choker asks.

"The big bang happened 15 to 20 million, or is it billion years ago? Anyway, creationists believed the earth was created just 6,000 years ago, hell the earth is four to five million, or is it billion years old? We know that just by the Grand Canyon.

"And, we know that because there is 3k radio energy flying in space. It's used by the Hubbell to judge the speed of the galaxies. Our Milky Way is moving at 400 miles a second. What is going to happen is the galaxies are going to run out of energy from the explosion.

"They are going to stop."

"So?" they both say together.

"So… then gravity is going to pull them back. It will be the big crunch. Then there will be a giant explosion. Another big bang will happen. We'll be gone, but life will start over, that's the good part."

"So… then why kill yourself and miss all the banging?" Choker says. "And, suicide is no different from abortion. Killing is killing. Right?"

"Indeed, Perspectivism," Marion says. "But shouldn't someone who is dying, someone who is in pain and has no hope, be allowed to employ a doctor assisted suicide?

"Who does a doctor assisted suicide hurt?"

Marion stands a bit wobbly. He doesn't answer his own question. "It's not like an abortion where society is hurt," Marion says as he reaches under his shirt and pulls out a paper bag. He hands it to Cresty; she opens the bag and pulls out a video.

"Take The Hearse back to the boat and go watch the video."

Marion starts to jog, but slows and then offers a friendly wave to the angry lifeguard as he walks down the bay beach.

"See you back at the boat," Choker yells to him. "Hope it's not raining in the morning, we got some trees to cut."

With the clouds even more ominous back on the boat, and the burger guy cooking on his new grill, sending even more smoke into the sky, Choker and Cresty pet Brennan, who doesn't stand up. He just lifts his head. Choker puts the videotape in the old TV player on the boat. It shows Marion instructing him how to save a baby from partial birth abortion. He must have just shot the video on the boat.

The tape shows Marion saying: “first, you use the choke hold you showed me on the doctor.”

Choker and Cresty put the tape on pause. Play it again. Pause it… play the tape again...

At the end of the tape, Marion shows how to deliver a baby with the head already exposed using the rolled-up Barney blanket as a baby prop.

He wraps his hands around the ball of the blanket, like the ball is the head.

Marion pulls real hard. Then soft. Then hard again.

Chapter 20

The boat is empty when Choker wakes up next to Cresty in the morning. There is no sign of Marion. They can only hear a wake from a passing boat ripple against The Byrd.

"I'll wake his tumor up," Choker says, sniffing the clammy low-tide air with a long snarling draw, "I'll bang it out of him like shooting a long 3-pointer."

Choker backs up The Hearse to the boat and cranks up the Fish Finder. Loud. The blare is the Stones' 2,000 Light Years From Home: "Breathing red fetuses turn to dark, lethargy here is in every part, it is so very lonely, I am thousands of blood smears from home," Choker sings.

Marion bounces up on the deck on "home." He unwraps the Barney blanket and jumps off the boat. He grinds with buckling knees toward The Hearse. but trips over a bench on the dock. Marion props up like nothing happened. Putting the blanket in The Hearse, he leans against The Byrd huffing.

"Let's go to work," Marion says revived

"Not me," Cresty says. "Drop me off at the beach, I'm looking for God today and I think I'll find Him in a tube with no spray."

"If He is down there today, we all should go," Marion says, pointing to his head like he knows something.

"I don't know if He is there, but I feel He is when I'm womping in some tubes."

Choker's smile is piercing like the early morning sun reflecting off car windshields in Utsch's parking lot.

"She's onto something, Marion, with this surfing," Choker says. "The rhythms of the oceans are the pulse of our liquid planet. As certain as the tides, the energy of the sea is a constant challenge, which can never be overcome, only respected. The dimension in which we coexist and flow with life-giving waters is the realm."

"Man, that is good, Choker. Sounds like wet water judo talk. That's deep."

"Yeah, deep from my closet. That is the slogan of the Realm Clothing Company."

Marion bangs a surfing pose.

"I got to get me some surfing shirts, dude."

"I got to get surfing," Cresty demands.

Repeating with a satisfied grin, "The dimension in which we coexist and flow with life-giving waters is the realm," Choker drives to the beach while Marion sits in the middle and Cresty lounges by the window. With rods by their side, the fishermen stand motionless on the jetty at Devil's Reach. The waves crashing into the jetty are powerful and the spray is submerging the rocks.

Cresty tucks her board under her right arm, waving to Choker and Marion, who drive away, slowly chugging through side streets to The Pointe.

"I was telling you about the Big Crunch and besides being a whole lot like my Big Squeeze, it's also like waves," Marion explains, sliding further down in the seat until suddenly rising when driving around the oval across from St. Agnes Church. "You just got to realize that with all the surfing talk. Just like a wave swell expands on its journey across the ocean, it runs out of room and goes crunch, then it squeezes back until it hits another wave with a bang.

"Over and over. The cycle continues. Round and round like the migration of the Monarchs, the Danaus plexippus.

Choker loops around the oval, making continuous laps as Marion continues, "The milkweeds around the dock flutter with the Danaus plexippus. The females with their yellow and black-veined wings are easy to spot from the males, with their orange and thinner black veins."

"The days are getting shorter now in early August," Choker interrupts. "Maybe the butterflies will leave soon."

"Our Monarch friends soon will migrate," Marion says on another lap as Cresty paddles into the surging surf on the other side of Devil's Reach. "The eastern North American Monarch will embark on its multigenerational southward swing to Mexico. The Danaus plexippus covers 1,000 of miles. It's their cycle of life."

"When do the Danaus plexipatapus return?" Choker asks.

"Plexippus."

"Who makes up these scientific names?" Choker asks, slowing down for a grandma pushing a baby stroller. "Who are these mad scientists?"

"The ancient Greeks," Marion smiles. "Danaus was the great-grandson of Zeus. Plexippus was one of the 50 sons of Aegyptus. There were no abortion clinics in Athens."

"Now they have 3-point yellow lines painted around them," Choker says with a disdainful puff. "Don't feel ready to surf after doing some up-and-downs, standing on the board in the shallow surf. We should go hit some 3-pointers," Marion finishes rambling nonsensically.

"We shall," Choker says, "we shall."

"Plexippus means a "charioteer" so indeed the Monarch butterflies here are telling you to ride, to ride on, too."

Halting his loops, Choker drives through the middle of Cape May Point, slowing down near the milkweeds growing around the fresh water lake where Blackbeard buried his loot. The Hearse parks at the lighthouse lot.

Putting their feet up against the pavilion rail, they see Cresty carrying her board out of the bay.

"The surf was raging, a wave pushed me into the bay," she explains. "I rolled with the water, and then I paddled to shore. Here I am."

They head out, driving in loops again around the St. Agnes oval since the milkweeds are covered with the Monarchs. Cresty shakes her wet head out the window. Her red hair is growing longer, like when she was younger.

"When do they leave, when do they come back?" Choker rapidly asks.

"Their range expands and contracts depending on the season. The eastern Monarchs migrate mostly to northern South America to the Cook Islands, the Solomons and New Guinea… all from little Cape May, New Jersey.

"But unlike the Big Crunch, they, the Monarch doesn't come right back. The Danaus plexippus actually skips at least one generation before returning from Mexico to eastern North America."

"Why?" Cresty asks from her window seat.

"No one knows, not even my wife. She came here to study the Monarch and find out why their migration is multigenerational.

"You talked to her?" Cresty asks excitedly.

"Read her blog," Marion says before adding, "Still, the Monarch on these milkweeds do migrate and expand like our Milky Way and then they do contract and come back to Cape May like our universe will someday contract."

"You really believe in the Big Crunch, don't you?" Choker asks. "You really think the universe will contract on our butts?"

"It's not just me, There was this guy, John Taylor, he taught at Kings College up northeast in Pennsylvania like 40 years ago and he wrote that after the Big Bang and during the Big Crunch, time would run backwards.

"He wrote people would start rising from their graves. We would *ungrow* and finally be unborn. That means in the end, we would meet God as unborn babies."

"That's way deep," Cresty says. "No way."

"Yeah, way, baby, that was his thinking… and it's mine, too."

"That means our baby is meeting God right now, he has already been through the Big Crunch,"

Choker says. "I like this John Taylor. I wish I knew him."

"You will meet him some day, even though he's dead" Marion smiles.

"Now, that would be some wild Rochambeau in the after foo-kin life," Choker says.

Taking a spoke of a road off the oval, Choker pulls The Hearse, filled with truisms, close to the nun house and up on the sand.

"I see *rideable* waves in the bay," she says. "We should get surfing in this life."

Unstrapping her board off the roof of The Hearse, Cresty says, "I'm going out here, below the lighthouse."

"I see a red flag, Cresty, maybe you shouldn't go out. We wouldn't be able to help you. Marion can't see and I can't swim."

"Yeah, we don't want another Mark Foo. I can only take one..."

"The red flag is for swimmers," she says. "And I have to, this is my righting moment. I need to live outside of me after the dying inside me. I have to get back to being myself. Pete would want me to be me again. I haven't been the last two years…"

Cresty waves at a nun on the porch of the house and marches down the beach with her board over her shoulder. She walks through a crowd of surf fisherman with uncasted lines. She dives into a wave and paddles through the choppy white water. A lifeguard on a jet ski is waving her back in. She keeps paddling.

"The waves are too big, especially for where the bay meets the ocean, she should come in," Choker says. "There are only two losers… surfers out there besides the lifeguard guy on the jet ski..."

The current pushes Cresty back toward the Devil's Reach Jetty away from Choker and Marion, standing with the nun on the porch and overlooking the bay.

"I can't see," Marion laments to the nun while squeezing his broken Aviator sunglasses, "what's happening?"

"But, the blind man can see…" the nun says as Choker pulls Marion to The Hearse.

The speed through the side streets of West Cape May and pull up to the jetty at Devil's Reach when a surfer dude slips over the lip of a sizeable wave and tucks immediately. But the surfer gets mashed by the breaker and is forced to dive into the foaming wave. The jet ski patrol picks him up.

"He better get Cresty. I can't see her."

"Me foo-kin neither," Marion says.

With waves splashing over the jetty, Choker climbs down the rocks. Marion sits near the beach on top of the jetty.

There is shouting below.

Being pounded by six-foot swells, the second surfer paddles in exhaustion to the jetty. The fishermen help him on the rocks. They all look beyond the spray of the crashing waves.

There is no one else surfing.

No Cresty…

An ambulance siren wails.

"It's the Doppler effect," Marion shakes Choker, standing on the edge of the jetty, "the siren is getting closer."

Choker is frozen looking into the shallow surf near the beach.

The emergency vehicle screeches to a stop next to The Hearse. Marion uses his hands to climb down the rocks and runs toward the paramedics, who are rushing up the beach. He squeezes behind a circle of gathered people.

Lying on the sand, Cresty is surrounded. The guard on the jet ski administers mouth-to-mouth. He is pushing on her chest.

Choker pushes through the crowd.

"Save her!"

Marion shakes him.

"It is my fault. I saw her in the backwash, but I couldn't, I didn't go in… after her."

Marion and Choker crawl on the knees through the crowd.

They can't get to her.

The legs of the people are like thick vines holding them back.

Choker squirms to his feet. He pushes to the outside of the circle of gawkers. He dives into a slither left by a third paramedic squeezing into the pack.

Marion squirms on his belly through the myriad of legs. Choker and Marion bump heads as they see Cresty is spitting up water.

Thank God. She is all right.

She springs up with eyes wide open, in a daze. Her smile is even wider.

"I saw my baby. It was the coolest feeling," she says to the two uniformed paramedics. "I was panicked at first, but then I felt so comfortable. I saw Pete. I wanted to go to them… mehr licht…"

"She is babbling," the one paramedic says.

"No, she isn't," Choker says, "She is saying mehr licht, more light."

The medics try to stop her from talking.

"I remember seeing a while light and then a baby's face, it looked like you, Choke, and then the baby. He was beautiful."

"So are you," Choker says, squeezing her.

After wanting to walk, Cresty rests on the beach under the lighthouse, not far from the bunker. The crowd of fishermen stare for a minute before going back to fishing. Choker and Marion sit on a lone dry rock half buried in the wet sand.

"Those waves were monsters, they were moving mountains," Choker sighs. "It's not your fault. God wanted Cresty to see her baby. And she did. We should get going. We have some beautiful work to do."

They pick up Cresty and climb through the sand to The Hearse.

"Go to the clinic," Marion orders.

The Hearse is already pointed north, toward the clinic.

Making a left off the Parkway, across the illegal cutover, Choker parks out back near Madame Palm's. Marion retrieves the long tree shears. He climbs up a tree between branches, slicing a few before he cuts the power line to the clinic.

It's a Saturday… no one is in the clinic… except a lone girl wearing baggy basketball shorts, the ones

Cresty used to wear. She knocks furiously on the side door.

"No baby brain surgeries will be done on Monday," Marion says. "It will take them a while to fix these lines."

Choker drives to the landfill. Marion sits down in the dandelion patch while they sit next to the grave of their baby.

"I think we should bomb the clinic," Marion declares, plucking out a dandelion from the sand. "Stealing babies and cutting the power won't stop them. We have to kill them. This is past the 40th anniversary of Roe vs. Wade now. What a better way to celebrate than to kill the ones doing the killing. And, plus, the Stones are touring again this year."

Marion plucks a pedal from the dandelion.

"Row vs. Way? I'm sorry I killed their mother, but that was before... before my Righting Moment," Choker says.

"No, R-o-e vs. W-a-d-e was a Supreme Court case that legalized abortions," Marion says. "I'm surprised you didn't know."

"I did."

Marion strums a fake guitar as he stands on the landfill.

"It was the first time in history that killing was made a law in 1973," Choker says. "Forty years after Pete left us."

"Indeed, 40 is a biblical number as crazed Catholics know," Marion says with glazed eyes and a strand of saliva stretched from the top of his inside lip to the bottom, expanding and contracting with each syllable. "Forty years in the desert for Moses, 40 days of advent, 40 days in the desert for Jesus…

"I'm convinced 40 years from now… well, 2,000 light years from now, history will judge our generation and society will be devastated how we allowed babies to be killed."

"Right. Then why kill anyone? Why bomb anything?" Choker asks. "Let the Big Crunch take care of it. God seems to have a plan.

"Didn't God tell the prophet Habakkuk that 'for the vision has its time… if it delays, wait for it, it will surely come … the rash one has no integrity, but the just one, because of his, shall live?'"

"I can't wait for your God," Marion says, "or your Rochambeau."

Back at Marion's boat, The Byrd, Choker tosses stones at a tree and then into the canal. The lady with the swimming pool in her front yard dips her feet in the shallow end while holding her baby. Cresty sleeps on the bow deck, resting her head on Brennan and holding Row and Way in her arms.

"If I plant a tree and then chopped down an older tree, is that right?" Choker asks Marion. "Don't you plant two trees every time you cut one down? Don't you say the beauty of the Stones is they love R&B, rock, country, and reggae? Didn't they even do that disco song 'Miss You?' Don't they respect all music?

"Shouldn't we respect all life?"

"There you go again with that gray area," Marion says.

"No, there really shouldn't be a gray area here," Choker snaps. "There's a problem with your thinking, man. How can you fight so hard to save a baby, but want to kill a person with a bomb? Isn't life, life no matter how old or young?"

Marion throws a stone at the tree. Missing badly. He doesn't answer.

"Aren't you the one against the Death Penalty?" Choker continues. "But you think it's OK for doctor's assisted suicide of old people in Oregon. Don't you have a set list anymore? Isn't the death penalty on your set list? Why isn't bombing an abortion clinic?

"Your set list is a cafeteria menu."

Marion stares across the bay at the lady and her baby.

"You know what's happening, I think the big crunch has started and you are thinking backwards. Is that what happens? Is that why I'm thinking like I do now?"

"You might," Marion hesitates, "be onto something."

"Then, in the big crunch, since everything is going backwards, and God has a plan, does the dead come back to life and live here with us before the bang?" Choker asks. "Do all aborted babies get born? Will my Pete come back to life? Will the cop in Sea Isle, the one in the coma who died, come back and meet… his killer?"

Choker drops his head into his hands and starts to cry. Marion reaches around and places his arm around his shoulder. He pets his head like Row or Way. He rubs his head real hard, then soft, then hard again.

Choker doesn't wait for Marion to console him.

"I'm afraid of heaven," Choker says. "What happens if someone you love isn't there? How can you be in heaven so to speak, or enjoy heaven if a loved one isn't there?"

"I mean… you would know they didn't live a good life, right? I mean now that animals go to heaven, how could Row enjoy heaven if Way wasn't there?"

"That's why I'm making my Righting Moment," Marion says.

Choker looks up. Marion stares at him. They slap a chokehold on each other.

"Perhaps, you know Goethe said, 'thinking is more interesting than knowing, but less interesting than looking.'" Marion groans through squeezed windpipes, "We should go looking."

"Indeed, mehr licht," Choker yells stirring Cresty and attracting a startled look from the lady holding her baby across the bay. "We should go find more light."

As Choker toys with Marion, grappling with him, keeping Marion's deteriorating mind distracted, Cresty scrolls through his phone. She stops when seven straight phone calls were made by Marion to the same number – a 650 area code – with just the letter "X" for a name. She googles 650… Palo Alto.

She dials the number on her phone. A lady's voice answers.

Chapter 21

The Three Horsemen are on a southbound train.

"It's August," Cresty declares, "we need a vacation."

Sitting in seats facing each other on the Amtrak coach, with Choker and Cresty on one side, Marion peppers them with questions.

"Where we headed?" he said continuously from the New Jersey Transit train in Atlantic City to Philadelphia. Now, he continues to ask to everything Cresty and Choker says, "Why are we going to Savannah?"

"I called your ex-wife," Cresty confesses. "The other day, when you two were wrestling at The Byrd… I apologized calling her but said we were friends and I was worried about you.

"She seemed concerned."

"Really? She did? Why did you call?

"I told her you were dying with guilt for talking her into aborting your baby. I told her the guilt has boiled, whatever, almost twenty years later… and you were… maybe going to do something… bad."

"What did… what did she say?"

"Here, read her text back to me the next day," Cresty says, handing Marion her phone.

"I can't read small letters."

"I'll enlarge them," Choker says, grabbing the phone.

The large letters say on the first screen:

Tell him while he was golfing

Choker scrolls to the second screen:

didn't have it

The next screen:

the late-term abortion

Marion reaches and scrolls to the end of the message, Choker pushes him away and scrolls to the next screen:

had the baby

Marion slumps in the seat as Choker shows him the next screen:

girl

Then, the next screen:

gave her up for adoption

Next screen:

in delivery room

Marion rubs his eyes. Real hard. He looks at the next screen:

she lives in Savannah

Marion dozes off around Washington, D.C. after downing a tall glass of Jameson, steadily sipping without any ice melting to simmer the sting.

Cresty, Choker and Marion all sleep through the Amtrak stop in Savannah. They debark in

Jacksonville at sunrise. The next non-stop north isn't until mid-morning. They need a car so they rent a candy red Toyota Corolla.

They drive northeast to Amelia Island in search of breakfast. They each order fried shrimp and hush puppies at Sliders on the beach. Over the grassy dunes, only 40 yards in front of them, SUVs park on the beach. Surfers dot the light blue water beyond the breakers.

"I'm upset me only rented a two-wheel drive truck... and declined the insurance option... but digging me foresight to pack a shovel in me airline carry-on bag to make my lovely daddy-daughter reunion following lunch on Amelia Island this afternoon," Marion says to the politely disinterested waitress with a double nose ring.

As Bob Marley wails, the 20-something waitress asks, "Are you vacating or vacationing?" Marion responds, "Both and neither.

"Are ya'll going to a destination wedding," Kristen K, the waitress asks and then says, "I was at six weddings in Savannah before 21."

"How long *youse* been here?" Marion asks.

"My whole lousy life," she smiles. "How'd bout ya'll?"

"Since when me look out on the beach and I helped dig out this man with his wife and four kids who got stuck driving on Amelia Island's in their two-wheel drive pickup," Marion rambles.

Kristen K. returns with the food and Marion resumes his story, "The man I freed up insisted on buying me a pint of gratitude... I accepted reluctantly... he insisted on buying me another... I accepted less reluctantly... and then another…"

The waitress refills everyone's water after helping Marion open the ketchup.

"The family man insisted on buying since he just lost his job, didn't know how he would feed his family and couldn't afford a tow truck... he said he came to talk to God when he got stuck and God sent me…"

The top of the ketchup pops off as Marion shakes the bottle. His hush puppies are smothered. The waitress scrapes the ketchup to the side of his dish with a knife from her pouch.

"Happens all the time," she says casually. "What happened next?"

"Just then the man received a text from his brother, who needed his old suffering horse put down and the vet wanted $500... he texted his brother and said he could fix the situation for $250... on the ride there he tells me he can't shoot a horse and asked if I can do it... I saw his four kids in the back of the pickup and agreed reluctantly..."

Kristen K. scoops the excess ketchup on Marion's plate with a spoon and tries to put it back into the bottle, but there is crust around the edge and the ketchup just runs down the side of the bottle.

"We drove a few miles to this Georgian House on a farm with a horse that looked like it could win the Kentucky Derby, prancing outside a sprawling barn... he handed me a shotgun from under the seat... I pulled the trigger... a man sprinted across the wraparound porch... I said, 'your brother sure is happy to pay you for shooting his old horse, but the horse didn't look that old'... the guy said, 'that's because the horse was his prized two-year-old thoroughbred and that isn't my brother... he's my old boss that fired me.'"

The waitress says, "You shot my dad's horse," as she squeezes the top back on the ketchup bottle with the ketchup dripping down the side.

Using a napkin to help wipe her hands, Marion says, "I plan to arrive in Wise Blood unless The Violent Bear Awakes... in that case If A Good Man is Hard to Find than take solace in Everything That Rises Must Converge."

Cresty says to her, "We are going to Midnight in the Garden of Good and Evil."

"I understood," Kristen K. says, tossing the messy ketchup bottle into the empty trashcan. "I read Flannery O'Connor… The Habit of Being and The Presence of Grace are my favorites… tomorrow, or is it tomorrow after tomorrow, or the tomorrow after, anyway August 3rd is her birthday."

Marion insists on driving to Savannah. Choker acquiesces. Marion stops for a Snickers Bar and large fountain coke at a rest stop outside Callahan, Florida.

"How will we find her," Marion asks when crossing the state line on I-95 into Georgia.

"Your ex texted me that she gives ghost tours," Cresty says.

"Sweet," Marion says, munching on the Snickers Bar before lamenting, "There must be a lot of ghost tours in the old Southern city with so much history and so many… dead."

Marion is enthralled by the Spanish moss hanging on the live oak trees in the squares of Savannah. "There are 22 squares off all sizes in the downtown," he says.

They go to Mrs. Wilkes House for lunch. Marion says he wants to eat "where guests sit at communal tables," but the line is a block deep on the cobblestone and tree-lined Jones Street.

"We can't miss the tour," Marion says as they walk into One Fish Two Fish next door to the Wilkes Dining Room.

They take an afternoon ghost tour with a girl in her 20-somethings. She tells them how Nathaniel Green "hated Spanish moss" and when the major general of the Continental Army during the Revolutionary War was shot and killed in Georgia, the "Savior of the South" was reinterred in Johnson Square. She points to his 50-foot white marble monument and says, "Soon after his reburial, all the Spanish moss upped and died."

The tour girl walks quickly. The pack hurries at an uncomfortable pace. Marion is in front. The guide turns around and stops at Chippewa Square as Marion is on her tail, almost knocking her over.

"This square is known for the famous park bench scenes from the Forrest Gump movie," she bristles. Then she adds before Marion can ask, "The park bench Gump sat on is now in the Savannah History Museum," but quickly injects, "Sir, I'm told Gump sat on that bench over there," pointing to the rear of the park.

Marion plops next to her, sitting in the grass.

She orders, "Don't sit in grass… ch… ch… chiggers."

After the two-hour tour of ghost stories, with Marion on her heels the whole time, she asks if anyone had questions. Choker asks, "What are *chiggers*?"

With the tour girl explaining to Choker that chiggers are a "thousand times worse than ticks" and saying how they "burrow into you" and adds how "they have babies under your skin" and how "even worse, some chiggers carry paralyzing parasites," Marion asks Cresty, "How will we find my daughter among the ghost tour guides?"

"Well, first off, she was born in California, right? In Palo Alto?" Cresty says.

"Yeah, that's right."

"Also, you ex texted me that her name is Jacqueline."

A feather floats above the oak trees and sweeps down and lands on a limb with Spanish moss.

Marion reaches up and clutches the feather. He hands it to the tour girl and asks, "Is your name by chance… Jacqueline? She shakes her head sideways and tells him she knows of a girl by that name who gives tours, but cautioned she isn't from Savannah."

"Us Savannah girls give the best tours," she says.

Marion scouts out the tour guide brochures. He calls two of them and finds a girl in mid-20's named Jacqueline.

The late afternoon ghost tour is filled with mostly senior citizens. Marion nudges close to the guide, Jacqueline, and tells her he is spending "tis lovely Antebellum Afternoon with his Georgia

Peaches... and hoping to find his Savannah Sweetheart."

The first stop is Flannery O'Connor's childhood home, which has its mailbox wrapped in a dark purple bow with fresh purple violets.

Marion tells Jacqueline back in college he had taken an American Literature course and thought the Southern Gothic style writer Flannery O'Connor was "a dude with a funny first name."

She smiles politely as he adds, "And today, August 3rd is her birthday."

"No, she died on August 3rd. We celebrate death in Savannah not birth."

Pointing to the purple violets and trying to regroup, Marion says, "Well, the viola is the largest genus of the violet family, but usually they grow in more temperate climates, like in the Northern Hemisphere."

Jacqueline doesn't bite for a conversation and so Marion adds, "You know, the viola sororia is the state flower of New Jersey, where I'm now living… and did you know most violas contain antioxidants, which contain cyclotides… used as anti-HIV, anti-insecticidal and anti-microbial agents."

They walk across the square to John the Baptist Cathedral where the baptismal font is at the front of the church.

"Fitting," Jacqueline says, "babies are baptized in their first days."

The last stop is Bonaventure Cemetery where the *faction* - or historical novel - Midnight in the Garden of Good and Evil's famed "Bird Girl" book cover was photographed. The tour droops in front of a tombstone of a young girl in a full button-down dress with her head tilted and her elbows on her hips and her hands out to the side holding bird feed bowls that look like the scales of justice.

Marion asks Jacqueline if she grew up in Savannah. She says, "Born and raised."

When asked, she tells Marion there are no more ghost tours until night, "after dark," she says.

They walk around a few more squares before registering for the Savannah St. Paddy's Parade next year on the way to buy night ghost tour tickets. There aren't any tour guides named Jacqueline, but there is one named Jackie.

Waiting down by the river for the tour to start, Marion reads a plaque that says the NS Savannah, built in Camden, which was the first nuclear powered merchant ship and was named after the SS Savannah, which was the first steamship to cross the Atlantic Ocean.

Marion immediately starts a conversation with the tour guide after her opening spiel about "using your cameras to capture images" to the 40 or so people in the crowd, including a wedding party after the rehearsal dinner. Marion tells her about the NS Savannah being built in Camden and she says in a pleasant tone, "I read the same plaque every night."

With Marion trailing Jackie 's every step on the night ghost tour of Savannah, they stop at the Colonial Cemetery. The lovely tour guide explains how headstones from the original burial ground behind the fence were reused by the indebted city as the sidewalks… and then Revolutionary War soldiers were buried on top of bodies with new headstones.

Turning and reaching to point to a tree in the graveyard, her back right shoulder reveals the top of a tattoo, of the head of a young girl.

Jackie asks the tour if anyone had a question.

Marion raises his hand from the back of the crowd, which is mostly families and the wedding party, and tells her, "I have a question but it was 'very deep.'" She says that's "just peachy because I'm a high school history teacher by day," while putting her hand on the graveyard gate's lock, and rattling it, scaring a few kids.

Marion asks, "If she knew why a fence was built around the cemetery?"

Jackie replies, "Oh… I thought you were going

to ask me about my tattoo… you keep staring at it…"

"Sorry," Marion says, "but the tattoo is fascinating…"

"That *she* is, which is why I keep *her* covered," she says. "What was your question again?"

"Oh… just why there is a fence around the grave yard… do you know why?"

"No, but do you?"

Taking a step into the pack of people, Marion informs her and the tour, "The fence is around the graveyard because people are dying to get in."

She starts laughing and falls into the grass around the fence. She pops up and says, "chiggers."

Marion asks if she was born in Savannah. She says, "No… near San Francisco… raised in Santa Cruz."

The next morning, the Three Horsemen drive 20 minutes to Tybee Island. The candy red car sticks out like the rising sun. Marion says he wants to "wake up the sleepy Savannah college kids on the main drag in the middle of summer to come out and play."

"Well, me will let them sleep a bit more since they must have studied late last night," Marion says standing at the end of a public pier jutting into the ocean, "and they left me baited fishing rods."

On the drive back into Savannah, Marion seethes the entire time about Jackie's tattoo, complaining why "would she do that to her sacred body… I wonder what is the rest of the… the young girl's head."

They wander down River Street and stop by the Paddlewheel Riverboat.

"Wish I could paddle back in time," Marion says.

"You can go back, like the Prodigal Son did," Cresty says, rubbing the top of Marion's head. "You are the Prodigal Father."

"Well," Marion smiles, "the Lord works in mysterious ways."

"Indeed," adds Choker, tugging on Cresty's long red ponytail, "Psalm 23."

"I will go back, but let's just do some Huck Finning around this day in downtown Savannah... done with adulting... the bathing and wearing a tie... the sitting up straight and speaking when spoken to... the not spitting for distance and cussin in front of company... yup tried to be civilized again last night but the suit didn't fit so Finning to the Territory Ahead... going down River in life."

They pull "ashore" at Kevin Barry's Pub.

"I think perhaps meself should retire here... and pull shipwrecks to shore for a sniff of the dark stuff and a whiff of laughter with us," Marion says, continuing his phony Irish accent. “Van Morrison asks me each afternoon ‘why don't we do this every day?’”

“I found my daughter,” Marion beams and then adds, “I just wish she didn’t desecrate her body with a tattoo.”

“I just wish,” Cresty says, swing her ponytail over her shoulder, “we can see the rest of her tattoo… someday.”

Chapter 22

Steam rises from the bay after an overnight thunderstorm rocked the marina. Cutting through the low-hanging haze, the sun is bright again this morning. So are Cresty and Choker after an early surf session. They wait outside Marion's boat, staring at the name Thomas Byrd while leaning against The Hearse.

"Who names their boat the Thomas Byrd? What are the chances? I know Rochambeau," Choker says, "you know with my last name being Byrd…"

Choker yells for Marion to come out. After a few minutes, Cresty screams for him.

"How did Marion meet his wife?" Cresty asks. "You said he told you at the hospital."

"Yeah, he was driving in Santa Cruz, leaving the hospital," Choker explains. "He was at the traffic light and the car to the left of him at the light had a young woman in the passenger seat. They started talking at the light. She was cute, and much younger. She told him she was going for her six-week follow up.

"The light changed. Cars were beeping behind. But he stuck out his hand and she wrote her number. He called and all that. Well that Friday night, he went to pick her up. When he rang the bell, the door open, but no one was there."

"He looked down and it was her. She was in a wheel chair. She had an ACL operation; she was a field hockey player at Cal-Berkley and tore up her knee."

"Well he meets her mom and dad, who were out visiting from back east at her off-campus apartment. They take turns driving her around to class; she had a tough major, biology. They tell him how they have been out here for six weeks, mostly alternating. They talked so long, they missed the movie starting time."

"So, Marion stops and gets wine. They go to the beach in Carmel. He takes her up to Pebble Beach golf course and Marion said shyly 'they started going at it, right in the 18th fairway bunker.' He said the dope made him feel guilty and he stared at the stars when she said she had to go, take a leak."

"He lifted her out of the bunker, grabbed her pants and underwear and started carrying her to the car. He said all of a sudden, she grabbed the branch of the Cypress tree in the middle of the fairway on the 18th hole. She hung on there and took a long leak."

"I like this chick," Cresty says.

"Marion took her back to the apartment and the dad was still up watching Letterman. The dad insisted Marion sit and watch Late Night. Marion said he felt all guilty and the pot just multiplied the guilt. The dad kept saying he was a great guy. To get the dad to stop complimenting him, he asked the mom if she wanted to see some card tricks. She was playing solitaire. The four of them sat around the table, the girl with her leg up in the brace on Marion's leg."

"The dad loved the card tricks. He kept telling Marion what a great guy he was. Marion felt more-guilty."

"Finally, Marion blurted 'I'm not a great guy.'

"The dad said, 'sure you are, son.'"

"Marion said, 'really, I'm not.'"

"The dad said, 'sure you really are, son.'"

"Marion said, 'no, really, I'm not.'"

"The dad said, 'you sure are son.'"

"Marion said, 'really, I'm really not.'"

"The dad said, 'sure you are, son, all the other guys out here left her hanging at the golf course on the tree.'"

Reaching inside The Hearse, Choker clicks on the music loud again, like yesterday as an alarm.

No Marion.

There is no Brennan either.

They check the boat. All his stuff is there. The Barney blanket is curled up on the bed. They go on deck and sit on bags of fertilizer stacked next to some boxes from Swain's, or Swan's Hardware store.

"He couldn't have," Choker says.

"Maybe he is up there at Stockton talking to the guard who makes bombs," Cresty says.

"Nah, mehr licht" Choker says. "He went to find more light."

"Goethe," Cresty smiles. "Perhaps he went to drink some of Hunter's wine."

"Maybe it's better this way," Choker says. "He was talking crazy, about bombing."

"Do you think he could've… like Pete?"

"He didn't change that much from wanting to save lives to take lives."

"He could've changed that much, you know. You did but the other way," she says. "You actually went from the Big Bang to the Big Crunch."

Walking through Utsch's parking lot and then down the pier, slumps Marion. He is carrying a small box - with BRENNAN written on the side - in his arms. He trips trying to get on the Byrd.

Ashes from the container scatter in the water.

"I had to put him to sleep across the street at Cape May Vets," he says. "I knew for weeks, it was bone cancer."

"We're sorry, why didn't you wake us, we would've gone with you like we did with Pete and his, our dog," Choker says. "He will go to heaven, like the Pope says."

"No, I'm sorry for you two. You just lost your baby. And you lost your dad," he says, patting Cresty's shoulder.

"Brennan's life is good too," Choker says. "All life is good."

"Well, he died good, the vet put him to sleep while I was holding him. I looked him in the eye till he closed them. He knows I didn't leave him.

"Like my baby," Cresty says.

"Let's take him to the canal and bury the rest of his ashes there," Choker says, scraping some ashes off the side of the container.

"Thanks, but I'm going to drop the rest right out front here where he used to poop, it's well fertilized and he loved the spot. I picked out a cornus florida rubra to plant."

"A pink dogwood tree," Choker says. "Good choice."

The digging goes quickly. Marion hangs Brennan's dog collar from the sapling. He then goes to The Hearse.

"I have the right song for the moment, it even has an animal's title, Wild Horses and he sings: "I know I dreamed you a sin and a lie, I have my friends but I don't have much time, faith has been broken, tears must be cried, let's do some living after we die."

"I loved Brennan, but I'm relieved he is gone. He was ill and I hated the name."

"Who was he named after?" Choker asks.

"Yeah, you name everyone after someone," Cresty adds.

"Chief Justice Brennan. He legalized abortion in 1973. I'm glad he is gone too now, but when I first became an abortionist, I started making money quick and easy and I got the big house because of CJ. I had no one in there so I got the dog and I named him Brennan because he's the guy that made me easy money. But now I know he legalized killing, I'm going to legalize blowing up abortion clinics. I bought the fertilizer and chemicals to make a bomb."

Cresty and Choker both grab Marion. Their horror is obvious to him.

"Marion, you are right, a terror generation has been borne out of abortion acceptance... and you are part of the terrorism," Choker says.

"I plan to get my truck back from Hunter and just park F150 where I usually do and let it blow on Monday morning."

"But, you love your truck," Cresty pleads. "And, anyway it is sacred remember? "It has probably the last working Fish Finder… beside The Hearse."

"Uh yeah, I don't want to destroy anyone else's property, but it is important. I'll stay in F-150 when she blows and ride straight to hell."

"How can you do that, I mean what is the difference between suicide and abortion?" Choker asks again. "Isn't killing, killing?"

"Perspectivism… I don't know anymore, the unborn can't be defended and they can't defend themselves," Marion moans. "I can't see clearly anymore… about anything, literally and figuratively. The gray area of what is life and what is not is getting grayer."

"It shouldn't be," Choker says. "It's not like these people at the clinic wronged you. Actually, Dr. Hyde likes you."

"Bam Bam, you mean… I'm dying anyway. The headaches are coming more often now. And I can barely see, it's only a matter of time before I see more light… mehr licht."

"Well since you can't foo-kin see, you can't drive The Hearse. I'm not driving, doing it."

Marion drops his head in his hands. He rubs real hard. Then soft. Then real hard.

"Sorry sir, this is for your own good," Choker says as he starts up The Hearse. Cresty nods in agreement as she slides into the passenger side.

"Where to?" Choker asks as he drives into town. "I just wanted to keep him away from these wheels."

"The lady," Cresty says. "Let's go see her."

Choker turns around at the railroad tracks, which cross in the middle of the projects on the right side of the road.

He slowly drives a block up past the old train depot, the final stop on the Cape May to Philadelphia line that runs straight up through The Villas and along the small bay towns for 60 miles to the big city.

The Hearse pokes over the Cape May Bridge and straight on Route 109. He stops at each traffic light. "What do we say?" he asks Cresty while making a looping left toward the ferry.

Choker drives down to the end of the road on the corner of Beach Avenue, to the blue house with pink-trimmed windows sitting on a diagonal facing the bay.

There is a minivan in the driveway. Across from the house, Choker parks on an angle.

Cresty dials. The lady, wearing another one-piece tennis outfit, answers. "You still have the minivan, huh?" Cresty says.

Choker and Cresty run toward the front door. The lady opens.

The three of them sit near the small white statue at the point of the front lawn.

"We saw, and met your baby," Cresty says, staring at the cherub with its hands cupped and open toward the sky.

The Hearse drives back to the boat, The Byrd. Choker pets Brennan's collar hanging on the newly planted pink dogwood tree.

"Marion," Cresty yells. Choker also screams, "Marion."

No Marion. They jump on board. Below, Marion is asleep, holding Row and Way.

Choker and Cresty dump the fertilizer overboard. When dumping, they see the name of the boat is changed. Painted. They shake Marion from a deep trance. He is holding the sitar from the F150.

"Why?" Choker asks. "Why change the name of his boat from the `Thomas Byrd" to the HR1122?"

"Simple as H-R-1-1-2-2," Marion spells out. "HR1122 is the president's veto act on the partial birth abortion ban."

Marion lets go of Row and Way. He continues, "It's no use trying to fight by writing to our senators and congressmen. I'm taking the HR1122 with me. I had a dream that in 16 years from now, society legalizes the killing of descendants of abortion docs, clinics, nurses, the drug manufacturers. Even friends. That would be justice. Chief Justice Brennan's gang better watch out."

Marion strums the sitar

"I don't want anyone to know we were friends. You will be safe. So, will your children. I could hear you dump the fertilizer. I guess I can't finish my job. I'll be going then. I will migrate with the Monarch butterflies.

"I always wanted to visit the Galapagos Islands."

"What are you taking up surfing?" Cresty says, humoring him. "There are some killer waves there."

"No, after living with the Monarchs in Mexico, I'm visiting the islands off Ecuador where Darwin developed his theory of the survival of the fittest. It's either that or joining an avalanche patrol in Lake Tahoe, but I can't see and I'm no good at saving people's lives."

Choker reads an 8-track cover on top of one of the boxes from the hardware store.

"Why not go? I'll never be one of the Stones," Marion rambles. "The Stones still make guys who can't dance, dance. They make guys with white-collared shirts and striped ties and tires for stomachs move and shake. They make middle age homemakers take off their bras and throw them on stage. And when the concert is over, they make a husband and wife turn and kiss like they were on their first date again. They are living, doing their thing at their age, and they are making people feel alive, they are life giving, and that is what life's about.

"I'm not alive anymore."

Choker struts over to Marion and shakes him. He hands him the 8-track. He points to a song.

"Stoned. It's an early Stones song, it is just an instrumental, no words," Marion says.

"Right, but what does that mean?

"He is pointing to the words 'Nanker Phelge.'"

"Oh, you didn't know? That is the nom de plume that Mick and Keith used to write some early Stones songs. 'Play with Fire' was written by Nanker Phelge, too."

"That's why I chose it as my email address, Nankerphelge@gmail which is why I knew it was more than Rochambeau that we'd be together after Uwrenski called you Phelge."

Marion smiles and whistles to the tune Play with Fire. He strums the sitar out of tune.

Outside by The Hearse, Choker bangs his head in his hands as Marion puts "Stoned" in the Fish Finder.

They listen. Marion is sort of dancing. Cresty is lying on the floor.

Why didn't you ever tell me? How come you didn't let me know what it meant? This isn't just a coincidence? You are right. This isn't just Rochambeau?

"This is much more isn't it?"

"I never said anything because I knew this, our lives, had to play out, together, No. From what you learned about the universe, there are no coincidences. God doesn't play rock, scissors paper. Mick and Keith didn't meet by coincidence either. They were put here to help me and you to save babies.

"That's the big picture in the Big Bang and the Big Crunch."

"You sure it can't be just a big dose or Rochambeau?" Cresty wonders. "This is too freaky."

"Not, gott würfelt nicht, neither," Marion says. "God does not play dice. God has made the Fish Finder to help us. He has made a Seal of the Fisherman between us."

Cresty says, “We met your ex-wife. We talked to her.”

Marion clicks on another song. No Expectations: “Take me to Savannah, put me on the train, I’ve got only expectations to see my daughter again, Once I was a rich man, now I am so poor, but never in my sweet, short life had I ever felt like this before.”

Chapter 23

As if in love, Choker and Cresty go chase butterflies. Marion says he is too tired. The Monarchs are migrating now in mid-August.

They stop at the Sunken Ship to see the butterflies and check on the army jacket man at the gift shop.

The store is closed. A sign says: GONE BIRDWATCHING AT THE POINTE.

The Super Bowl of bird watching runs now through the end of November. This is the height of bird watching season. The Atlantic Airway route of migratory birds, funnels over Cape May State Park.

The bird-viewing deck along the dunes near the lighthouse at Cape May Pointe is one of the best spots in North America to see migratory birds.

"More than 60,000 birds of prey migrate the Atlantic Flyway each autumn," the leader of the Audubon Society tells a pack of birders near Choker and Cresty.

On this muggy Sunday, 140 different birds are spotted overhead. To help "birders" identify birds, "counters" from the Audubon Society shout out the species flying overhead.

Worldwide authorities on birds can be seen counting at Cape May. Officially, the experts first started in 1976 counting on the dunes at The Pointe before the construction of wooden structures, which hold hundreds of birdwatchers.

Looking for Vane, they see a familiar looking guy wearing a turban. Looking through the binoculars, he tells Cresty and Choker that he saw "more cooper's hawks fly than in all of 1976" this weekend.

He is the parking guard from Stockton, where Choker last fought in judo before taking the summer off.

"Hey it's you, "Cresty says, "Nivek Nahalac. Don't you surf anymore?

"I'm a b-man now. Ask me anything about the B's. I'm a birder now," he says.

"B is for bird?" Cresty asks.

"What did you think?"

"Bomb," she states as if she is simply naming a bird. "You talked about getting fertilizer for..."

"For the trees," he says. "To fertilize the young trees… so the birds have a home to live."

"Where's the old guy, Marion?" he asks.

"He's gone," Cresty says.

"Gone?"

"Well, going," Choker says.

"Tell him to stop and see me here, I can teach him… things… how during the months from

September to November, there are 'epic days' - to see hawks, eagles, falcons, vultures and other birds of prey.

"The park here is called the Raptor Capital of North America because of its bird-watching reputation. But in addition to providing birders a hobby, the migratory birds are counted for scientific reasons, too. That's what I do.

"Hawks, for instance, are predators perched at the top of the food chain, so a change in their population has an effect."

Cresty drifts away, looking toward the ocean. "She doesn't seem to want to hear about predators and the population of birds," Choker says. "Not after her loss."

But Choker listens. Another voice interrupts next to him.

"Although it's difficult to predict the traffic of the birds south, one clue to look for early in the season is whether a cold front has come through the previous night. The cold air sparks the birds' desire and interest in traveling to warmer spots," Vane tells them.

"Birdwatchers look for clear conditions so you can see high above where the birds often hover before flying across the Delaware Bay.

"Although autumn is the best time to see

migratory birds, there's never a time when birds are not migrating.

"One of the reasons Cape May State Park is so renowned for bird watching is because many of the birds hover, before flying over a large body of water, like the one between Cape May and Delaware."

Choker and Cresty stay all day after their birding lesson… and night. They sleep on the spot they did with Marion not long ago.

"We seem to be hovering, too," Cresty says, "like the birds above."

When they awake, even before the sun is up, there are already a dozen birders with cameras and binoculars at the ready. Both the man, Nivek, in the turban and Vane in the army jacket, lift their binos in birding position.

Hawks, maybe a dozen, circle above the bay.

"The food chain must be healthy," Choker says, shaking Cresty to head out. "The strong eat the weak.

"We should go eat. We should go protect the weak."

They drive The Hearse back to the HR1122 without stopping to for food.

"Where's the boat," Cresty screams.

Choker drives to the end of the marina.

The boat is gone.

In the slip, the red boat is docked, The rich man, Daddy Starbucks, stands at the pulpit.

"Where's the boat?" Cresty yells to him out the window.

"The pier owners said the owner shipped out abruptly yesterday afternoon. I was on the waiting list. I came early this morning and rented the vacant slip. I needed to be closer to the action. I was docked way out past Dividing Creek… on Money Island where the tides, the water levels, are rising…

"The pier owners said your blind pirate did leave cargo, a cage, with a note there on the dock."

Cresty and Choker both sprint, stumbling onto the dock. There is a handwritten note taped to a book on the cage with Row and Way. The Aviator sunglasses hang from the cage, below a thick book. With the rich man staring, they haul Marion's cargo back to The Hearse.

Gasping, Choker reads:

"Studies have shown that a fetus is able to learn and remember things during the last six weeks in the womb. Babies show a greater familiarity with songs that they have heard from a microphone pressed to the mother's belly. That is why one-day old infants respond more strongly to their mother's voice than to a stranger.

"Tell Cresty to play music to your baby… the next time. There will be a next time. Play Lady Jane, that's one of my favorite Stones songs."

Choker and Cresty sit inside The Hearse with the rabbits. He puts on Fish Finder. It plays Lady Jane. He continues to read:

"Congress talked about repealing the Hyde Amendment and allow the federal funding of abortions for decades. The amendment's defeat would allow taxpayer money to be used for abortions. That would mean your tax dollars would be spent on killing babies.

"The new immigration law Obama pushed through allows the undocumented to receive care from Planned Parenthood, which is funded by tax money, which means we pay for abortions.

"I can't kill anymore," Choker continues, "I had to migrate," before handing the note to Cresty.

She reads: "Anyone who accepts killing babies is barbaric. You know that. But, you also know there is a larger reason why you can't let the killing to continue. We didn't meet by Rochambeau."

Choker turns off Lady Jane as Cresty reads more, "I did indeed go off to Mexico with the Monarchs, then perhaps the Galapagos Islands. But we know only the strong survive, of course… and this country doesn't allow the weak, the dying to die with dignity, to pass on with the help of doctors."

Choker studies the 8-track cover of Stoned.

"He knows he will never get there," Cresty says. "He can't see. He had no food. He went out to sea to die."

Leaning over Cresty and the rabbits, Choker reads the end of the letter: "Go find some lost girls who need your help. Help them, like you helped me find my girl.

"We are one, with love, Nanker Phelge."

Choker slaps down the note on the American History book, next to where the note was taped. It's opened to a page with the two words highlighted: Thomas Byrd. Choker reads, "Really, what's the fookin chance, the odds that Byrd is my name, too? Rochambeau?"

Cresty looks over his shoulder and reads from the book:

"Thomas Byrd was the first man executed in the United States. He was hung in Portland, Maine. He was just 22 years old and was in jail for a year before meeting the gallows. That year, he became a dear friend of the jailer and his family, six children. The jailer would leave his kids alone with him to play.

"On the morning of his execution, the family cried saying good-byes, especially the kids. They didn't understand why he was hung. They could not go and watch. Byrd was hung because he was accused of mutiny on the high seas. He stuck to his story that he never killed the captain of his sailing vessel. It was a gang killing, but he admitted he never stopped it."

Damn, that sounds familiar.

Choker grabs the letter and reads Marion's manifesto: "Thomas Byrd's killing started the lawful execution of Americans. The Roe vs. Wade ruling just continued the lawful killing of babies. What Amendment will be next? We already have the Oregon law where old people can be axed legally. Will that law become the law of the country? Now they are looking at cloning embryos for stem cells. When will the killing end? But we can't be assisted in killing ourselves?"

Chapter 24

Choker and Cresty speed toward Avalon. "What would Pete do?" they say to each other.

The August late afternoon son is scorching. Cresty sits in The Hearse. Choker sits on the white fence by the basketball courts. He cuts his hand on the fence. His blood drips on the bloodstain already there.

Choker talks to Catrina - still a perfect lady - pushing her kid in a swing. They talk about the race riots in Ferguson.

"Nice wheels," she says. "Last we talked… last summer… you were red-face pissed for a black guy about the Trayvon Martin case in Florida, remember?"

"You look much older now. You look worried."

Catrina tells Choker she is a lawyer besides "still having perfect boobs."

"Do you need help dealing with the race riots in Ferguson?"

"Maybe," Choker says. "Confused… just came up here to think, to find the Righting Moment here… not having the energy to think about Ferguson…"

"Well," the lawyer lady continued, "the Brown v. Board of Education Supreme Court decision in 1954 that declared states which established separate schools for blacks was unconstitutional," she said pushing her kid wearing a Notre Dame sweat shirt on the swing. "The decision overturned the Plessy v. Ferguson decision of 1896 which allowed state sponsored segregation in public schools."

"Ironic, huh? Plessy v Ferguson and now race riots in Ferguson, Missouri. Or just luck, huh?"

"No such thing as Rochambeau, not gott würfelt nicht neither," Choker says as he wanders over and shoots baskets with a young kid wearing a Larry Bird jersey. They knuckle punch.

"How is your shot?" Choker asks the 12-year-old or so kid, who shoots an air ball.

"Remember I told you, a few months ago, back in April, the last time I was here… how you have to shoot into the wind," Choker says, sounding like Byrd again. "You got to use the resistance to get to your goal."

The kid dribbles down to the other end of the court where the wind blows in his face.

"You can't let anything stop you from reaching your goal," Choker says, following him. "You know life is really like the last seconds of a tied basketball game… a game you train your entire life to win… but the other team has the ball… so you defend like a madman… force a tough shot… you, box out like your life's goals depend on getting the rebound…

exhausted, you somehow fight to pull down the ball in a pack… there is not any time to think… you start to dribble up the court… using all your moves you ever practice, the spin dribble, behind the back, around the back, stutter step, between the legs, just to get around the defenders… but there are two more at the foul line… exhausted, you use the spin dribble, behind the back, around the back, stutter step, between the legs, just to get around the last two defenders… you are at the basket… you have your shot to justify your existence… you take your shot…"

"Does it go in?" the kid asks as Choker bounces back to The Hearse, turning around to say," Doesn't matter… you did everything you could to take your shot… you took your shot."

Choker squeezes the steering wheel.

"You cut your hand here," Cresty says, pointing to the blood smeared on the steering wheel. "That's no Rochambeau. You are one with Marion … and Pete."

Choker runs in a circle around the court. He goes out and lies in the middle of the field. Cresty follows.

"Don't be sad," she says.

"I'm sad about Marion. I'm sad because Marion never got to meet the Stones. I'm sad because Marion wanted to be buried where the picture for the cover of Hot Rocks was shot. It looked like a castle. It looked like a good place to lie to rest."

"Hey, if you can't be buried in a castle," Cresty says, "floating off to sea was a noble way to go."

Choker smiles and spits in the grass.

"I know, he didn't live like he wanted, but he is dying the way he wanted."

They both run back to The Hearse holding hands and drive right to the clinic. Choker knocks on the front door. No answer. He goes in. He comes out with Dr. Hyde. They walk to The Hearse. He gives her Row and Way.

"I know you wanted these bunnies, they are yours."

"Well, thank you, Choker. The rabbits are beautiful."

"So is our universe," Choker says. "Take care of them."

"I know, but why did you say that?" Dr. Hyde says.

"The Earth and moon circle the sun," Choker spouts. "The sun circles the core of the galaxy at 175 miles per second. The Milky Way galaxy is hurling around other galaxies. There is a lot going on out there. What makes this planet different? Life.

"That's all."

"That is why I want pets," Dr. Hyde says. "People don't kill them. My husband and six-month old son were blown up at the Twin Towers. I had to move down here, near my older brother... and help other girls not go through the same pain."

"I'm so sorry," Cresty says. "That's too fookin sad."

"My mom went through the same pain," she continues sniffing. "Her oldest son was drafted and went to Vietnam. He came back in one piece, but had PTSD before they even knew what posttraumatic stress disorder even was.

"He has spent his life dying, watching birds at The Pointe and selling old shit at the gift shop by the sunken ship and trying to raise funds to raise the Atlantus."

"We know Vane," Cresty says. "He's a good guy."

"He could've been a great guy. A family guy. A father," the doctor says. "Yes. No, this world isn't safe for people let alone beautiful babies. I'm helping girls keep their babies from being hurt.

"Hey, where is Marion?"

Choker pounds his chest.

"He is here," Choker says.

Dr. Hyde looks confuse as she pets the rabbits.

"By the way, did you ever hear of the Hyde Amendment?" Choker asks?"

Dr. Hyde points to her nametag.

"Of course, and it's not named after me, if that is what you are thinking. It is, what do you guys say, Rochambeau, just luck of the draw that was have the same name."

"No such thing as Rochambeau, not gott würfelt nicht neither. Gotta split."

Dr. Hyde stands with her mouth open. There is dry saliva connected from the top of her lips to the bottom. She holds the rabbits tight. She watches Choker rev up The Hearse and hears him puts on Fish Finder to Street Fighting Man and sings:

"Everywhere I hear the sound of stabbing, changing feat boy, 'cause summer is here and the time is right for fish finding in the street boy."

Chapter 25

After Doc Hyde goes inside, The Hearse turns around at the illegal crossover on the Parkway, into Madame Palm's place.

Cresty goes inside Madame Palm's while Choker waits in The Hearse alone. He sees a familiar girl, the lone girl wearing baggy basketball shorts, the ones Cresty used to wear who knocked furiously on the side door just when Marion cut the power lines. She is bigger when they saw her on the quick drive-by.

Choker approaches her. Intercepting her in the parking lot of Madame Palm's.

"You want to listen to the Stones," Choker asks nervously. "I'm not trying to pick you up."

"Get lost."

"Don't do it. I can help."

"Don't even talk to me."

Choker clicks on Fish Finder as she hurries to the clinic. He turns the Stones up and sings: "Have you seen your mother, baby, doubting in the shadow, will you have another baby, doubting in the shadow, I hope I open your eyes."

She goes in the front door of the clinic. Choker waits in the front seat. Some time goes by.

After an hour, Choker goes in the side door. He sees an opening in one room. He goes in the room. He washes his hands and leaves. The halls are empty. One room has a "Do Not Disturb" sign. He goes in.

Dr. Hyde is in front of the girl, who is under anesthesia. Her legs are in the air in ropes. Dr. Hyde turns around when the door shuts. Choker puts his index finger up to his mouth, shushing her.

"No one is allowed in here. What do you want? Take the rabbits back, just get the hell out of here."

"I'm here to help. This is your Righting Moment."

Choker approaches her. He puts his hands under her neck.

"This is the juji-jimi, it's a front choke in case you ever need it to fight off the devil."

"You don't have to choke me out. She drops the scissors she is holding on the floor. The baby's head is visible. Choker picks up the scissors."

"If I was still living in the gray days, I would kill your baby for you. But, I know better. Life is life. Fish Finder here is going to save a fish and throw it back."

Choker pulls hard, then soft, and then hard again. He delivers the baby without any trouble. The girl is woozy and is speaking weirdly. Choker opens the scissors. He cuts the umbilical cord. Dr. Hyde ties the cord.

The baby is breathing.

"Don't cry yet," Chokers says to the baby.

Choker wraps the baby in a sheet and leaves the room. Still no one is in the hall. The path to the side door is open. Dr. Hyde opens the door for him.

He goes outside. It is raining.

"It's a good day to be a Fish Finder for babies."

Inside The Hearse, Cresty stares at her right palm. Without looking up, she says, "Madame Palm said I would get a baby."

Choker hands the baby, wrapped in the white sheet, to her. He starts up The Hearse.

Chapter 26

The next morning, Choker carries the baby from the butterfly boat, the one he used to work at before he ever met Marion. The boat hasn't been used for fishing since Choker left. But the frig is stocked with food.

There is fresh fruit on the captain's chair with decorative dandelions, freshly picked, in the bowl.

Mr. Hallward appears on the dock. "Hey, I knew you would be back. I hope you ate. I did have to hire a new guy, but he doesn't start until tomorrow. You both can still sleep on the boat."

"Thanks, sir," Choker says politely.

"I had my law enforcement pals do checks on Marion Francis, too, just like Francis Marion before, but none were found," Mr. Hallward says. "I used Promis Gavel to check for charging documents and charging disposition, Motor Vehicle for his Drivers Abstract, did a NCIC warrant check for a criminal history in both single state and multi states, I searched for a FBI number or a SBI number."

"I checked ACS for a complaint summary, a narrative, or a payment and checked FACTS for juvenile 2:C charges, but nothing," he adds, walking away.

"Did you check his real name?" Choker asks, "Nanker Phelge?"

With Mr. Hallward left scratching his head, The Hearse drives away. The baby lies on Cresty's lap where Row and Way used to sit. They drive to Devils Reach.

"Thanks for the baby," Cresty says.

"Your welcome," Choker smiles.

"We can make a baby again," Cresty says. "This baby should go to… is for… is for… you know who…"

"No," Choker wails. "Not fair, for you."

Choker shuts his eyes after Cresty hands him the baby.

Cresty reaches over to pat the baby in the front seat as she gets out. The baby is asleep in a blanket.

Some time goes by before Choker goes up to two surfers kneeling by their boards sharing a joint.

"Where's Cresty? She said told me she wanted a quick romp in the waves."

"Dude, she is gone," the first surfer says. "I think for good."

"Yeah, bro, she just started paddling out past the breakers. We went out after her, but she said she wanted to paddle."

"Don't worry, man," the other surfer says. "She said she'd be Okay. I'm not worried, bro."

"She looked happy man," the one surfer says. "Said she was going to Rochambeau."

"I never surfed there, bro. I surfed Half Moon Bay, Waimea Bay in Hawaii and Todos Santos off Ensenada, Mexico, but never Rochambeau," the other surfer says.

"Don't even know where it's at."

"No one does," Choker says.

Choker gets in The Hearse and drives over the Cape May Bridge and straight on Route 109. He doesn't stop at any traffic lights. He makes a left. He drives toward the ferry.

He drives down to the end of the road on the corner of Beach Avenue, to the blue house with pink-trimmed windows sitting on a diagonal facing the bay.

There is a minivan in the driveway. Choker parks hastily, but straight across from the house. Staring at the bay, he takes the crying baby's head out of the sheet. He kisses the roaring baby's cheek.

"She still has the minivan, huh?"

Choker runs up toward the front door.

He stares at a small white statue at the point of the front lawn, the ornament of a baby angel. The cherub has its hands cupped and open toward the sky and its legs are crossed. The birdbath behind the angelic statue is on its side laying broken.

He places the baby in the small wooden boat now used as flowerpot on the side lawn.

Choker stops, and stares. The cherub's wings are wide. A seashell is placed in the statue's lap. The John Deere hat is still on the baby statue's head.

He slowly turns and walks back to The Hearse, saying to himself, "Indeed, Kilroy was here."

Choker is shaking.

Choker drives down the road. He speeds up Lincoln Boulevard and crosses the canal. He speeds up the dirt path to the hill overlooking the bay and the canal. He whizzes over and stands near the dandelions. He fixes the flowers and the tree saplings. He pats the sand where the seed was planted.

Choker dials Cresty's cell phone.

He can see the house.

He hears the lady's voice. He can see the lady step out the front door in her tight tennis outfit.

Choker says, "Read the note."

She reads the revised words from the Stones single, Good times, bad times: "We had our good times, we had our bad times, I have my share of dread times too, but you lost your faith in our world honey when I hurt you," love Nanker.

"This, the baby in the flower pot, is from your husband."

"Where is he? Who are you?"

"On his way to the edge of a black hole somewhere. He would want this for you. He won't ever be back here, but I'll see him someday."

The baby screams. She races over to the flowerpot.

"When you see him, say I'm sorry too," she says, holding the baby. "Tell him I am lucky to have a baby to love."

"No Rochambeau, not Gott würfelt nicht neither. There is nothing lucky about you having a baby. God does not play scissors, paper stone or dice."

Choker clicks off the cell phone. He drives in The Hearse back over the canal bridge.

"Life can be like a sunken concrete ship," Choker says to himself. "Sometimes relationships just can't be salvaged… but life can."

He drives back into Cape May to Utsch's Marina. No sign of Cresty. He can see the lady, the one who Marion aborted her baby, out front playing with her new baby.

He sits on the rich man's empty red boat and watches.

The sky turns dark.

He drives back to the dune across from the cherub house. He sees Nanker's …Marion's wife rocking with the baby through a window.

He lies next to the grave of his baby.

"I will be with you some day. With you and Marion."

With one dandelion dangling in his mouth, Choker drives back to the butterfly boat.

"I must save the fish out there who will be caught tomorrow."

He dives in the water and swims to the other boats. The bait boxes are hanging in the water. He cuts them lose. He does this to every boat in the harbor.

He goes over to the nets hanging in the water. He pulls out a knife from the fishing box and gets ready to cut the net. Inside the net is a fish, conjoined at the head.

"He pulls the fish out of the net and throws into the water. He climbs on board his old boat with the Butterfly. He then paints HR1122 on the side with the blood of the blue fish bait on board.

"This will remind everyone to write to their congressmen and women to vote to ban partial birth abortions," he says to no one.

Choker stands on top of the deck and screams.

"I'm out of this, I did all I can. Like Mick said, 'what can a poor boy do?'"

Choker fakes strumming a guitar.

"Tomorrow, I'm going back to judo," he says to himself. "No more Fish Finding for me. Marion will understand. I found one. When Cresty comes back, I'll be in school. She'll be f-in proud."

Choker walks to The Hearse and clicks on Fish Finder. The song, the Last Time, plays. Choker sings along: "Well, I'm sorry girl who I can't sway, feeling like I do today, it is too insane and too much horror, guess I'll feel the same sad sorrow, this will be the last rhyme, this will be the last crime…"

Choker drifts asleep in the front seat with the music playing. A young kid goes to the boat of his old boss. The kid is slamming things around on the boat. It is gray out. Choker slides down the hill. He grabs a handful of sand and throws it into the wind. Some of the sand blows back. He picks up another handful of sand.

He walks up the pier to the boat. The late teenage kid is looking up toward the skies. Choker approaches him with his hands out and cupped up.

"Dude, this is my first day, what should I do, should I fish or not. My boss will be pissed if I go out, and have to come right back because of the rain and waste all that gas and has to pay me for a half day. Damn, what should I do?"

Choker smiles, shakes his head, sticks out his hand.

"What's your name?"

"Taylor."

Choker's eyes pop open in amazement.

"Don't tell me your first name is Mick, as in Mick Taylor of the Stones, the guy who replaced Brian Jones and then for some crazy reason left the greatest band?"

"No, just Johnny, as in John Taylor."

Choker tries to jump into the boat. One foot goes in the water. The sand he has in his hand spills into the bay. He pulls himself on board. He sits down near the steering wheel. He puts his feet up.

"Quit. Quit this job and come with me."

"And do what? I need money for college. My Dad used to be a teacher but he got expelled or something and I need the money."

"Be a Fish Finder."

"I do that now. Just not well."

"Right. You know what Keith would do right now?"

"Who is Keith?"

"He would want to be a Fish Finder if he knew about it. He would join us. Shake it here. This will join us as one. It is the Seal of the Fisherman."

"How is the pay?"

"Better than money. You can't bring the stuff with you anyway."

"What will we do that is better than money?"

"All we will do is find as many fish as we can and throw them back into the ocean."

"That ain't hard, but you ain't going to make any money doing that. You might get f-in shot."

"We won't need any money, just when the Stones put out a new 8-track, we'll need some loot to buy it."

"What's an 8-track? Who are the Stones?"

"You'll learn. You'll be a rich man."

"Sounds like I'm a lucky man to meet you."

"No Rochambeau, not Gott würfelt nicht, neither."

They walk up the hill to The Hearse. Choker starts showing him the chokehold. They hear a voice off in the harbor. It is Cresty paddling to them. She paddles to the beach. Hoists the board on her back and carries it with two hands behind her back and up the hill. She looks right at the boy.

"This here is Johnny Taylor, the grandson of John Taylor, perhaps, the Father of the Big Crunch."

Cresty drops the board. Then hops into her surfing pose. She shakes her head and smiles.

"No Rochambeau."

Choker slides into The Hearse and clicks on the Fish Finder. They all sit down on the hill and watch the sun break out above the clouds. Below, on the marina's small beach, is a young couple with an infant playing in the surf.

As an unfamiliar song plays, Choker says, "This is Marianne Faithful, she was Mick - and Keith's - girlfriend at one time. She could sing too. This is what she sang at the Stones' Rock N Roll Circus on Dec. 11, 1968, it is called 'Something Better.'"

For the final chorus, Choker sings: "Say hey, have you heard Fish Finding is the rage, I will send you a hug in the morning, it is all right to live in a cage, you know the mask isn't something better."

Chapter 27

With their arms around each other, connected by more than names linking people and seemingly coincidental events, Choker and Cresty drive past the clinic. There is a John Deere hat hanging on the back post of the empty bench outside the clinic's door.

He wheels down the sandy road winding between Willow Creek Winery and Rea's Farm. The grape vines on both sides are tangled and overgrown, wrapped around posts on both sides of the narrow path. Choker drives through the green tunnel of vine leaves, scrapping both sides of The Hearse before stopping in front of the white shed.

With only a nod, Hunter gives him keys, tied to the end of a leafy vine, and points to the shed where the white truck rests inside with a bottle of Goethe wine on the hood.

On the door is painted NANKER PHELGE, surrounded by a black rose.

With the summer crowd waning as kids head back to school, Choker drives the truck right onto the ferry without waiting in a line. The motorcycle isn't strapped in the back anymore and the Fish Finder is still broken.

Slumped in between Choker and Cresty, Taylor examines the Fish Finder, holding a wire not attached to anything under the dashboard.

"That's my Fish Finder," Choker says proudly. "You're a fisherman, right? You should know what they are for."

"I know what a fish finder looks like, and this ain't one," Taylor snaps.

Choker looks away and rubs his eyes with both hands as if he is wiping away a maddening memory.

"He just calls it a Fish Finder for some silly reason," Cresty injects.

"Some might call this an 8-track player, but to me it is a Fish Finder," Choker says. "When we used to play music, good things happened."

Under the piercing wail of the ship's whistle, they embark on the ferry to Delaware. Leaving the canal, they can't see a missing rock in the jetty anymore. A gray rock fills the hole, mixing with the black ones.

The ferry motors pass debris in the water below. Standing on the bow, they see a deflated aqua gray rubber raft and a blue gray rubber dolphin with its fin slashed off, leaving a gash, floating ahead. They turn and rush to the back of the boat, the stern. They look in the ferry's wake for the raft and the rubber dolphin, but the water is empty.

"I hear someday you will be able to take a ferry from Lewes to Camden New Jersey," Choker says. "From there you have a view of Philadelphia, where it all began…

"Where the Constitution was written and where the Declaration of Independence was written. Where are forefathers said all men are created equal...

"Just not the unborn."

The ferry, still basking in its 50th anniversary year, glides across the bay without resistance or worries.

"We never got to see the great De-rek Je-ter play in his last season," Cresty says.

"Yeah, no we didn't," Choker says softly, "there will never be another De-rek Je-ter."

They do see the inviting view across the bay, where the land ahead always seems better than the shore you leave.

Perspectivism.

No, there are no laws to say you can't dream of a better life on the other side even if the land ahead is only better because life's *sunken ships* can't be salvaged on the land you are leaving.

The wake behind the ferry divides the water evenly. The ripples just roll on, touching both shores with the same harm and with the same care, endlessly covering the Atlantus… and Atlantis.

Chapter 28

In Delaware, the first state, they drive south, pulling off of I-95 to take a leak near Bear, where a dude riding a new bike gets a flat tire and tosses the entire bicycle over a spiked-metal fence and into the high grass of an un-kept graveyard.

They stop at Dover where the interstate is backed up with campers going to the NASCAR race. They turn toward the city, the capital. They sit in front of the Georgian-style Old State House where a husband and wife who look alike push a baby carriage filled with thick hardback books.

"Let's go find our sunken ship," Choker says.

"We can salvage him," Cresty says.

On I-95 South, they drive through the night and pass countless motorcycle gangs before they reach the Georgia border at dawn when Cresty says, "they are anti-society, but all dress the same."

Driving in the middle of the twin towers across the Talmadge Memorial Bridge, with a barge packed to the captain's deck with tractor trailer containers, they spot Marion's boat docked on a Savannah River pier outside of Kevin Barry's pub.

Inside, the bartender tells them Marion spends his mornings here drinking 'seagull milk" and making up words to Stones' songs on the jukebox and his afternoons and evenings going on ghost tours, but this morning Marion told him he was going "gumping."

They connect with Marion at the Savannah History Museum, sitting on the bench where Gump sat. He is reading Vonnegut's Tomorrow and Tomorrow and Tomorrow.

"If you could take a pill and live forever, would you?" he asks. "Would you want to be 172 years old, living in a three-room flat in New York City on the 76th floor of Building 257 with 20 relatives who call you Gramps?"

"No," Cresty says, "but if they called me Grammy…"

"Hey Smiles," Marion says, looking up at Choker, "why you smiling?"

"We figured you'd be here," Choker says, 'either here or Jerome, Arizona, trying to resurrect the old mining town in the desert."

On the ghost tour of Savannah, their third stop is at the Colonial Cemetery where a lady with shoulder white hair, like an English judge's wig, is talking into her cell phone, but talking with both hands so she needs to keep repeating herself. Jackie patiently waits for her to finish before she explains how headstones from the original burial ground behind the fence were "reused by the indebted city as the sidewalk and then Revolutionary War soldiers were buried on top of bodies with new headstones."

Jackie asks the tour if anyone has a question. Marion raises his hand from the back of the crowd and tells her, "I have a question… but it 'was very deep.' She says that's 'just peachy because I'm a high school history teacher by day.'"

Marion asks, "If she knew why a fence was built around the cemetery?"

Jackie replies, "I do... whew, I thought you were going to ask me about Higgs boson and how the universe would be cold, dark and lifeless without the God particle…

"But do you know why a fence surrounds the cemetery?" she asks playfully.

Moving toward the front of the pack, Marion informs the tour "the fence is around the graveyard because people are dying to get in."

She feigns an amusing laugh and flops into the grass around the fence.

"Watch out for chiggers," Marion pleads, reaching for her shoulder, brushing away her hair covering the top of her tattoo.

At night, they go back to the ghost tour. Jackie isn't there.

They go to a brewery where a motorcycle gang guy looks like Marion.

"Cool catchin' up with this Doppelgänger guy," Marion says leaving, "the double dude said plurality is better for beers and people... but this couplin' creep smelled twice as bad as meself and wasn't nearly as multiple schizophrenic."

They go back to Bonaventure Cemetery. They walk around, illuminating the hanging moss with their cell phone lights.

"I saw him again shadowing here with the other ghosts of Savannah at Midnight in the Garden of Good and Evil," Marion says to himself while walking out of the cemetery.

The next day, they visit the Sisters of Mercy School and the home of Juliette Low, the founder of the Girl Scouts. They stop at the Great Indian Trading Road, which is also called The Philadelphia Path.

At night, they go back to the tour.

Again, Jackie isn't there.

Under his breath, Marion calls the elderly lady with the judge's white wig look who is giving the tour a "toothless, bearded hag."

Marion demands to wait for the 9 o'clock tour to see if Jackie is working. "I will wait with you," Choker says with sudden compassion.

"I will look around town for her," Cresty says, walking away, pulling moss from a tree and wrapping the weed around her neck like a scarf. "Good fookin luck."

The 9 o'clock tour starts with the "toothless, bearded hag" leading the pack out of the square as Marion's cell rings – the screen photo is Cresty.

A man's voice says, "Sir, this is officer Tilton, you have to go right to the hospital."

"What? Is Cresty ok? Tell me she is Ok…"

"Sir, you have to go right to St. Joseph's Hospital on Mercy Boulevard – now!"

Driving wildly, Marion cuts off the tour crossing the street. The "toothless bearded hag" types the license plate number in her cell. Marion steams as the candy red car idles at a traffic light that is green since a horse carriage with a family of four pokes across the intersection.

"Whip that horse," Marion orders the cart driver.

"You know, on your death bed, you probably will never remember all the hours being stuck in traffic in your life… but I'll remember this one," Choker reasons.

Cutting off a horse carriage with a newlywed couple, Marion sings out the window: "I see a red floor and I want it painted black, no colors anymore I want time to turn back, I see the girls walk by dressed in their surgery clothes, I have to save the dead until the darkness goes."

In the emergency room, Marion and Choker freeze when they see the stone somber faces of the ambulance drivers and nurses.

"I guess, Cresty is in God's hands now," Marion says calmly to Choker, who drops to his knees. "Indeed, "mysterious ways…

"Psalm 23," Marion continues solemnly as Cresty bursts through the swinging doors.

"Hurry," she says, "Jackie is in a coma."

"How could God do this to me," Marion screams as the three of them run back through the swinging doors that haven't closed yet.

Outside of the curtain in intensive care, Cresty explains: "I found her slumped on a bench in the Gump park… Chippewa Square… tried to stir her… she was unconscious so started carrying her… cop saw me and called 9-1-1… I jumped in ambulance and asked cop to call you… doc told me her oxygen level in blood is down to 60 percent… needs to be 300 for normal…"

Marion washes his trembling hands in the emergency room, using the dispenser on the wall. Wiping his hands, he uses his 'doctor card' to confer with the emergency room doc, a middle-aged man with a round face. Dr. Bell tells them how "the chiggers caused meningitis."

Jackie had lapsed into a coma.

"She is in a black hole," the doctor says. "We don't know anything more…"

"A black hole isn't mysterious, although we don't know much more about the holes in space as the ones in Middle Earth," Marion rambles, but in his confident professorial tone. "We do know that there are giant black holes in our universe and on their extreme edges, time actually stands still."

The doc says, "She needs medication but her adopted parents can't be contacted."

Marion tells the doc, "I'm her real father."

The doc asks for proof.

He can't prove he's her father.

"I need her in my life now," Marion says.

The Doc explains how she is a Mennonite. Says she refused medication before lapsing into the coma.

"The Mennonites believe… they have strict laws," the hesitant doc says.

"Force her… IV her, inject the meds," Marion orders, shaking the doc's shoulders.

"But, Marion," Cresty injects. "Just think for a moment, the earth and moon orbit around the sun, the sun travels 175 miles a second around the center of the Milky Way galaxy, and our galaxy is circling under the influence of other galaxies in the universe as it expands.

“That's a lot of movement. And, unlike man, which forces laws on people, laws that kill other people, gravity rules not by force, but by inducement, or persuasion.

“Man doesn’t rule by anything but force,” she continues, kicking both feet in the air.

“Gravity lays convenient paths for planets and galaxies to travel through time. We are traveling through time, just like the planets. It’s just that we flow in God's time.”

“Yeah, I told you, Pete taught us a Greek word for God’s time,” Choker adds, “Kairos.”

“Let gravity play out,” Cresty adds.

Marion slumps against the wall. He slides to the floor.

“I tried to talk her into taking meds,” the doc says, “but she mumbled ‘aborted babies come back reincarnated to kill’ and lapsed into coma.”

Marion washes his trembling hands in the emergency room waiting area, wiping incessantly and reciting…

“In the grayness of life, we’re all splashing, but not all of us are swimming… “

He rubs his hands real hard and then soft and hard again. He continues, “Some of us find fish in life’s pool, some even save fish… protect… from the ones who eat fish.”

He lies on the hallway floor, flanked on either side by Choker and Cresty, flopping fitfully through the night.

"I know," Marion screams, waking up at dawn. "She can't take meds, but she can take natural ingredients. You know, the viola sororia, the violet flower, contain antioxidants, which contain cyclotides… used as anti-HIV, anti-insecticidal and anti-microbial agents."

Marion sits and picks at his toenails. He peels the top of each toenail, trimming them with his thumb and forefinger. He cups the clippings in his right hand as he jumps to his feet and screams, "give her viola sororia…"

A weary Dr. Bell stares through the glass of the swinging door. His eyes tell them Jackie has died.

Falling on his knees, spilling his toenails onto the tile floor, Marion screams… but there is no sound.

He rolls up in a ball on the floor.

"I didn't have the choice to help her," Marion then laments. "The doc gave me no choice."

"We need… a pink bag…" Choker says as Cresty reaches to console Marion and says, "Extra-large."

Jumping up on his bare feet, scattering his toenail clippings on each side of the hallway, Marion sprints through the swinging doors and into the intensive care unit. He turns the corner and sees the doctor rolling Jackie's body over.

He slumps against her bed.

Choker and Cresty help him to his shaking feet. He says, "I already had planted a sapling on the dune for her… never knowing I would find her."

Using the hand dispenser next to her bed, Marion washes his trembling hands, wiping incessantly.

Between the untied medical gown Marion can see her right shoulder… the head of a young girl is visible.

Marion begins petting her hair, moving the strands from her shoulder, he sees the tombstone tattoo of the young girl in a full button-down dress with her head tilted and her elbows on her hips and her hands out to the side holding bird feed bowls… like the scales of justice…

The End

www.ingramcontent.com/pod-product-compliance
Lightning Source LLC
Chambersburg PA
CBHW031610160426
43196CB00006B/75
* 9 7 8 0 9 9 9 0 3 7 2 4 9 *